Explore th

NELLES

BERLIN
AND POTSDAM

Authors:
Eva Apraku, Manuela Blisse, Ellen Brandt,
Matthias Eckolt, Reginald Hanicke, Adrienne Kömmler,
Armin Lehmann, Regina Mönch, Constanze Salm,
Jürgen Scheunemann, Birgit Schönberger, Martin Schrader,
Petra Steuer, Hans-Joachim Wacker

*An Up-to-date travel guide with 142 color photos
and 13 maps*

**Third Revised Edition
1999**

Dear Reader,

Being up-to-date is the main goal of the Nelles series. To achieve it, we have a network of far-flung correspondents who keep us abreast of the latest developments in the travel scene, and our cartographers always make sure that maps and texts are adjusted to each other.

Each travel chapter ends with its own list of useful tips, accommodations, restaurants, tourist offices, sights. At the end of the book you will find practical information from A to Z. But the travel world is fast moving, and we cannot guarantee that all the contents are always valid. Should you come across a discrepancy, please write us at: Nelles Verlag GmbH, Schleissheimer Str. 371 b, D-80935 München, Germany, Tel: (089) 3571940, Fax: (089) 35719430.

LEGEND

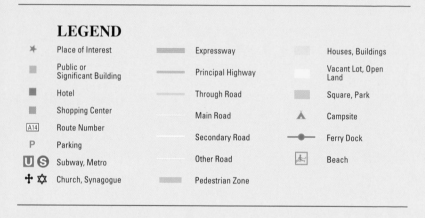

✳ Place of Interest	▬▬▬ Expressway	Houses, Buildings
■ Public or Significant Building	▬▬▬ Principal Highway	Vacant Lot, Open Land
■ Hotel	▬▬▬ Through Road	Square, Park
■ Shopping Center	▬▬▬ Main Road	▲ Campsite
A14 Route Number	▬▬▬ Secondary Road	● Ferry Dock
P Parking	▬▬▬ Other Road	Beach
U S Subway, Metro		
✝ ✡ Church, Synagogue	▬▬▬ Pedestrian Zone	

BERLIN and Potsdam
© Nelles Verlag GmbH, D-80935 Munich
  All rights reserved

Third Revised Edition 1999
ISBN 3-88618-029-8
Printed in Slovenia

Publisher:	Günter Nelles	**Translation:**	M. Cohen, R. Rosko
Chief Editor:	Berthold Schwarz	**Cartography:**	Nelles Verlag GmbH
Project Editor:	Jürgen Scheunemann	**Color**	
Editor in Charge:	Marton Radkai	**Separation:**	Priegnitz, Munich
Editor:	Chase Stewart	**Printed by:**	Gorenjski Tisk

No part of this book, not even excerpts, may be reproduced without prior permission of Nelles Verlag   - X08 -

TABLE OF CONTENTS

EXPERIENCING BERLIN

BERLIN BY NIGHT

FEATURES

GUIDELINES

GREATER BERLIN

0   5 km

LIST OF MAPS

BERLIN

A New European Metropolis

It is said that you are not born a Berliner, you *become* one. Those who quote this old quip are usually "foreigners" who have moved to Berlin from elsewhere and like to think of themselves as real Berliners. What is true, however, is that Berlin has always been more than just a city; the name Berlin has always stood for an idea, a feeling and ultimately for a powerful myth that all too often obscured the city's real character.

The Berlin myth originated during the Roaring Twenties; what consolidated the legend was the basement culture of the post-war period, the Berlin Wall and the Cold War, the Kreuzberg riots and being the "Capital of East Germany" and, finally, the fall of the Berlin Wall and reunification. In recent years, the "Wild East," with its experimental galleries and bars and the avant-garde scene in Berlin Mitte, has had the public spellbound.

All this makes up Berlin, but it isn't the whole truth. Berlin, on its way to being a modern European metropolis, gives the impression of being a city searching for its own identity.

Berlin seems to have gotten lost somewhere between its glorious and legendary history, insecure present and by no means safe future. Some say that the Berlin Bear is spinning on its own axis, directionless and dizzy as a result of the many rapid changes.

Berlin's unsuccessful application for the Olympic Games in the year 2000

showed how clumsily the city's powers that be acted in trying to innoculate Berlin with a vision of a meaningful future as the capital of the Federal Republic of Germany, as a "turnstile between western and eastern Europe," and as a European "cultural metropolis." These ideas must be provided with content and action – and it's proving to be Berlin's Achilles heel.

The hopeful longing with which Berliners are waiting for the Federal Government and its Parliament to move from Bonn to Berlin and the way they are welcoming new investors shows how far removed Berlin is from the relaxed confidence of other metropoles such as Paris or London. Is Berlin simply a city in historical free fall?

Berlin – the Unified City

A decade after the fall of the Wall, Berlin itself has still not been unified. The people in the east and west of the city still think and live differently, even if their children are growing up as Berliners. If the past appears to be such an omnipresent topic these days, it's because of the very difficult experiences each half of the city went through during the three decades of brutal separation.

There was West Berlin, which, after the Wall went up on August 13, 1961, became an artificial island in the middle of the Communist sphere of influence, an outpost of democracy and open-mindedness. It was often called the "window on the West." In reality, this is where the Cold War was fought, and it formed the interface between East and West. For Berliners in both parts of the city, the experience was at first hand and took place on their own doorstep, making it an intimate part of their everyday life.

But over time, West Berlin learned how to live in the shadow of the Wall: young students and artists who had moved to Berlin from West Germany had

Preceding pages: Grooving to techno, thousands come to the Love Parade from across Europe. Gedächtniskirche at night. Winter landscape on the Havel. Left: Keeping an eye on the Love Parade.

not left any family and friends on the other side of the Wall. Hence West Berlin became a niche for drop-outs, a place where people experimented with new life-styles and shaped a different future for themselves. Almost all the important alternative impulses that eventually spread throughout the whole of West Germany came from Berlin: student revolts and the so-called APO (extra-parliamentary opposition), the Green Party, squatters and punks. West Germany, the "Old Republic" – and the rest of the world, too – was hardly noticed by the Berliners.

West Berlin imagined itself to be the hub of the universe – after all, the world was watching, even if the intervals were becoming longer and longer. At the same time, West Berlin was becoming more and more provincial. Building speculators and narrow-minded politicians

Above: Anything (artistic) goes in Berlin.
Right: A typical Berliner: eccentricity against the anonymity of the big city.

dominated city life, scandals and affairs became the order of the day.

Meanwhile, on the other side of the Wall, a completely different city was evolving. East Berlin was artificially redesigned in a vacuum to become the representative "capital of the GDR." In the East, the other part of the city was simply disregarded. West Berlin – or Berlin (West) as GDR jargon had it – only existed on the subway charts and city maps as a large, blank area. The other part of the city beyond the Wall was no-man's-land for the GDR.

Unter den Linden, an avenue with a long and honorable tradition, was converted into a parade ground for the cheering working masses. Alexanderplatz, with its new high-rises from the 1960s, was to become the center of the peaceful, socialist Republic.

But East Berlin's outlying areas told a different story. The old, 19th-century tenement blocks fell into disrepair, the infrastructure remained on the level it was during the 1950s – East Berlin was sad, drab, and stank of brown coal smoke and two-stroke fumes. The pomp of the GDR regime was staged one last time in 1987 during the city's 750-year celebrations. Two years later, everything was in shambles, as policemen marched against the rebellious "we-are-the-people" demonstration on Unter den Linden.

The peaceful GDR revolution triumphed on the night of November 9, 1989, when the border crossing at Bornholmer Strasse was opened. During the following days, people danced exuberantly on the broad Wall in front of the Brandenburg Gate, broke through the Wall at various points, and celebrated wild parties on the streets. Once again, the world was watching Berlin.

During the two years after the Wall fell, Berlin became the testing ground for Germany's reunification. Something was happening to the country – and at first the change passed virtually unnoticed, as the

geographical distance between Bonn and Frankfurt/Oder was too great. The ones who were the first to feel it – once again – were the Berliners. The transports of delight of the autumn of 1989 did not last long. After a short period of getting to know one another, the Berliners West and East retreated to their own neighborhoods in rapidly growing disillusionment. The reunification celebrations in October 1990 were the last joyful event in the process of getting back together, and a sobering act indeed.

Coarse Charm: Berlin Mentality

Berlin and the Berliners have become the victims of their own clichés: their lippiness and bellicosity, Berlin nights and Kreuzberg, *Laubenpieper* (weekend gardeners) and islanders, cheekiness and provincialism. People come to Berlin expecting a city that will confirm all of their preconceived notions.

These people then stroll along the Ku'-damm and are in for a surprise: they come across the cheeky bus driver and the square but affable *Laubenpieper*, the man with the warm Berlin heart and the busy old lady who may well have cleared away rubble after the war (the legendary *Trümmerfrauen*).

However, in recent years, this cliché has turned stale. Only since the reunification has Berlin's charm revived, mainly thanks to the East Berliners. The neighborhoods of East Berlin had managed to maintain the kind of working-class and petty bourgeois culture as well as the sharp wittiness of rebellious big-city types no longer heard in West Berlin. Drinking *Molle mit Korn* (beer and a shot of spirits) and taking the family out to the country (*ins Grüne*, as it's called) or to the city swimming pools on Sundays is a habit that has not changed in a hundred years. Genuine Berlin dialect can be heard once again, quite different from the ostentatious, phony dialect used by those who had moved to Berlin to cover up their true origins (Swabians, in great part, with their broad, slow dialect).

So the Berliners' *Schnauze*, their sharp tongue, has returned to Berlin, but it has become more international. Just as Berliners have been pasting together their own dialect from the languages of immigrants to the city, nowadays they accept the lingual acrobatics established in everyday life, particularly Turkish and Polish. Perhaps the Berlin mentality is changing back to what it used to be. Crude yet spirited, cheeky and rebellious, Berliners are again behaving the way they did before the war. This is also a result of reunification; the new fast pace of everyday life in a metropolis is so overwhelming that people instinctively use coarser manners to protect themselves.

Today, as one hundred years ago, Berliner *Schnauze* is a kind of protection which all too often hides a genuine friendliness. The nature of the Berliner differs drastically from the reservedness of the northern Germans, the loud heartiness of the inhabitants of the Rhineland or the cosy conviviality of the Bavarians.

Berliners are unpredictable. Perhaps that is why Goethe referred to them as an "audacious race," and to Berlin as a place where "you have to have hair on your teeth and occasionally be a bit coarse to keep your head above water." The visitor to Berlin has to come to a decision: one either loves Berlin or hates it. Berlin keeps a firm grip on its visitors and citizens, as life in the city is too fast-paced and the intensity of urban life too overwhelming.

Repeat travelers to the great capital on the Spree River may notice that at each return, the welcome will be a bit different. Their sojourn will be truly delightful on occasion, the next time he may feel repelled by the city and its people, probably because Berlin is such a chaotic and contradictory place.

Right: Construction work goes on 24 hours a day at Potsdamer Platz, where a whole new city section is in the making.

The fact that people totally disagree about Berlin may be its greatest forte: as long as a city is provocative, it is also bound to be interesting.

The Future is Already Waiting

Great things are in store for Berlin: if you take a trip to Berlin in the 1990s, you will immediately notice the large numbers of construction cranes on the horizon. During the course of its history, the city has often been remodeled and rebuilt. But the construction boom that Berlin is presently experiencing is the greatest one to date. By the year 2000 almost 50 billion Deutschmarks will have been spent on construction in the newly unified metropolis; at present, whole new districts and centers are being drawn up from scratch.

The most celebrated construction site is the historical Potsdamer Platz, where Daimler-Benz and Sony are now erecting huge office-cities. The new government and parliamentary buildings are being planned around the Reichstag in the Tiergarten district. Several corporations are also erecting department stores and service centers on Friedrichstrasse, once the capital's most prestigious shopping street. The idea is that Friedrichstrasse should regain its full glory as Berlin's Fifth Avenue in a few years.

Much of the anonymous architecture carelessly plopped around Alexanderplatz by the GDR is being torn down and replaced by new, elegant high-rises. All in all, the area being demolished and rebuilt is about the size of an average city district. Simultaneously, Berlin is undergoing a difficult transitional period: the Cold War had given it a special status, which it has now lost. When the Allied troops and the Red Army left their respective sides of the city in 1994, the postwar era ended very symbolically. Yet the West Berliners confess that they miss the Allied troops. In spite of sporadic ten-

sions arising over the years, the Berliners had gradually learned to like "their" Allies.

Since then, Berlin has become even more "normal," which is something particularly visitors notice – the change doesn't seem quite so marked to the Berliners. Maybe they don't really want to know. It is more than obvious that Berlin lost some of its special flair and status when it started to resemble the majority of other German cities.

The planned merger of Berlin and Brandenburg into one large state will probably completely redefine the character and role of the city: as yet, many Berliners still only have a vague perception of their immediate surroundings.

Nevertheless, Berlin is still larger, more diverse, more aggressive and closer to eastern Europe than any other big city in Germany.

Since the fall of the Berlin Wall in 1989, the city and its 3.5 million inhabitants have attracted even more immigrants from Germany and elsewhere. It's getting crowded in Berlin. Life is becoming more colorful, more diverse and more cosmopolitan, and, unfortunately, somewhat more inhospitable.

The crime rate in the city has stayed almost the same since the beginning of the 1990s, yet most people feel increasingly unsafe and threatened in subways and suburban trains, or out on the streets at night. The social problems in Berlin have undoubtedly intensified: the city is bankrupt, yet it is faced with an army of unemployed people, especially in east Berlin; and tourists cannot help but notice instances of extreme poverty, even on the prestigious Ku'damm.

Maybe these are all the first harbingers for the metropolization of a major city: in the coming years, Berlin may outgrow its role as the "little sister" to the world cities of New York, London and Paris. Berlin is still sustaining itself on its historical myth, and yet it is on its way to becoming a European metropolis, not least of all as an intersection of newly open air and land routes across the continent.

TWO VILLAGES ON THE SPREE

The present-day area of Berlin had already been settled by various Slavic tribes as early as the 6th century A.D. They came from the east during the great migrations, and gradually reclaimed the swampy, remote forest regions along the rivers. The Hevellers, named after the river Havel, constructed a fortress in the proximity of today's Spandau, and the Sprewaners, named after the river Spree, built a castle on the present Köpenicker Schlossinsel, or Castle Island.

Around 1100, more and more land throughout Germany began to be cleared and settled, and German princes also attempted to expand into the territories east of the Elbe River. The Ascanian Prince Alfred the Bear subjugated the Slavs in a single campaign and, in 1137, took their most important fortress, the Brennabor on the river Havel, making it into his residence. He and his successors settled their new lands systematically and extended it as far as the Oder River: the March of Brandenburg thus came into being.

Then, sometime during the first half of the 13th century, the towns of Berlin and Cölln were founded between Spandau and Köpenick. They were both located on an especially narrow and shallow spot on the Spree, ideally suited for a ford and a harbor both. There were no articles of incorporation for either of the cities. The name Cölln first appeared in 1237 on a document referring to a witness, a priest named Symeon of Cölln. Incidentally, this document provided the basis for the celebration of the city's 750th anniversary, even though the name Berlin does not appear at all. That name was first mentioned in a document dated 1244. Berlin officially became a city in 1251; Cölln was so designated ten years later.

Left: Elector Joachim II (1535-1571), oil painting by Lucas Cranach, about 1551.

Just where the name Berlin originated is unknown. Possibly it is a compound of the Slavic words *bar* (pine forest) and *rolina* (farmland). But another theory suggests that settlers brought the name with them from the west.

Soon, Berlin and Cölln became economic centers, in that they stood on the intersection of the important trade routes linking Frankfurt on the Oder to the west, and the route from the Baltic coast going south. Both towns served as shipping points for lumber and rye from the March, fish from the north, pelts from Russia and increasingly precious spices. The Ascanians accelerated economic development by granting merchants exemptions from duties and giving Berlin the right to its own mint, supreme jurisdiction within its boundaries, as well as the depot laws which decreed that traders who were travelling through should sell a portion of their wares in Berlin.

Civic Freedom and Royal Seat

In doing so, the Ascanians undertook nothing against the interests of the city's patricians, who generally came from merchant families and dominated the Magistrate (the municipal authority). During the 14th century, the roughly 8000 residents of the twin city could, despite great obstacles, proclaim their dominant position in the March of Brandenburg. In 1307 Berlin and Cölln merged, even building a third city hall on the Lange Brücke (Long Bridge) which connected the two cities over the Spree. Nonetheless, the twin city must have seemed rather modest when compared to the episcopate cities on the Rhine.

Berlin was almost completely leveled by fire twice during this period, and the Black Plague that ravaged Europe also paid a lethal visit. Nevertheless, in spite of these calamities, the city was able to survive relatively intact the feuds raging between the noble houses in the March of

Brandenburg after the passing of the last Ascanian prince in 1319. At the beginning of the 15th century the battles in Brandenburg became increasingly fierce. Of course, the land was elevated to an electorate in 1356, but robber barons invaded and plundered Brandenburg, and they did not overlook Berlin, either. The militia was defeated and the city occupied. In 1412 King Sigismund sent his closest advisor, Burgrave Friedrich von Hohenzollern of Nürnberg, to Brandenburg with the task of pacifying the rebellious noble families. Friedrich defeated the robber barons, liberated Berlin in 1414 and was named margrave and elector for his efforts. His rule signalled the beginning of the 500-year-long ties between Berlin and the Hohenzollerns, under whom the city lost many rights. His successor, Friedrich II, used internal conflicts among the citizenry as a pretext for subjugating the city's proud and inde-

pendent patricians: the Magistrate was stripped of power; old rights of the city abrogated, goods and estates seized. The Berliners did not put up with the situation for very long. In the famed *Berliner Unwillen* (indignation) of 1448, they decided to rise up against the elector. However, their militia was again defeated and the city had to publicly declare its vassalage. The electoral soldiery thereby put an end to all attempts at autonomy on the part of the citizenry. The elector also had his position of power vividly portrayed in a new seal for the city of Berlin: naturally it showed the Berlin bear, although the Hohenzollern eagle was perched in a victorious pose on its back.

Berlin was then systematically expanded into a royal seat: Friedrich I had already started with the construction of a castle in 1443, which his successors constantly remodelled. The Hohenzollerns had hunting lodges built in Grunewald and Köpenick and recruited court officers from their homelands Franconia, Swabia and Thuringia. The assemblies of the

Above: The Great Elector Friedrich Wilhelm welcoming the French Huguenots to Berlin.

March also took place in Berlin starting in the mid-15th century.

By 1550, the population had grown to about 12,000, and the luxury of the royal court also made its way into the city. The intellectual climate was enlivened by the first schools, printing presses and a newspaper. Indeed, in the course of the 16th century the Berliners managed to regain some of their erstwhile municipal rights, in particular their own jurisdiction, since the electors needed money and sold many rights back to the city.

The Reformation swept through Berlin more peacefully than elsewhere. In 1539 Elector Joachim II converted to Lutheranism, albeit under pressure from the estates of the March. The Plague raged in Berlin several times during this period, and the Thirty Years' War (1618-1648) also exacted its tribute. Because the local rulers could not quite decide which side they were on, Protestant or Catholic, Swedish troups and imperial armies repeatedly invested Brandenburg. The outlying areas of Berlin suffered as a result, half of the population fled and gradually the city fell into decay.

The Great Elector and the Huguenots

Elector Friedrich Wilhelm acceded to the throne in 1640 at the age of 21. During his rule he attempted in particular to strengthen the economic power of the province and extend its influence. The weakened Brandenburg of the day consisted of the March as well as regions in Westphalia and the Duchy of Prussia in present-day East Prussia. In this disjointed land, the Great Elector (so named after his 1675 victory over the Swedes at Fehrbellin) established a centralist administration. He curtailed the rights of the landed estates and the cities. He installed a military governor in Berlin and Cölln in 1658, who, as highest-ranking officer of the electorate in the twin city, took over many municipal duties besides

police power. Friedrich invigorated construction activity with tax reductions and a new building code. For his officers he even founded two new, independent cities: Friedrichswerder to the southeast of Berlin and later Dorotheenstadt. These plans were certainly quite expensive, so that in 1667 he had to introduce a general excise tax, the *Akzise*. In addition, Berliners were forced to take on construction tasks at the new fortifications which had been laid in a star-shaped form around the city. The economies in these new cities flourished, however. The first manufacturing plants based on the French example were established and crafts became increasingly specialized.

In 1669 the Baltic and North Seas were connected with each other via a new canal between the Spree and Oder rivers: the traffic of goods between the coastal cities and wealthy Silesia could thus also be carried out via Berlin.

The Great Elector also understood how the economic upswing could be given an additional stimulus with a skillfully thought-out immigration policy. Starting in 1671 he admitted wealthy Jewish families from Vienna into the March (who could, however, only practice their religion under certain conditions) and, following the famed Edict of Potsdam (1685), primarily Huguenots. 20,000 of these French Protestants fled from their Catholic homeland to Brandenburg; 6000 settled in the Berlin area, particularly in the two new cities. The Huguenots formed an independent society, but their culture, language and especially their skills as craftsmen influenced the life of Berlin. You can still find traces of the Huguenots today. Some examples are the French Cathedral and the French *Gymnasium* in Berlin (1689), which is the oldest extant school.

Friedrich also directly supported the arts and sciences. His collection of paintings created the basic stock for Berlin's future museums, and he established the

first public library, which in 1686 already included some 20,000 volumes. By the time of his death in 1688, he had created four blossoming cities on the Spree, of which Berlin alone numbered 20,000 inhabitants. His wise policies put Berlin on the road to becoming the capital city.

The successor to the Great Elector, Friedrich III, continued in the same vein as his predecessor. In 1701 he elevated himself to the rank of king and ascended the Prussian throne as Friedrich I.

In 1709 he consolidated the four cities of Berlin, Cölln, Friedrichswerder and Dorotheenstadt into the greater municipality of Berlin; in so doing he cleverly succeeded in setting limits on the old civic rights by giving the larger city a new, restrictive municipal constitution. He had the old city castle beautified, bringing the most important master builders of his time to the Spree: Andreas

Above: Frederick the Great, quintessence of the enlightened despot. Right: The Tea-house in the Sanssouci complex.

Schlüter, Arnold Neuring and Eosander von Göthes, who all shaped the new appearance of the city with their Baroque structures. The cultural life also changed, becoming more that of a capital city. In 1694 the Academy of Arts was founded and later the Academy of Sciences, whose first president was the philosopher Wilhelm Leibniz. When Friedrich I died in 1713, he left behind a city with upward aspirations, a population of 60,000 and numerous magnificent buildings. However, the price for this urban development was a gigantic mountain of debt.

Berlin as the Center of Prussiandom

The new king, Friedrich Wilhelm I, introduced a strict and frugal rule to the court. Court officials were reduced in number, servants released from their duties, officers' salaries cut. Where once the court had shaped the face of the city and its economy, it was now requirements of the army for which the city lived and produced. Friedrich wasn't named

the "soldier king" for nothing. He enlarged the Prussian army from 40,000 to over 80,000 men, turning it into the fourth most powerful military force in Europe. Berlin soon took on the appearance of one big military camp: many soldiers were housed in private quarters, the pleasure gardens and the Tempelhofer Feld were turned into exercise grounds.

In 1740 Friedrich II (Frederick the Great) ascended the throne. Old Fritz, as he came to be called, had a dual personality: on one hand he was a flute-playing king who received Voltaire in Sanssoucci, a modern monarch under whom the Enlightenment gleamed in Berlin with such personalities as Friedrich Nicolai, Moses Mendelssohn and Lessing; he was the kindly and humane leader who abolished torture and paved the way for the founding of a constitutional state, the art-lover whose architect Wenzeslaus von Knobelsdorff improved Unter den Linden to a boulevard with such magnificent buildings as the Opera and St. Hedwig's Cathedral. However, Friedrich had

another, darker side. He was also the absolutist monarch, who, with high import duties and systematic state support, geared up the Prussian economy for war. Berlin's new weaving mills made it Germany's most important center of textile manufacturing. However, this policy ultimately served the military.

Friedrich proved to be a cold-blooded power politician who wanted to propel his country into the circle of Europe's great powers at all costs. To this purpose, he put his subjects through a series of grievous wars that almost ruined the country. When Friedrich II died in 1786, Berlin was nevertheless still the center of Prussia and, with its 150,000 residents, could claim membership in the club of the great cities of Europe.

The next decades, though, brought about the collapse of Old Fritz' state. The French Revolution caused the downfall not only of monarchies, but also of the very idea of an absolutist state.

Ultimately Prussia succumbed to the attack of Napoleonic troops. In 1806 the

Grande Armée staged a triumphal march right through the Brandenburg Gate and occupied Berlin. The French reorganized the city administration and even set up the forerunner of a city parliament. These ideas were picked up by Prussian reformers, such as Baron von Stein in 1809 after the French had withdrawn. With his legislation the interests of the state and the city were separated by the institution of Berlin's own assembly of councils. This resulted directly in the first mayoral elections of 1809.

The cultural life of the city gained noteworthy luster, side-by-side with those new political and civic structures. In 1810 the Friedrich Wilhelm University was founded by Wilhelm von Humboldt. Its registration soon numbered 2000 students, making it, at the time, the largest university in Germany. Berlin attracted the greatest minds of the era, such men as Alexander von Humboldt, Hufeland,

Above: Men, women and children on the barricades in 1848, fighting for civil rights.

Hegel, Schleiermacher and Neander. This development continued into the following decades, when writers such as Heinrich Heine, E.T.A. Hoffmann or Bettina von Arnim, the painter Adolph Menzel and philosophers such as Leopold von Ranke or Johann Gottlieb Fichte flocked to Berlin. In the field of architecture, it was Karl Friedrich Schinkel who, beginning in 1815, finally turned Unter den Linden into a boulevard worthy of a capital.

The years following the wars of liberation were rich in all matters artistic; cafés, operas and concert attendance epitomized the spirit of the period. And brilliant, intellectual conversation animated the salons of Rahel Varnhagen and Henriette Herz. However, a retreat into culture was also the resigned answer of the citizenry to its unfulfilled political hopes. For this was by no means an era of enlightened and liberal politics in Prussia. As the Restoration increased its grip, the reformers of yesterday suddenly found themselves to be the persecuted.

1848: The Failed Revolution

When the new king of Prussia ascended the throne in 1840, a great hope for political reform swept through the expectant society. His liberal gestures were only of short duration: soon the land was being governed by the same tyrannical Prussian regime that suppressed each and every political activity of the citizens and took no note of the interests of most classes. Dissatisfaction among the people became greater, especially in Berlin, where many associations were formed allegedly to cultivate sports or the intellect, but in truth as a way to solidify a political opposition.

As discontent festered, social tensions also increased. The 1844 rebellion of weavers in Silesia also reached Berlin, where large sections of the populace also lived in great poverty, especially in the city's outskirts. In 1847 the city had to devote 40 percent of its expenditures to relief for the poor. Yet the urgent social problems continued to grow unabated, a fact which was then made public in newspapers and books as well. In the same year, the *Kartoffelrevolution* (Potato Revolution) took place: After a bad harvest had pushed up prices, enraged Berliners stormed the market stalls.

One year later, influenced by the new revolution that was shaking France, the citizens, craftsmen and workers of Berlin plucked up their courage. They wanted to negotiate with the king about changes in the constitution, but the Prussian crown showed no inclination whatsoever to waste its breath discussing polital matters with its people. A demonstration before the Brandenburg Gate resulted in the first casualties when the police advanced on the crowd. The military marched into the city in order to re-establish law and order. Once again, on March 18, 1848, a large demonstration took place at which the freedoms of assembly, press and speech were demanded, as well as a pull-out of the military from the city. As these demands were called out, troops advanced against the crowd and opened fire. The demonstrators set up barricades, and in turn attacked the soldiers. The fighting lasted almost a full day. Finally, the king called on the citizenry for peace in a proclamation beginning: "To my dear Berliners." As a symbol of his good faith he had the military withdraw and promised reforms. How heavy the pressure must have been on the monarch became readily apparent when he paid his last respects to the 183 people who had been shot, and who were laid out in state on the Gendarmenmarkt.

Friedrich Wilhelm IV actually kept his promises, guaranteeing the freedoms of assembly and press. Even the uneven voting system was reformed, giving the less fortunate more power for their ballot. The Berliners revelled in the new freedoms. Newspapers flooded the city, and people openly discussed politics in the cafés; in the salons political associations were formed, the forerunners of the future parties. However, the experiment of the first German Parliament in Frankfurt fell apart in May 1848. Nor could the Prussian National Assembly, dominated as it was by conservative merchants and industrialists, come to any sort of agreement on a new constitution.

In December 1848 Friedrich Wilhelm IV brought the experiment to an abrupt end by forcing the Prussian National Assembly to adopt a new constitution, containing liberal elements which his successor later rescinded. Furthermore, this second version reintroduced the tax-based voting system, which now applied to Berlin's Municipal Parliament as well: only five percent of the roughly 430,000 inhabitants were thus allowed to cast their ballots. Chief of Police von Hinckeldey suppressed the liberal opposition with rigorous censorship of the press and police terror. The reactionaries had claimed victory in Berlin.

SPLENDOR AND MISERY

Beginning in the mid-19th century, Berlin grew to become Europe's largest center of industry. No other city in Europe underwent such headlong and turbulent industrial development. The political and social results were also more blatant here than anywhere else. Engineering and metal working especially contributed to the city's economic upswing. The factories required an ample supply of workers; as a result the population increased at first to 450,000 (1860), then to one million (1877) and, ultimately, to two million (1905).

However, the shadow side of this growth loomed ever larger. The workers were exploited to the hilt, with toil of up to 16 hours a day, frequently under inhumane conditions; the wages were only enough for survival when all members of the family worked, and child labor was no rarity in those days.

The rapid population growth posed immense problems to the city, since it had to build affordable housing as quickly as possible. Between 1860 and 1870 the total number of residences doubled to 166,100. On the outskirts of Berlin entire quarters such as Moabit, Wedding or sections of Schöneberg popped up out of the ground as if by magic. Land speculators and contractors became wealthy by throwing up cheap housing complexes and leasing them at excessive prices. Berlin became the city of rental barracks, in which the families of workers often had to live in one room. On top of that, most of the apartments were very dark due to their small interior courtyards, and they often lacked sanitary facilities.

After its victory over Austria in the Austro-Prussian War (1866), Prussia had put the second great German power out of the running. In the same year the North

Left: A working-class family in a Berlin tenement at the end of the 19th century.

German states also consolidated into the North German Confederation, which was dominated by Prussia. The chancellor was Otto von Bismarck, whose goal, however, was the unification of all German states – a goal he was able to achieve by 1870/71. The German states – again under Prussian command – won a victory over France in the brief but fierce Franco-Prussian war. This most important and dramatic of 19th-century European wars of unification forced the German states together and led directly to the founding of the German Empire. In the Hall of Mirrors in Versailles, on January 18, 1871, Wilhelm I, King of Prussia, was proclaimed Kaiser of Germany.

The Berliners themselves remained quiet on receiving the news of German unification. The prospect of their city becoming the capital of Germany didn't spark great euphoria. Furthermore, Berlin's hospitals and sick bays were full of Prussia's wounded; the economy of the city had also been crippled by the rapid conversion to and from war production.

As the capital of the Reich, Berlin attracted emissaries not only from the other German states, but also from foreign countries who constructed their embassies here. In addition, political parties established their central offices in Berlin. Social democracy, with a major following in Berlin, was especially successful and important for the city. One of the main reasons for the easy propagation of Socialist ideas was the poor living conditions of the city's proletariat. Despite Bismarck's *Sozialistengesetze* (Socialist Laws), which banned the Social Democrats, the party continued to enjoy great popularity in Berlin. Its leaders, such as August Bebel and Karl Liebknecht, were among the most important politicians of the Reich. Bismarck was also unable to fully coopt the proletariat with his – for those days – modern social laws. Conditions in the poorer quarters of Berlin were too miserable for this. In sharp con-

trast to the rest of the Reich, support for the Social Democratic Party (SPD) among Berliners persisted. In 1890 the party received more than half of all the ballots in Berlin, and after 1893 five of the city's six representatives in the Reichstag (Parliament) were Social Democrats.

The founding of the German Reich, which created a gigantic unified economic region with millions of consumers, also coincided with a steep economic upswing. Germany experienced a tremendous boom, which was further enhanced by five billion francs in war reparations exacted from the French. Berlin, as the new capital, profited most heavily from these founding years of the new Reich. Banks, insurance firms and joint-stock companies moved to the Spree or were founded in Berlin – in 1872 alone some 250 firms, 40 of which were in the construction business.

Above: Prussia's pomp and glory – Emperor Wilhelm I at a parade in Berlin.

In the second half of the 19th century the city underwent increasingly rapid industrialization. Appearing alongside the traditional branches of industry, such as engineering and the processing of textiles, were new sectors, such as electrical engineering and the chemical industry. Siemens & Halske introduced the first electrically-powered locomotive in 1879; the AEG (Allgemeine Elektrizitäts-Gesellschaft) was founded; chemical giants like Schering took their places beside older companies such as Borsig.

The industrial upswing was accompanied by correspondingly rapid, and not altogether easy, development of the city. Since the middle of the century Berlin had become more self-assured with regard to the Prussian state. Berlin's pride manifested itself in the new representative *Rotes Rathaus*, the Red Town Hall (thus named after the color of its bricks), which was constructed from 1861 to 1869 near Alexanderplatz.

Since Berlin had become the capital, many things also improved for its citizenry. A sewer system (still functioning) was finally installed, as well as a new water works and, in 1885, the first power plant went into operation. The city now added the construction of roads and street cleaning to its tasks, busied itself with laying out parks and gardens, and arranged for better stocking up of food supplies by the building of a new market and a central stockyard and slaughterhouse. In 1873 the first municipal hospital was opened in Friedrichshain.

Berlin's transportation system changed along which the growth and modernization of the city. Increasingly, the old horse-drawn omnibuses disappeared; by 1902 all routes had been electrified. By 1877 the *Ringbahn (*ring railway) had already been put into service. It connected the various main railroad stations with each other. At first the carriages were pulled by steam locomotives, later electric ones. And, starting in 1905, the first automobiles appeared in the streets; in 1913 the first German *Autobahn,* the AVUS, was constructed through the Grunewald district.

Berlin and the Wilhelminian Era

During the period Berlin developed into a world-class metropolis, Germany was first ruled by Kaiser Wilhelm I; in 1888 – the so-called "year of the three Kaisers" – Friedrich III ruled for 99 days. He was succeeded by the man who was to be Germany's last Kaiser, Wilhelm II (1859-1941), and whose name left its stamp on an entire epoch.

The young, energetic Kaiser, whose first act was to fire Chancellor Bismarck, had himself and the dynasty celebrated with parades and marches before the *Stadtschloss* (City Castle). The Berlin of this epoch consisted of plucky officers with spiked helmets who displayed their militarism for all to see, and of timorous Philistines of the sort described by the chronicler of the times, Heinrich Mann,

in his 1918 novel *Der Untertan* (*The Subject*). There was, however, also another side to Berlin, with artists both real and fake, corrupt politicians, money-hungry financiers of dubious repute, and social climbers whom Heinrich Mann parodied in his 1900 novel *Im Schlaraffenland* (*In Never-Never-Land*).

The literary world of Berlin attracted many talents, among them Theodor Fontane (1862-1914) and Gerhart Hauptmann (1862-1946). In painting, Berlin artists also forged new paths: in the *Brücke* (Bridge) movement, expressionist artists such as Emil Nolde, Ernst Ludwig Kirchner and others joined forces. The leading exponents of the Secession, Max Liebermann (1847-1935) and Walter Leistikow worked in Berlin. Max Reinhardt produced numerous works on the city's stages. The Philharmonic Orchestra was founded in 1882; new theaters and opera houses opened. Scientists such as Max Planck (1858-1947), Albert Einstein (1879-1955), Fritz Haber (1868-1934) and Robert Koch (1843-1910) – many of them Nobel Prize winners – taught at Berlin's universities.

Berlin seemed to have a great future ahead of it. However, with his aggressive foreign policy and tremendous arms build-up Wilhelm II brought the German Empire into ever sharper conflict with the other great powers of Europe. With their equally aggressive arms build-up, France, England and Russia did their share to make Germany feel hemmed in. A chain reaction lead to the outbreak of World War One in August 1914.

Kaiser Wilhelm II called out to the jubilant Berliners in front of the Stadtschloss: "I no longer know any parties, I know only Germans." However, belief in a quick victory soon fell apart and German patriotism began to waver as the initial successes of the Great War gave way to the muck and the mire. Besides the enormous blood toll, fighting a slow-moving, material-intensive war on two

31

fronts against a much larger enemy exhausted the country's moral and finances. The winter of 1917 was the hardest the Berliners had ever seen. Everything was rationed: an adult received only 70 grams of meat and 20 grams of butter per week!

In April 1917, 300,000 workers at Berlin's armaments plants went on strike; in August the populace plundered the weekly markets; the victory of the Russian Revolution helped to mobilize the proletariat. As Germany's military situation became increasingly hopeless the seamen of the German fleet mutinied in November 1918, thus precipitating events. On November 9 Kaiser Wilhelm II had to abdicate, workers and soldiers took up arms and councils were formed. Germany and Berlin looked to the Reichstag, but its members were unable to act until, on the same day, the Social Democrat Philipp Scheidemann pro-

claimed the German Republic in the Reichstag. At the same time, the Spartacist leader Karl Liebknecht proclaimed a Socialist Republic from the City Castle.

The Twenties: Days of Gold and Chaos

The political confusion in the new Republic lasted until late March 1920. Up until then the Communists, Social Democrats and reactionaries struggled for power in the country. In January 1919 the so-called Spartacus Rebellion broke out in Berlin's newspaper district on Kochstrasse and Friedrichstrasse. It suffered a bloody defeat at the hands of troops loyal to the government.

In the process, two of the most important ringleaders, Karl Liebknecht and Rosa Luxemburg, were shot by soldiers of the Freikorps, a militia made up of World War I veterans with reactionary leanings. The 1919 elections to the National Assembly had turned out a solid majority for the democratically oriented

Above: Fighting during the Spartacus Rebellion in January 1919. Right: Bustling city life on Friedrichstrasse (around 1930).

parties, but in March of the same year it became apparent how unstable the new order was. Units of the Imperial Army, led by an unknown officer by the name of Kapp, carried out a putsch and occupied Berlin. The rest of the Imperial Army refused to obey the government and did nothing to stop the rebellion. It was a strike by Berlin workers that ultimately brought an end to Kapp's political ambitions.

The first years of the Weimar Republic continued to be tumultuous. On June 24, 1922, Foreign Minister Walter Rathenau (1868-1922) was shot on the street by assassins from the extreme right wing. This attack was the climax in a wave of 376 political murders which shook the Republic from 1918 to 1922. By the way, 354 of these murders were committed by right-wing extremists; most of the perpetrators were never convicted.

On November 9, 1923, a group of arch-reactionary politicians and army officers around the still obscure Adolf Hitler attempted a putsch in Munich. This

time he could be headed off, sentenced and sent to prison.

The economic situation reflected the political disorder: Germany had to come to grips with millions of soldiers returning from the fronts, an exhausted industry that had been adapted for war production, and heavy reparations. The German economy stumbled from one crisis to the next. In 1923 the galloping inflation hit its peak, with the US dollar costing 170,000 reichsmarks (July), then 12 million (August) and finally 12 billion (October), until ultimately a new currency, the *Rentenmark*, was introduced.

After the new currency was put into circulation the economy slowly began to recover and the unemployment rate dropped. Berlin was ready for a new start. An urban reform in 1920 drastically increased the size of the city. Berlin and seven additional cities in the vicinity, almost 60 villages and 27 farming communities were consolidated into a single, gigantic administrative district called Greater Berlin. At this point 3.8 million

33

people lived here; only ten years later the population crossed the four million mark.

The face of the metropolis was transformed yet again. As ever the housing complexes remained the dominant feature. On Alexanderplatz and Potsdamer Platz, modern office high-rises in the lucid Bauhaus style were erected. In the outlying districts model residential complexes were built following the same principles, an example being the renowned *Hufeisensiedlung* (Horseshoe Settlement) in Britz (1925-1927). The transportation network in the city was finally brought up to world-class level. Ernst Reuter, then responsible for the city's transportation, rapidly extended the subway system (U-Bahn) and managed the amalgamation of all the transportation firms into the joint-stock *Berliner Verkehrs-Aktiengesellschaft*, the BVG, which, in 1928, united all of Berlin's means of transportation under one roof. During those days Berlin became the "little sister" of the great metropolises of Paris, London and New York. In some aspects, too, Berlin even came to set examples for these cities.

The few years between 1918 and 1933 gave rise to the myth of Berlin, identifying the city with an entire epoch, referred to as the "Golden Twenties." Berlin's unique reputation was justified in many ways. But alongside its distinguished rank as a nucleus of culture, technology and the sciences, there was the suffering of the thousands forced to exist in conditions of abject poverty, the constant yo-yoing of daily politics and the equally unstable economy. Berlin was marked with blatantly clashing social contrasts. All the glamor and misery of an epoch came together here. Perhaps it was these contrasts combined with an aggressive, hectic atmosphere which attracted artists and literary figures.

Right: Monetary inflation and loose living – scenes from the Golden Twenties.

They met together in Berlin's countless cafés and restaurants, the most famous of which was the gloomy Romanisches Café on Auguste-Viktoria-Platz, where the Europa Center stands today. There were "swimmer" and "nonswimmer" sections (so to speak) for the regular guests and the curious upstarts wishing to begin their careers here. In fact, such literary figures as Arnold Zweig, Bertolt Brecht, Walter Benjamin, Leonhard Frank, Wolfgang Koeppen, Klaus and Erika Mann, Kurt Tucholsky, Joachim Ringelnatz and Erich Kästner drank their coffee in the Romanisches Café. Journalists like Carl von Ossietzky, Herbert Ihering and Alfred Kerr sometimes wrote their critiques and articles there. With the nearly 150 newspapers and countless magazines which were being published in Berlin, the city became the center of the German press.

Just as in literature and political journalism, all directions of the visual arts were also represented in Berlin. Some of them, such as the anarchistic Dadaism and the austere Futurism, first unfurled to their full impact in the city. Such painters and sculptors as Karl Hofer, Max Beckmann, Ernst Barlach, Georg Kolbe, Fritz Klimsch and George Grosz found their motifs here. Like no other artist, Grosz captured the rise and fall of the Golden Twenties with his Berlin collages.

Berlin's music scene was very much that of a world-city as well: Wilhelm Furtwängler, Bruno Walter and Otto Klemperer directed the Berlin Orchestra; Erwin Piscator and Leopold Jessner directed their great theater successes here. Berlin was also the capital of German film. The UFA built Europe's largest film studios in Babelsberg. UFA's film stars resided there and in Potsdam, but they took their entertainment in Berlin. Heinrich George, Elisabeth Bergner, Fritz Kortner, Werner Krauss and many others stood before the camera here. Future Hollywood stars Greta Garbo, Marlene Die-

trich and Peter Lorre, among others, also began their careers in Berlin. Political cabarets and large-scale variety shows were other new developments. The two largest houses, the Wintergarten and the Scala, constantly tried to out-do each other with their rather daring revues. The Berlin of the Weimar Republic knew no closing hours, no censors, no stultifying morality laws. As a result, the city quickly acquired a reputation as a den of iniquity where everything was allowed. However, the shrill and colorful hedonism and craze for amusement of the period began to seem more and more like a dance on a volcano because the political situation was growing more threatening.

Berlin and National Socialism

After 1926 the German economy gradually weakened. In the following years increasing numbers of firms went bankrupt, resulting in mass firings. In October 1929 the Western industrialized nations were shaken by the crash of the New York stock exchange. Black Friday was the final warning signal of the approaching crisis.

The collapse of the financial system ultimately had its nefarious effect on the German economy. Even major Berlin firms like the Borsig plants released all of their employees. After a hard winter, in February 1930, there were 450,000 unemployed in Berlin; in May the first riots took place, in which 30 people died.

The state unemployment benefits were too low to prevent a political radicalization of the masses. In the Rotes Rathaus and the Reichstag the elections of that year produced no solid majorities, while the first street-fighting broke out between Nazis and Communists. In 1932 the number of unemployed rose to 600,000. A full 25 percent of all Berliners were living on welfare by then.

In the same year the National Socialists (NSDAP) reaped their best results in the elections of July 31: 37.4 percent of eligible voters cast their ballots for the "brown" party (only 28.6 percent in Ber-

lin). Thus the NSDAP became the strongest party, and after the Reichstag was again dissolved and new elections held – with two further governments miscarrying – President Hindenburg named Adolf Hitler the new Chancellor on January 30, 1933.

On the evening of that same day the SA, Hitler's paramilitary organization known as the Brown Shirts, marched in a torchlight procession through the Brandenburg Gate, passing before Hitler, who was standing at a window of the Chancellery. Max Liebermann, the Jewish painter and president of the Prussian Academy of the Arts, lived nearby and on this occasion is supposed to have said: "*Ich kann gar nicht so viel fressen, wie ich kotzen möchte.*" (I can't eat nearly as much as I would like to vomit). Several days later the torchlight parades were repeatedly staged for the cameras of the weekly film news *Wochenschau*. The Nazis used ter-

ror to increase pressure on the ministers and other politicians of the democratic parties. On February 27, 1933, the Reichstag burned down. Up to this day no one knows exactly who set the fire, but all indications point to the Nazis, who exploited it for their own propagandistic purposes. Indeed, that very night Hitler declared that the Communists had set the fire and that an overthrow from the left was looming in the immediate future. Under this pretext some 5000 members of the opposition were arrested in the following nights, especially in Berlin. Also, on the next day the Reichstag passed an "emergency decree for the protection of the people and the state" that gave Hitler comprehensive powers.

In March 1933 elections were held anew, since the National Socialists wanted to have public approval of their policies. However, the turnout was disappointing for the Nazis: they received only 43.9 percent of the ballots; in Berlin only 34.6 percent – the Communists were still the second-strongest party in the city!

Above: A perfectly arranged mega-spectacle: Jan. 30, 1933 – Hitler seizes power.

Nonetheless, Hitler also managed to cripple the parliament with the *Ermächtigungsgesetz* (Law of Empowerment). Only the remaining Social Democrat ministers voted against it; the mandate of the 81 Communist members of parliament had been withdrawn beforehand. With the death of Hindenburg in August 1934, Hitler designated himself *Führer* and Chancellor of the Reich.

Terror and Resistance in Berlin

Already in the first days after Hitler's appointment as chancellor in January 1933, the Nazis in Berlin had established spontaneous holding camps and opened a big concentration camp in Sachsenhausen to the north of Berlin.

There were about 150,000 Jews living in Berlin at that time (by comparison, there were only 500,000 in all of Germany). Only 5000 of them were able to hide in Berlin; some 55,000 were killed in the concentration camps; the others succeeded in fleeing.

Many of Berlin's intellectuals and artists were of Jewish extraction. They and members of the opposition had to either flee or go underground. Kurt Tucholsky, Max Reinhardt, Else Lasker-Schüler and Hans Sahl managed to leave Germany in time. Other prominent people, such as Carl von Ossietzky and the major Berlin publishers Samuel Fischer and Rudolph Mosse, were killed by the Nazis or died embittered.

Step by step, starting in 1933, the rights of Jews were restricted, until they lost all rights under the 1936 Nürnberg Laws. And, on the so-called *Reichskristallnacht* (Night of Broken Glass) on November 9, 1938, Jewish businesses were ransacked and plundered, and synagogues set ablaze. 12,000 Berlin Jews were deported that night and in the days following.

Berlin had become the center of power for the Third Reich. The headquarters of the SS and the Gestapo were located on Prinz-Albert-Strasse and on Wilhelmstrasse in Kreuzberg; the Luftwaffe was situated in a monumental new building, and on Vossstrasse Hitler had a new chancellery constructed.

These palatial buildings were only the beginning. Starting in 1937, Hitler's chief architect, Albert Speer, began taking his plans for the future Berlin from the blackboard to reality. As "Germania," the city was to become the capital of a National Socialist world empire; the center was to be a 4.5-mile (seven km) north-south artery cutting straight through Berlin. It was to be lined with immense government buildings; at each end great halls were to rise skyward. With their heights of around 1000 feet (300 meters) they would have had room for 180,000 people, the perfect arena for the massive propaganda productions of the Nazis. Compared to these proportions the Brandenburg Gate would have seemed like little more than a side-entrance. These phantasmagoria of Hitler's grand delusion were destroyed by the war.

While the Nazis in Berlin fanned the flames of state terror, the city simultaneously became the center of the (albeit limited) German resistance. Alongside the SPD and the German Communist Party (KPD), which were active in the underground distribution of leaflets and illegal publications almost until the beginning of the war, the two churches stirred up opposition.

Officially, both confessions had come to some agreement with Hitler, but some priests and theologians of the *Bekennende Kirche*, an opposition church movement, struggled against the Nazis. Ministers like Martin Niemöller, who preached in Dahlem, Dietrich Bonhoeffer and others paid for their courage with long internments in concentration camps or with their lives. Parallel to them, secret organizations such as the *Rote Kapelle* (Red Chapel) smuggled Jews out of the

country, and members of the opposition found kindred spirits in the "Kreisau Circle."

The most significant source of resistance gathered around Carl Goerdeler, the former mayor of Leipzig. Besides Goerdeler it was particularly the upper ranks of the military, such as Colonel-General Ludwig von Beck and officers in the various ministries, who planned putsches against Hitler. Effective they were not, except perhaps to salvage Germany's conscience. The assassination attempt on July 20, 1944, committed by Colonel Claus Schenk Graf von Stauffenberg, failed. Members of the Kreisau Circle were arrested; on the same evening Count Stauffenberg and others were summarily shot in the inner courtyard of the Bendlerblock. Almost 200 people paid with their lives for the attempted assassination of Hitler.

Above: Roland Freisler in the People's Court. Right: Berliners search for food among bombed-out houses.

A Hail of Bombs and Chaos

While Hitler spread terror across Germany, he systematically built up the armaments industry. In matters of foreign policy he increasingly took the initiative; with the propaganda slogans of *Lebensraum* for Germany he demanded concessions from the neighboring European countries. With a mixture of skillful demands for peace and coldly calculated threats, he managed to impose his will on Europe before turning to open aggression. However, the Berliners didn't rejoice when German troops attacked Poland on September 1, 1939. In contrast to 1914, there were no huge parades on the streets of Berlin – the people were stunned, frightened and depressed.

This slowly changed with Germany's victories up to 1941, although during these years life in Berlin became progressively more difficult. Even in the first year of the war, rationing coupons were introduced for foodstuffs; the economy had also been converted to war produc-

tion. The stylish, pleasure-seeking Berlin of the prewar years was already a vague thing of the past by 1940. More and more the city resembled a grey military encampment with nightly blackouts.

In the summer of 1940 the German Luftwaffe began bombarding civilian targets in England. The Royal Air Force struck back; on August 25 and 26, 1940, the first bombing raids on Berlin took place. Some 222 Berliners had lost their lives in these bombardments by the end of 1940; from then on the British, and later American, bombers flew one mission after another. The heaviest attack of all took place in February 1943, when 2643 tons of bombs were dropped on the city. In that year 400,000 Berliners became homeless. During the entire war some 49,600 people died in the hail of bombs in Berlin alone.

In April 1945 the Red Army accelerated its advance on Berlin from the east; the bombed-out city had meanwhile sunken into chaos, the infrastructure was destroyed, the administration disinte-grated. Straggling troops, civil militia and refugees wandered through the devastated streets and put up a last suicidal house-to-house battle against the Red Army in late April 1945. Meanwhile, the upper echelons of power of the Thousand Year Reich cowered in their bunkers. Adolf Hitler finally shot himself on April 30, 1945, in his bunker beneath the chancellery. The other Nazi commanders and generals either died or fled. The fighting in Berlin continued until May 2, when City Major General Weidling surrendered. Six days later the German army was just about finished; on May 8, Germany's unconditional and total surrender was signed at the Soviet headquarters in Berlin-Karlshorst.

However, the suffering of Berlin's population was to continue into the last days of the war: the Russian army plundered, raped and often wantonly murdered civilians as well. This was in revenge for the gruesome massacres that the Wehrmacht and the SS had committed in the Soviet Union.

FROM ZERO HOUR TO THE FALL OF THE WALL

At the end of the war Berlin constituted the largest single uninterrupted area of ruins in Europe. Of all its former power and splendor, this was the only superlative that could possibly apply to the one-time imperial capital. Eleven square miles (28.5 sq km) of densely constructed urban area had fallen victim to Allied bombing and shelling by the Red Army; 246 million cubic feet (75 million cubic meters) of debris were piled high in the streets. The true scale of the destruction was only discernible from the air. The bottom line looked as follows: Of some 250,000 buildings, a meager ten percent had made it through the war unscathed. Almost 48,000 were completely destroyed or irreparably damaged; the remaining 70 percent had suffered more or less serious damage.

On assuming the highest authority in the city, the Red Army had also taken over primary responsibility for both the woes and well-being of the civilian population. Approximately 2.5 million people, of which there were almost twice as many women as men, were hovering on the edge of a catastrophic famine in this city of ruins. Peoples' Commissar Mikojan, acting on behalf of the Moscow War Commission, organized on-location deliveries of aid. "Everywhere women, children and the elderly are begging members of the Red Army for a piece of bread," he reported on May 18, 1945, in *Pravda*. " The people are eating grass and the bark of the trees."

Families of refugees from the East, who had left their homes and belongings to flee from the Red Army, strayed through the desert of rubble in their search for food and shelter. Hygenic conditions were catastrophic, dysentery and

Left: The memorial to the Berlin Airlift in Tempelhof, a symbol of freedom.

typhus raged. Cut off from the outer world, shattered and pillaged, Berlin had reached the nadir of civilization. That it was able to get back on its feet was due more than anything to the indefatigable nature of its inhabitants.

The Russian troops had scarcely moved on when the huge clean-up began in the outlying areas. By the end of May the first subways and streetcars started running. Gas and electricity were restored, though intermittently at best. The new cultural stirrings were promising. In the Titania Palast in Steglitz the players of the Philharmonic gathered for a memorable concert under Leo Borchard on May 26. One day later, the Renaissance Theater celebrated its postwar première, and in mid-June the *Kammer der Kunstschaffenden* (Chamber of Creating Artists) opened an exhibition with the works of painters and sculptors who had been ostracized under the Nazis. The *Reichstrümmerfeld*, or "Imperial Field of Rubble" as the Berliners called their home town with a healthy portion of black humor, had once again come to life.

The City of Sectors

For two months the Soviet conquerors ruled Berlin single-handedly. Exiled German Communists, purposely flown in from Moscow, recruited reliable party activists for the new city administration. They were supposed to represent all of the anti-Fascist powers – at least for the sake of outward appearances – under an impartial mayor. However, the decisive posts were filled with their own.

On June 5, 1945, the Allies established a Supreme Control Council for occupied Germany, with its seat in Berlin. The city was put under the supervision of the Four Powers, as had been decided by the Big Three on September 12, 1944. The governmental protocol decided in London with regards to the zones of occupation in Germany envisaged a status as "special

41

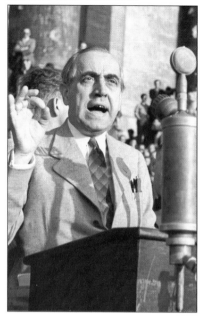

military governors met at regular intervals. Their adjudication served as the basis for all questions affecting Germany as a whole.

The Inter-Allied Command in Dahlem played the same role for Berlin. Unanimous decisions – there was no other kind – were conveyed to the Mayor, Arthur Werner, for implementation. At the very first meeting the Soviets were able to push through their position that prior orders of their military command would remain in effect until further notice.

The Allies subdivided the entire Berlin occupation zone into sectors for the quartering of the various troops. As might have been expected, the Western Allies took over the western half, with a total of twelve districts. Remaining in Soviet hands – almost the same size in area – were the eight eastern districts, including the traditional center of the city.

The miseries of the postwar period continued to be the same, regardless of which victor ran what sector. Chronic hunger was written on the faces of many people. Adult men had an average weight of 125 lbs (57 kg), women 116 lbs (kg). Out of dire need, tens of thousands of Berlin women hired themselves out to clear the rubble, clean and stack the salvageable bricks, and so on. In the graduated rationing system, rubble clearers were given *Class Two* ration cards. For the rest of the population there was the notorious *Class Five* "graveyard card," providing only 1200 calories per day. The only way to survive was either to go to the country to scrounge for food, or to barter on the black market. The winter of 1946/47 was particularly harsh, with the mercury stuck at -4° F (-20° C) for weeks. Coal ran out, transportion, the economy and culture came to a standstill; the municipal council established public warming shelters. 1142 people were found starved and frozen in their homes.

region" under international law for the territory of Greater Berlin under inter-Allied administration. In contrast to the other zones it was to be occupied by the forces of all three powers (four, after the inclusion of France).

Even before the end of April, General Eisenhower's forward line had pushed up to the Elbe through the Red Army's planned occupation zone. On July 4, in the course of an exchange of troops, the Americans were the first to march into Berlin, followed by the British and the French. The Control Council moved into headquarters in the former Supreme Court in the Schöneberger Kleistpark. The large conference hall, where, in August 1944, the notorious Nazi *Volksgerichtshof* (Peoples' Court) had passed the death sentence on the men who had attempted to assassinate Hitler on July 20, 1944, became the place where the four

Above: Mayor Ernst Reuter on November 9, 1948. Right: The Anhalter Railway Station, still a ruin to this day.

For the first time since May 1933, Berlin elected a city parliament: on October

20, 1946. Meanwhile, in the surrounding Soviet occupied zone, the Socialists had been put out of action as an independent political power as a result of their forced unification with the Communist Party. The Social Democrats were successful in resisting the merger by means of a strike ballot, but only in Berlin's Western Sector. The newly-formed Communist SED suffered a humiliating defeat in both the overall results and in the Soviet Sector. With 19.8% – compared with 46.4% for the Social Democrats – they wound up back in third place behind the CDU (Christian Democrats), which received 22.2%. The LDP (Liberal Democrats) received 9.3%. Thus, the bottom line was that a convincing majority had decided in favor of the West and a social system based on individual liberty.

The Soviets didn't take their loss of power in the democratically-elected legislative body sitting down. On June 24, 1947, the municipal assembly elected Ernst Reuter, the leading spokesman of Berlin's Social Democrats, as governing mayor. But the Russian commander thwarted his assumption of office with a veto, so that Reuter's deputy, Louise Schröder (SPD), had to take on the difficult post. The Soviet Union transformed its zone into a people's democracy on the Stalinist model. The Western powers aspired toward a parliamentary federal government. In the Council of Foreign Ministers, the Soviet Union insisted upon unreasonable war reparations and a say in the future of the heavily industrialized Ruhr River Valley. On the other hand, within his sphere of influence Stalin blocked the Marshall Plan for the reconstruction of Europe, leading to the division of the continent. As a result, the Western powers decided to merge their zones – as the initial political stage in founding a state with a unified economic and currency system.

Blockade and Airlift

Against this background, trouble arose in the Allied Control Council on March

43

20, 1948. As a protest against the Western powers' unilateral decisions to hammer together a modern German state, Marshall Sokolowski declared the work of the Four Powers' supreme committee ended. The Soviet delegation in the commanders' headquarters cleared their desks – for good – on June 16.

Meanwhile, the Communists' war of nerves against the presence of Western troops continued full blast. Since the lines of communication ran through the eastern zone, the Soviet Union clearly possessed the greater direct leverage. Traffic to and from Helmstedt depended upon previous arrangement with the military commanders. The supervision and maintenance of the Autobahn and railroads was the exclusive reponsibility of the eastern side. Only the use of the three flight corridors had been formally regulated by arrangement within the Control Council at the end of 1945. The system-

Above: Montgomery and Zhukov in Berlin.
Right: A "raisin bomber" about to land.

atic impairment of military and civilian interzonal traffic signalled the beginning of the first Berlin crisis in the spring of 1948. It escalated into an open test of strength on June 23, when Marshall Sokolowski decided to enact a currency reform for the greater area of Berlin analogous to that of the eastern zone. The Western Allies declared the order null and void within their areas of command. They simultaneously arranged for the introduction of the new Deutschmark in the Western zones of occupation as the legal currency in their three sectors.

At midnight, the lights went out in the Western Sector – the electricity coming in from the other zone had been cut off. In the same night, the Soviet military administration called a halt to all road and rail transportation between the Western zones and Berlin. Inland navigation also fell victim to this arbitrary blockade.

Military Governor Lucius D. Clay warned his superiors in Washington that if Berlin should fall, West Germany would follow. On July 1, President Harry

S. Truman announced the decision that the Allies would be staying in Berlin. The western half of the city, with a population of 2.1 million, had food supplies to last 30 days. There was still enough coal on hand for 45 days. For the necessities of survival, Allied experts calculated a transportation requirement of at least 4500 tons per day. If it was to be done at all, the defense of Berlin boiled down to an airlift. From the outset, both the Americans and the British were in the same boat. Mayor Ernst Reuter vouched for the steadfastness of his fellow Berliners. The situation certainly helped the victors and the vanquished of the besieged city to pack away their enmities and become allies.

"Operation Vittles" developed from an improvised shuttle operation to a major logistical undertaking. To relieve pressure on Tempelhof and Gatow, a third airfield in Tegel was hastily built from scratch in a record three months. With meager rations of dried food, but with unbroken morale, the "islanders" endured their fourth postwar winter without coal or light. Less than 100,000 Berliners registered in the Soviet Sector for food and fuel. On the "Easter Parade" of April 15 and 16, 1949, the Airlift reached its climax: 12,940 tons of supplies were flown in on 1398 flights. Behind the scenes, at the United Nations building in New York, secret talks were already underway to end the deadlock. On May 12, at one minute before midnight, the barriers swung up again.

Altogether during the nine months of the blockade, the Western Allies had transported 1.7 million tons of supplies into the city on about 213,000 flights. Seventy Allied airmen and eight German assistants lost their lives in service to a common goal. In the democratic world the name Berlin won a new reputation. At the war's end it was associated primarily with the monstrous crimes of the Hitler regime, during the blockade, however, it

became a symbol of the Western stance against tyranny. The price, however, was the division of the city.

The Cold War in Berlin

The unified municipal administration of Berlin had broken up in the autumn of 1948 in the midst of the maelstrom of the currency dispute. The Communist SED drove the majority of the parliamentary assembly out of the East Berlin city hall with the help of pre-arranged demonstrations. In the constitutionally mandated new elections of December 5, which could now be held only in the Western Sector, 64.5% of all voters confirmed Ernst Reuter as Berlin's spokesman. Meanwhile, hailing itself as the vanguard of a "Democratic Bloc," the SED had wrested unto itself the sole authority in the Soviet Sector. Friedrich Ebert (SED), son of the former president during the Weimar Republic, became the head of the East's separate municipal council. For the next 41 years Berlin remained a divided city. This process was accentuated by the founding of the Federal Republic of Germany and the German Democratic Republic. Each half of the city was linked with one of the two different states, which belonged to two opposing geopolitical camps.

The Parliamentary Council had included Greater Berlin in Bonn's area of authority. The Western Allies suspended the corresponding amendment in Article 23, with the proviso that Berlin would have no voice in the national houses of Parliament "and will not be governed by the federal government either." Thus West Berlin could not become a full-fledged state under the Four Powers Agreement of 1944/45.

Five months after the Bonn constitution took effect, the German Democratic Republic celebrated its founding with a torchlight parade on Unter den Linden on October 7, 1949. All of the Soviet zone's administration, political authorities and cultural establishments had already been concentrated east of the Brandenburg Gate. According to the second amendment of the GDR constitution, all that was needed was the proper label to proclaim East Berlin the capital of the second German state.

The municipal government of West Berlin made its temporary offices in the Schöneberg *Rathaus*, which features a liberty bell donated by the American people. On October 1, 1950, the new constitution took effect, defining Berlin as a "German *Land* (federal region) and city at the same time." The subsequent elections to Berlin's Chamber of Deputies on December 3 resulted in a tripartite Senate of SPD, CDU and FDP (Free Democratic Party), under the leadership of Ernst Reuter. During the preceding dangers, he had become a charismatic father-figure for the people of Berlin. A sudden heart

Right: Workers defend themselves against Soviet tanks on June 17, 1953.

failure felled the "man with the beret," as he was popularly known, on September 29, 1953, in the midst of his work.

The political divisions and West Berlin's isolation became increasingly perceptible during the 1950s. The East-West conflict even overshadowed everyday life. In May 1952 the Soviets prohibited residents of the three Western zones from entering the Soviet Sector. Tens of thousands of West Berliners found themselves shut out from their garden houses and family gravesites on the other side of the city border. During the same year the inner-city telephone lines were severed. In the following year, bus and streetcar transportation followed suit. However, the subways and suburban trains continued crisscrossing the city. Hundreds of thousands commuted daily (from the east) over the open sector borders, and such repeated trips from one system to the other encouraged comparisons.

After the blockade, West Berlin faced a huge mountain of economic and social problems. It had lost its function as a capital city, its hinterlands and the greatest portion of its industry. In 1950 every third person was on welfare. The island-city was declared an official distress area, but was then primped up into the "showcase of the West" with financial shots-in-the-arm from the federal government and the USA. Once again, the Kurfürstendamm with its palatial cinemas shone in its old neon gleam. The alluring shop windows and the unrestrained Western lifestyle exerted their magnetism on the people in the East.

The SED regime, for its part, adorned itself with a showpiece boulevard: 262 feet in width (80 meters), with eight- to ten-storied residential complexes constructed in the Stalinist monumental style, the "first Socialist street of Berlin" – the *Stalinallee* – rose from the rubble of the old Frankfurter Allee. The workers' rebellion of June 17, 1953, flared up right on this prominent construction site, as a

protest against a drastic increase of their expected job-performance quotas. On the previous day masons and carpenters had marched from Strausberger Platz to the ministry headquarters on Leipziger Strasse. They aired their built-up anger over the repressive regime of the despised SED General Secretary Walter Ulbricht ("Pointy-beard – *Spitzbart* – must go!"), called for free elections and the resignation of the government. A general strike was announced for the next day.

On the morning of June 17, tens of thousands of striking workers flooded into East Berlin's governmental district. Two young demonstrators took the red banners down from the Brandenburg Gate. Violent clashes occured with the *Volkspolizei* (People's Police); shots were fired. At 1 p.m. the Soviet military commander declared martial law. Russian tanks bloodily crushed the uprising in East Berlin and other places in the budding Communist "workers'and peasants' state." The number of fatalities is unknown to this day.

The Construction of the Wall

There was only one way left for the residents of East Berlin and the GDR to demonstrate their dissatisfaction. "Voting with ones' feet," as it was called, was most easily done through Berlin. During 1953 a solid 332,000 refugees turned their backs on the GDR.

From 1954 until the end of 1958 the loss of population to emigration reached some 1.5 million, of which half were in the 25 and under age group. Nearly two-thirds of these people had been gainfully employed: jobs in industry and trades were particulary affected. This resulted in an increasing shortage of workers and specialists in East Germany, much to the detriment of the state treasury and the planned economy. SED boss Ulbricht later estimated the losses at 30 billion marks.

Republikflucht (*Flucht* = flight) was declared a punishable act; crossing the border into the Federal Republic became more difficult from year to year. The

Volkspolizei intensified their border checks for traffic to Berlin, however, the loopholes into the "four-sector city" could not be plugged so easily. Night after night at the close of the late news, RIAS, Radio in the American Sector, broadcast the number of refugees that had reported to the official agency dealing with asylum-seekers in West Berlin in the past 24 hours. 90,862 came in 1959; in 1960 there were 152,291. The majority were flown to West Germany at the cost of the federal government.

The SED leadership urged their protectors in the Kremlin to eliminate the "troublemaker West Berlin." The USSR took a second run at driving the Western powers out of Berlin. The land blockade had become a dulled weapon. In response to the wishes of the Allies, the Berlin Senate stockpiled enough supplies to last a year. The Soviet government and party leader Nikita Khrushchev demanded the transformation of West Berlin into a "free, demilitarized city." Simultaneously, in a memorandum from November 27, 1958, to that effect, Moscow sent the Western Allies an ultimatum to negotiate the retreat of their troops within six months. Khrushchev let the ultimatum expire, but the situation remained tense. In 1959 a conference of foreign ministers in Geneva broke up without results. At a summit meeting held in Vienna in early June 1961, with the new US president John F. Kennedy in attendance, Khrushchev threatened to solve the "West Berlin problem" within one year by means of a separate peace treaty with the GDR.

In the US Senate, Kennedy proposed additional military expenditures of US\$ 3.4 billion and boosted the army from 870,000 to one million men. In order to eliminate the last trace of doubt about US determination, he summarized his administration's position on Berlin on July 25 in the *Three Essentials*. These consisted of: 1) Allied right to maintain a presence in Berlin; 2) free access to the city; and 3) Berlin's ability to survive and the freedom of its population. A hysterical war of propaganda on both sides caused the number of refugees to increase explosively in the summer of 1961. From mid-July on there were no weekdays with fewer than 1000 new arrivals. The economic collapse of the GDR was imminent. In early August, at a secret conference of party leaders from the Warsaw Pact states, the decision was made to build the Berlin Wall.

In the night of August 12/13, the border of the Eastern Sector was transformed into a huge army camp. Armed groups of factory workers, the *Volkspolizei* and soldiers of the National Peoples' Army mounted guard. Under the protection of tanks and armored vehicles, rolls of barbed-wire were laid out, pavements torn up and concrete posts driven. Aroused by radio news reports, Berliners

Above: Erecting the wall on August 13, 1961. Right: John F. Kennedy and Willy Brandt after Kennedy's famous speech.

hurried to the scene of events. In impotent fury they had to look on as a bustling, lively city with its familiar, interwoven neighborhood tapestry was torn apart. Erich Honecker, then in charge of security matters in the Central Committee of the SED, directed the action, which had been prepared by the General Staff. The West was taken by surprise, quite literally in its sleep. On this critical Sunday morning in the conference room of the Allied Command, three perplexed city commanders waited in vain for instructions from their capitals.

The Allies confined themselves to belated protests. That they sat still – practically without lifting a finger – during the forcible division of the city, was deeply shocking to the Berliners. It demonstrated that, in fact, the American guarantees ended at the sector boundaries. As a symbol of encouragement, President Kennedy sent Vice President Johnson to Berlin in his stead. The Pentagon also sent a 1500-man task force over the interzonal Autobahn. Former general Clay,

the steadfast hero of the 1948/49 Airlift, returned on special assignment from Kennedy to the focal point of the Cold War. Disputes with GDR border posts concerning the uncontrolled access to East Berlin for American civilians heated up to a critical confrontation by October 1961. US and Russian tanks faced off at the Friedrichstrasse border crossing.

Here, at Checkpoint Charlie, which later became an almost mandatory feature in any spy thriller from the Cold War, Nikita Khrushchev waved affably over the borderline. Five months later President Kennedy appeared on the opposite side. His triumphal visit on June 23, 1963 – which attracted 1.3 million people – reached its peak at a rally before the Schöneberg City Hall with his world famous proclamation: "*Ich bin ein Berliner!*" (I am a Berliner!).

The Divided City

More than ever the residents of the walled city needed moral encouragement

during these years. The trauma of August 13 and the feeling of isolation weighed heavily on peoples' minds and souls. After almost 28 months of division a complicated agreement between the Senate and the GDR was reached on passes permitting West Berliners to visit their relatives in the East for Christmas 1963. In 1966 another agreement established six visiting periods. After this, West Berliners were only permitted to travel "yonder" for urgent family matters.

Through a "Tristate Concept," which treated West Berlin as an "independent political unit," Soviet diplomacy tried to separate the island-city from Bonn. When, despite protests from the East, the Bundestag conferred in the new *Kongresshalle* on April 7, 1965, Russian jet fighters terrorized the population with sonic booms. Carefully planned pin pricks directed against transit and air traffic – just short of a blockade – repeatedly

Above: The annual SED party conference in East Berlin, the proud capital of the GDR.

made plain the vulnerability of the western outpost, which could survive economically and financially only through billions of marks in subsidies from the Federal Republic's capital Bonn.

The GDR's economy stabilized in the shadow of the Wall; the reconstruction of East Berlin began to make visible progress. The immense 1197-foot (365-meter) television tower, visible from every point on the compass, ushered in the "new Socialist design" of the city center around Alexanderplatz. Year by year the GDR perfected the 102-mile (165-km) long fortified line surrounding West Berlin. By the fourth generation the Wall had grown to a height of 13.7 feet (4.2 meters). Like a grotesque tapeworm, the ugly and monstrous inner-city concrete wall cut a swath 28 miles (45 km) in length through the sea of buildings.

Nonetheless, inhabitants of the GDR repeatedly managed to overcome the militarily-secured border installation, some in rather adventurous ways. The number of memorial crosses on the West

Berlin side grew from year to year. The first year of the "anti-fascist protection wall" was especially bloody. Of the 10,315 days of the Wall's existence, 30 of the altogether 80 known or nameless escapees who paid with their lives died during that first year. Reality and symbol in one, the Wall has gone down in history as a monument to inhumanity and – only on the western side – as the largest graffiti gallery in the world.

In the years of greatest threat a rigorous anti-Communism had smothered all of the internal contradictions inherent in the society of a city on the Cold War front. This changed when, in the mid-1960s, a world-wide youth revolt with roots in the US broke out. The generational conflict with the older "blockade-Berliners" flared up particularly over the issue of Americans in Vietnam. The anti-authoritarian university students went out into the streets against the protecting power of the US. With its fresh impetus, the rise of the protest generation revitalized the anachronistic island city. The subculture of the alternative scene had its wellspring in the turbulence of the 1968 rebellion. Its members became involved, through public initiatives, in the politics of the city, and by 1981 could boast for the first time a representative in government from their own list of candidates.

The front lines of the Cold War also started to move. The superpowers began pursuing a policy of détente. Under Willy Brandt, the Social-Liberal coalition government introduced a "New Eastern Policy" (*Neue Ostpolitik*). During the bilateral treaty discussions held in Warsaw, Moscow and East Berlin, the ambassadors of the victorious powers came together in the old Control Council buildings in order to defuse the political crises in the center of Europe. Regardless of their varying legal positions, in the Berlin Accord of September 3, 1971, both sides accepted the status quo as the basis for a pragmatic balancing of their respective interests. They put their common responsibility for the whole of Berlin into practice through establishment of an alternating dispatch of military patrols and co-operation in inter-Allied air traffic. Additional agreements on the inner-German level provided for a regulated coexistence in practical matters. One of the agreements finally secured the unhindered operation of through-traffic.

The GDR authorities agreed to refrain from arbitrary checks on people and cars. In the following 15 years the number of travelers to and from Berlin using the roads tripled from 7.8 to 23.9 million annually. Telephone connections were restored between the two halves of the city, and restrictions on visitors from West Berlin were eased. The exchange of permanent missions normalized relations between Bonn and East Berlin. From a showplace of confrontation the city was transformed into a test ground for peaceful coexistence, but the gash through Berlin remained. Tourists from the West visiting the divided metropolis during the 1970s and 1980s found two fundamentally different political communities. Despite everything that separated them, though, the two Berlins were attached to each other like Siamese twins.

On the one side was a big city pulsating around the clock, an open-minded cultural metropolis of two million people. West Berlin, still Germany's largest industrial center and the seat of numerous federal agencies, sought and found new tasks as a super-regional center for service industries. Politically, legally and economically incorporated into the structure of the Federal Republic, by international law the city-state was under the sovereignty of the three Western powers, a fact which was reflected in a number of occupation laws, for example, the "temporary identity card" for West Berliners and the omission of compulsory service in the armed forces. East Berlin, with another 1.2 million resi-

dents, was the showcase of the SED state. Erich Honecker, who took power in the State Council offices after Ulbricht was deposed, interpreted the preferential improvement of the GDR capital as a "concern of the entire republic." Prussian heritage came back into favor under the native Saarlander, whose principal aim was to indoctrinate the citizens of the GDR with a separate national identity. In 1981 the equestrian statue of Old Fritz returned to its customary place in Berlin's historic center, and the great architectural monuments of classicism rose again in their old magnificence. "Socialist Berlin" selfassuredly held separate festivities for the 750th anniversary of the city in 1987.

Berlin – Unified Again

The senescent SED leadership stood firm on its policy of separation, although

Above: Selling GDR flags at the Brandenburg Gate – symbol of the collapse of the GDR. Right: A job well done!

entirely different signals were coming from Moscow's General Secretary Mikhail Gorbachev. While the world around them was changing under the banner of *glasnost* and *perestroika*, the population of the GDR waited in vain for reforms. Blind to the mistakes of "real existing Socialism," on January 18, 1989, Honecker boasted that the Wall through Berlin would "still be standing in 50 and even in 100 years, if the reasons at hand had not yet been eliminated." However, power slipped away from the obstinate cronies in the SED Politburo more rapidly than expected. Honecker and the old guard made their last public appearance on October 7 at a pompous military parade for the 40th anniversary of the German Democratic Republic. No real mood of jubilation could be drummed up, however, due to the spectacular mass exodus underway at the time. At the beginning of September Hungary had opened its western borders to citizens of the GDR. Each day thousands took advantage of the chance to flee. Others followed the route through the Federal Republic's embassies in Prague and Warsaw, and in the GDR the rapidly sprouting opposition would not allow itself to be intimidated any more with police terror. A powerful movement guided by peace and environmental groups protesting Stalinist conditions spilled into the street with the cry: "*Wir sind das Volk!*" (We are the people!). On November 4 more than half a million people marched through the streets of East Berlin's inner-city in support of democracy and freedom of expression. At that point, Czechoslovakia became the second "brother country" to open up the Iron Curtain. Egon Krenz, Erich Honecker's successor, saw that a radical change of course was necessary.

In the early evening of November 9, 1989, the GDR television network broadcast a press conference following the 10th plenary session of the SED Central Committee. Toward the end, SED Politbureau member Günter Schabowski mentioned almost in passing that the GDR had opened its borders. "Private travel abroad" could be applied for immediately, without special preconditions. It took several more hours before the sensational importance of this news got around, but from then on there was no stopping the flood. The East Berliners hurried *en masse* to the sector border crossings; everyone wanted to be among the first at the opening. The border guards finally capitulated before the onrush. They opened up the gates and let everyone through. On the same night tens of thousands from the eastern section of the city took the chance for an excursion across the Wall. On the other side they were received by jubilant throngs of West Berliners. Champagne corks popped, complete strangers embraced one another, and nobody was ashamed of shedding tears. Soon the Ku'damm was full of Trabis and Wartburgs, the automotive symbols of the GDR. Before the Brandenburg Gate the crowds danced

atop the Wall. The whole event was broadcast to the wider world via live television. Berlin celebrated the "most jubilant people's festival in its history." Walter Momper, governing mayor of West Berlin, rejoiced over the end of the city's division: "This is the day we've awaited for 28 years." Those who hadn't learned of the historic events of the previous night until listening to the radio the next morning thought they had awoken in another city. The Wall was gone.

This was the end of the Cold War and the postwar period. Since then Berlin has grown back into being one city again. And with the 1991 decision of the German Bundestag to move parliament and government to Berlin, the city has regained its status of national capital. However, the Berliners don't expect the arrival of the first members of parliament until the next century. As a sovereign, free and unified city and, since 1994, with no special status under occupying powers, Berlin is on its way to becoming a normal European metropolis.

BOULEVARDS AND SQUARES

KURFÜRSTENDAMM

BRANDENBURG GATE

UNTER DEN LINDEN

ALEXANDERPLATZ

KURFÜRSTENDAMM

There is scarcely anyone who does not associate Berlin with the **Kurfürstendamm** almost immediately. Every larger German city has its own distinguishing landmark, usually a church, a cathedral, or a castle. Only Berlin is identified with a street – the Kurfürstendamm, a chic avenue familiar to the globetrotter.

A classy strip, shopping El Dorado and entertainment hub in one, the Kurfürstendamm is simply and insolently referred to as the **Ku'damm** by locals. Since the reunification of Berlin the Ku'damm has been polishing its glamor again. The old mix of cosmopolitanism and parochialism had led to its gradual decline. Now, however, hotels, cinemas, department stores and shops are undergoing expensive renovations in order to keep up with Friedrichstrasse in the east, which is recapturing its prewar flair.

History of a Boulevard

The Ku'damm already existed in 1542, though it was known back then as the

Preceding pages: The ICC at night. The Zehner Bridge spanning the Tegeler Fliess. Left: Skyline showing the Gedächtniskirche and the television tower.

Knüppeldamm. It consisted of a scarcely paved riding path for the electors who rode from the *Stadtschloss* (City Castle) on Unter den Linden to their hunting lodge in Grunewald. This state of affairs remained unchanged for centuries, until 1871, when the chancellor of the newly-founded German Empire, Otto von Bismarck, returned to Berlin from Paris. He had seen the Bois de Boulogne in the French capital and admired the Champs Elysées. He wanted to create an equally splendid boulevard for the German capital as well. The Iron Chancellor fought for almost ten years until, finally, the "Kurfürstendamm Association" was established in 1882 with the aim of transforming the riding path into a showpiece avenue.

Bismarck had a very precise conception of his magnificent road: it was to be 2.3 miles long (3.8 km) from Grunewald to the Zoo, with a width of 184 feet (56 meters), featuring a riding path in its middle and lined on both sides with splendid apartment buildings. These lordly edifices, richly decorated with balconies and turrets, ornamented with cornices and intricate stucco work, provided an ideal living situation for well-to-do tenants. The marble staircases and columned halls richly decorated with mirrors and sculpted figures showed off the wealth of the occupants. Only Bismarck's fondest dream, an equestrian monument of himself on "his" boulevard, has remained unfulfilled to this day.

Around Breitscheidplatz

Those who want to truly experience the Ku'damm and the city of Berlin ought probably to begin their stroll at **Breitscheidplatz**. This square was formerly called Auguste-Viktoria-Platz, but after World War Two it received the name of the SPD Reichstag representative Rudolf Breitscheid, who was killed in a concentration camp.

The plaza is dominated by the **Gedächtniskirche** (Kaiser Wilhelm Memorial Church), constructed between 1891 and 1895 in memory of Kaiser Wilhelm I, and almost completely destroyed in the war. The ruins, which are called *Hohler Zahn* (Hollow Tooth) by tongue-in-cheek locals, would have been torn down after the war if things had gone according to the wishes of the then-Senator for Housing and Construction. However, polls taken at the end of the 1950s turned out in favor of preserving the church. In 1961 a new church, designed by Prof. Egon Eiermann, was constructed on the ruins of the tower. You might argue over the beauty of the new structure, but not over the fascinating play of bluish light in its interior.

Today's church-ensemble is not meant to commemorate any monarch, but rather the horrors of war. Its steps have been used as a forum for vigils, rallies and happenings for many years. These gatherings have frequently had a rather unreal appearance before a background of glowing advertisement signs. Across from the church, the Mercedes star shining on the roof of the Europa Center is brighter than all the other illuminated billboards on the plaza.

In front of the Europa Center stands the **Weltkugelbrunnen** (Globe Foun-

tain) designed by Joachim Schmettau. It is believed to circulate some 105,000 gallons (400,000 liters) of water per hour. In the summertime there are swarms of people at, in front of, and not infrequently *in* the fountain; sometimes the atmosphere recalls that of a popular festival. People meet each other here, chat, watch performances of street theater, and cool their feet in the splashing water. In short: everyone does just about as they please and no-one gets upset about it. The same applies to the punks and the homeless who wait around here, often the whole day long, and ask passers-by for a spare mark or two.

The people of Berlin are tolerant and aware of the fact that a big city has many

THE KURFÜRSTENDAMM

0   750 m

faces, including those of poverty, which can be seen here right alongside the extravagant world of consumerism of the **Europa Center**. By the way, a genuine Berliner never says center, but always *Zenter* ("z" is pronounce "ts"). In the 19th century the Wilhelmshallen, which featured the renowned **Romanisches Café**, stood on this location. In the Golden Twenties, Berlin's bohemian culture, the poets and thinkers, caricaturists, designers, theater critics, actors and actresses all came together here.

In the postwar years, life on Breitscheidplatz was a good deal quieter. The Romanisches Café had succumbed to the hail of bombs, and on the barren plot surrounding the plaza there were wooden shacks and the tent of a traveling wrestler. The Europa Center wasn't built until 1965. Incidentally, it was also the first write-off speculation project in the city. About 100 stores, restaurants, the cabaret **Die Stachelschweine**, the **Royal Palast** (five movie theaters under one roof, allegedly with the largest projection screen in Europe), and the **Tourist Office** (entrance on Budapester Strasse) provide an ample variety of diversions and amusement here.

Certainly there are a great number of shops and boutiques in the Europa Center and on the Ku'damm, but the small retailers are being increasingly forced out by high commercial rents. DM 400 (approximately US $225) per square meter

(10.7 sq feet) is about the norm, which is second only to Paris. This did not put off the U.S. movie colossus, Warner Brothers, which opened the largest **studio store** on the continent in the Europa Center. Even if you don't like stuffed animals, you should drop by: the four-horse chariot from atop the Brandenburg Gate and the Victory Column are interpreted here in a novel way, namely as animated comic-strip figures.

Today a stroll around the various levels of the Europa Center is enjoyable in any weather. In earlier days you often had to brave the bad weather in the drafty yard and be properly bundled up for your contemplation of the shops. As compensation, there was a skating rink in the middle of the courtyard. Later, the entire area was covered with a glass dome and the skating rink gave way to an artificial waterfall.

Above: Breitscheidplatz, the heart of the western part of the city. Right: The "Clock of Flowing Time" in the Europa Center.

Another eye-catcher in the Europa Center is the **Uhr der fliessenden Zeit** (Clock of Flowing Time), a technological artwork constructed by the Parisian physicist Bernard Gitton. In this 13-meter-high sculpture various colored liquids demonstrate drop-by-drop how quickly time slips away. The Berliners' predilection for jocular nicknames didn't stop here. They call this the *Fruchtsaft-Automat* (Fruit-juice Machine).

The building with the flat roof extending along the north side of the plaza on **Budapester Strasse** is the former *Staatliche Kunsthalle* (State Art Gallery), under which there is a shopping arcade with various souvenir and jewelry shops, as well as a bookstore and the office of the **Berliner Festspiele** (festival).

Also on the north side of the square is a futuristic blue spherical building. A fair number of shops and cafés have been opening here, only to close down soon afterward. ARD, one of Germany's public television stations, started producing a program on this location in 1998.

Wittenbergplatz and the KaDeWe

Breitscheidplatz connects the Ku'-damm and the **Tauentzien** (as the Berliners call Tauentzienstrasse); the latter leads to Wittenbergplatz and the *Kaufhaus des Westens* (Department Store of the West), called simply KaDeWe by Berliners. Tauentzien is strictly a shopping street with a wide range of shops from the branch stores of cheap fashion chains to Berlin's finest lamp shop.

The crowning glory of this shopping strip is the **KaDeWe**, whose labyrinthian interior extends over 258,000 square feet (24,000 sq meters) of retail space (equivalent to the Olympic stadium and four soccer fields). When the store was opened in 1907 by businessman Adolf Jahndorf, the Berliners warmed to it very quickly, although the city's west side was not yet the shopping paradise it is today. In 1927 the department store merged with the Hertie chain, becoming its flagship and having continually expanded

since then. Even its almost total destruction during World War Two couldn't shake the reputation of the store, and by 1956 it again shone with its old luster. Over the last few years this most financially successful of German department stores has been renovated once more: two great atriums which had been walled up since the war have been reopened and clad with sandstone slabs. Glass elevators glide silently up to the 7th floor where the store's conservatory, with its palms and waterfalls, offers gastronomic pleasures high above the roofs of Berlin. A huge glass dome lets in light from the blue sky.

Wittenbergplatz is dominated by the building of the **U-Bahn** (subway) **station**. The station was constructed from 1911 to 1913 after plans by then star architect Alfred Genander. After the first subway line was built between Stralauer Tor and the Zoo, the spot was occupied by little ticket booths, which were also designed by Genander. When he then received the contract to build a "first class high-speed railway station," he designed the structure in neoclassical style. Unfortunately, the beautiful stone building fell victim to the bombs of World War Two. The heaviest of the damage was not repaired until 1951.

At the beginning of the 1980s the station was finally put under historical preservation and painstakingly renovated for some DM 3.5 million. Using old photographs, the Art-Nouveau ornamentation and the yellow and turquoise majolica tiles were faithfully restored.

A Stroll down the Ku'damm

The way back to the Ku'damm leads by a gleaming metallic sculpture on the median strip at the corner of the **Marburger Strasse**: two oversized chain links, each broken in two places. This work of art, entitled *Berlin,* was created by the artist couple Matschinsky-Denninghoff and symbolizes the long division of the city. The sculpture is on long-term loan from the Deutsche Bank to Berlin; it was a contribution for the city's 750th anniversary festivities. In 1987 eight sculptures virtually transformed the Ku'damm and Tauentzien into an open-air gallery. Most of these artworks – valued at DM 1.8 million in all – were dismantled.

Our stroll down the Ku'damm begins at Kurfürstendamm No. 11, behind Breitscheidplatz on the right side of the street. The first house numbers disappeared in a wondrous manner as a result of a re-routing of the street. Until 1925 the Ku'-damm began behind the Europa Center, and the present-day Budapester Strasse was its last section.

All the construction sins committed during the 1950s and 1960s are, unfortunately, all too plainly visible on both sides of the street, creating a regrettable backdrop for the present-day Ku'damm.

Right: Café Kranzler, one of the great institutions of Berlin's social life on the Kurfürstendamm.

Alfred Messel, the builder of the old **Wertheim Department Store** would no doubt holler for a return to the good old days of architecture in the presence of the present edifice on the Ku'damm. Nevertheless, next to the department store stands one of the few examples of the old glory of Berlin: the **Marmorhaus** (House of Marble), a multi-screen movie theater, is a fine place to take a break. Cafés and the big first-run cinema houses have made the Ku'damm an attractive entertainment boulevard since the 1920s. The Marmorhaus is one of Berlin's oldest cinemas. It was opened in 1913 as a palatial luxury cinema and until recently had declined into a lackluster assemblage of projection halls. Today this movie palace, now renovated, is once again popular with moviegoers.

Café Kranzler, diagonally opposite, is famous indeed, but don't bother looking for the elegance of days of yore. The Kranzler – a Berlin institution for 150 years – has lost much of its polish since moving from Friedrichstrasse to the Ku'-damm after World War Two. Irate critics even claim that the Kranzler has degenerated into an egregious cake-and-coffee joint for Berlin's retirees, primarily the famous widows from Wilmersdorf, and a revolving door for groups of tourists. Nonetheless, going to the café-bakery is still among the Berliners' favorite activities, and what is better than lounging around in front of **Café Möhring** or the Kranzler in the summertime and experiencing the tumult on the Kurfürstendamm?

The unsightly **Ku'damm-Eck** opposite Joachimstaler Strasse, a collage of porno cinemas, cheap stores, the Berlin Panoptikum and the **Café des Westens** (known as "Café Megalomania" in its heyday after World War One) is about to be torn down to make way for a brand new edifice with shops and a hotel.

Café Kranzler is not far from the **Kempinski Hotel Bristol Berlin**, another

Berlin institution. On the way is the new **Aschinger**, formerly located at the Zoo. It was once famous for pea soup, but then fell victim to the age of fast food. Nowadays it continues to satiate fans of hearty Berlin food at its new location in the **Haus Wien** right on the Ku'damm.

The Kempinski is situated on the corner of Fasanenstrasse, possibly the most stylish side-street leading off the Kurfürstendamm. Many luxurious businesses have established themselves here in the last few years, especially in the **Fasaneneck** and the **Uhlandpassage**. Berlin's **Jüdisches Gemeinde Zentrum** (Jewish Community Center) is located on the way to the Kantstrasse. Berlin's largest synagogue once stood here, but only the arched doorway remained after the temple's destruction by the Nazis in 1938. It was incorporated into the current modern building. In the opposite direction are the **Käthe-Kollwitz Museum**, which honors the Berlin artist with a permanent exhibition, and the **Literaturhaus**, which caters to literary fans with readings and

exhibits. Those seeking a break from the overfilled Ku'damm cafés can withdraw to the dignified **Café Wintergarten**.

On the corner of the Ku'damm and Fasanenstrasse is the cozy **Café Leysieffer**, which was opened in the former Chinese embassy, and then there is the **King's Teagarden**, where you can make a selection from among more than 200 varieties of tea to strains of classical music. Next door, the **Astor** beckons to a night of film-viewing in its splendid halls.

Further on, in the direction of Halensee, is **Uhlandstrasse**, on the corner of which stands the **Maison de France**, the French cultural center in West Berlin. In the same building, **Cinéma Paris** (one of the better cinemas on the Ku'damm) presents Gallic film culture. **Galerie Brusberg**, one of the most renowned art galleries in Berlin, is housed in a gleaming white building opposite.

Twinkling in tones of orange and red on the median strip just past Uhlandstrasse is the **Mengenlehre Uhr** (Set Theory Clock). Across Uhlandstrasse is

the **Ku'damm-Karree**, a shopping arcade with pubs for tourists, small stores, and even popular stages, **the Theater am Kurfürstendamm** and the **Komödie**.

Rising up from the median strip on **Bleibtreustrasse** stands the **Pyramide** by Josef Erben, with a height of 42 feet and a breadth of 131 feet (13 by 40 meters). This sculpture is one of the few remaining from the 750th anniversary festivities. International fashion designers have opened a slew of exclusive boutiques between Bleibtreustrasse and **Leibnizstrasse**.

The buildings on the four corners of the intersection of **Wielandstrasse** have either been reconstructed or are in original condition. One of these buildings was almost totally destroyed by a hotel fire in 1988, just after it had been renovated at a huge cost; only the façade remained. It has since been completely restored.

Above: View of the Ku'damm. Right: Enjoying the weather at a Ku'damm outdoor café.

One block further on, on **Leibnizstrasse**, there is another magnificent example of a manorial residence of old Berlin, the **Iduna Haus**. In this case, however, only the façade has retained its original condition, the rest is all a brand new construction.

Passing by **Olivaer Platz** and **Adenauerplatz** you arrive at **Lehniner Platz**, where you can scarcely overlook the architecturally remarkable building of the **Schaubühne** designed by Erich Mendelsohn between 1926 and 1928. The renowned Schaubühne is without a doubt one of the best theaters in the world.

Finally, where the Kurfürstendamm ends beyond the **Halensee Bridge** at Rathenauplatz, the Grunewald residential area begins. At Rathenauplatz there is one further monument from the "art-boulevard": action artist Wolf Vostell set some old Cadillacs on end next to each other and embedded them in concrete. The demolition costs have been estimated at about 60,000 DM; when added to the artist's honorarium (DM 50,000)

and the installation costs (DM 120,000), the yield is quite a large sum, exceeding the value of the work itself by a large margin. It's too bad that the East German Trabant in concrete, which some practical joker put next to the Vostell sculpture one night, has disappeared: someone paid a substantial amount to give it a loving home.

Via Kantstrasse to the Zoo Station

Another important street to see in Berlin is **Kantstrasse**, which runs parallel to the Ku'damm and can be reached by any Ku'damm side-street you choose.

Savignyplatz, which straddles Kantstrasse, is well worth a more careful investigation for its numerous shops and cafés – especially under the S-Bahn viaducts. This rectangular park was named after the Prussian Minister of Justice and legal scholar Friedrich Karl von Savigny (1779-1861). The plaza was given a fresh shine for Berlin's 750th anniversary celebrations. The 19th-century pavement mosaic was carefully restored all around the square. The small park was also given a face-lift. And so Savignyplatz has once again become an oasis providing a calm spot in the middle of the city.

From Savignyplatz, two narrow pedestrian streets lead past the **S-Bahn Arches**, towards **Bleibtreustrasse**, and also towards **Uhlandstrasse**. The two thoroughfares now house cafés, art galleries and exclusive stores.

A little further on is the imposing structure that houses the **Theater des Westens** (Theater of the West), designed in 1896 by Bernhard Sehring and elaborately restored in 1984. Since 1987, artistic director Helmut Baumann has managed to transform the theater into one of the best stages for musicals in Europe, with such productions as *Cabaret* and *La Cage aux Folles,* and Broadway guest performances like *Porgy and Bess.*

Around the corner, on Fasanenstrasse, is the Ludwig-Erhard-Haus; a steel and glass construction resembling an armadillo which houses, among other things,

the stock exchange. Right opposite, a new trademark of Berlin soars up to the heavens, the **Kant Dreieck** (Kant Triangle) of the KapHag Group. The shining white metal sail on top of this office skyscraper is certainly a matter of taste. At least it does turn with the wind. To make way for this modern piece of architecture, a number of rundown stores that once gave Kantstrasse a rather shabby appearance were demolished. But Kantstrasse still does not look perfectly polished in spite of the new building. Some sections in the proximity of Bahnhof Zoo look quite dilapidated. Cheap import and export shops from eastern Europe give the streetscape its dominant colors.

This could change radically in the future if some of the planned construction projects are carried out. For example, the Victoria insurance company is planning a 524-foot-long and 180-foot-high (160 by 55 meters) complex stretching between

Above: Berliner Weisse with syrup – something every visitor to Berlin should try.

the Kant Triangle and Café Kranzler. And the Zoo-Fenster, or Window on the Zoo, a 377-foot (115-meter) office and retail building is being planned for the Kantstrasse, Hardenbergstrasse, and Joachimstaler Strasse triangle at a cost of DM 350 million.

Bahnhof Zoo (Zoo Station), located near Kantstrasse, has been thoroughly renovated in recent years, although with its gloomy passageways and generally seedy surroundings it is still a far cry from being a high-class train station. Nonetheless, you should take a look around here, even though the days of the notorious drug-scene at the Zoo – setting for the poignant film *Christiane F., We the Children of Zoo Station* – are a thing of the past. Nowadays this station is a gathering place for many of the city's poor and homeless. The crime in this area is basically limited to petty offences, however. It is not dangerous for tourists, either. In addition, the plaza in front of the gold-colored wall clock is a thermometer of social change in Germany worth checking on: before the currency unification of July 1, 1990, money was exchanged here at black market rates and minor deals were also made. In the same year gypsies and other refugees from Romania begged here for the bare necessities of life. Today the city's stranded are again among their own kin.

One of the most unpleasant shopping arcades in Berlin is on **Joachimstaler Strasse**, which connects the Zoo to the Ku'damm. It is lined with cheap pubs, porno cinemas, shish-kebab stands and a 24-hour flower stand. After crossing Kantstrasse and bypassing the Karstadt-Sporthaus, which is located in the former discount department store **Bilka**, you will arrive back at the Ku'damm.

If you are not up to continuing your tour of the city on foot, you can pick up a sightseeing tour in a double-decker bus between Joachimstaler Strasse and the intersection of Uhlandstrasse.

KURFÜRSTENDAMM

Transportation: The U-Bahn lines No. 2, 9, and 12 stop at the Zoo; lines No. 9 and 15 at the Kurfürstendamm, lines No. 1, 2, 12, and 15 at Wittenbergplatz, and line No. 7 at Adenauerplatz.

Slower but more interesting are the bus rides in the *Grossen Gelben* (Big Yellows): lines No. 119, 129, and 219 go from Halensee to Wittenbergplatz down the entire Ku'damm and stop very frequently.

Cafés and Restaurants

There are countless cafés, snack bars and restaurants around the Ku'damm (see pp. 187, 193; hence here is a small selection only).

Aschinger, Kurfürstendamm 26, tel. 882 55 58, daily 9 a.m.-1 a.m., Fri, Sat to 2 a.m.

Bovril, Kurfürstendamm 184, tel. 881 84 61, Mon-Sat 11-1 a.m.

Café Adlon, Kurfürstendamm 69, tel. 883 76 82, daily 8 a.m.-midnight.

Café Kranzler, Kurfürstendamm 18/19, tel. 882 69 11, daily 8 a.m.-midnight.

Café Leysieffer, Kurfürstendamm 218, tel. 885 74 80, daily 9 a.m.-10 p.m.

Café Wintergarten, in the "Literaturhaus Berlin," Fasanenstr. 23, tel. 882 54 14, daily 9:30 a.m.-1 a.m.

Glaskuppel Restaurant (with glass cupola) in the KaDeWe, Tauentzienstr. 21, 8 a.m., 7th floor, tel. 212 10, Mon-Sat, 9 a.m.-6:30 p.m.

Gosch, Kurfürstendamm 212, tel. 88 68 28 00, Sun-Fri 11 a.m.-10 p.m., Sat till midnight.

Hard Rock Café, Meineckestr. 21, tel. 88 46 20, daily noon-2 a.m.

Le Marché, Kurfürstendamm 14, tel. 882 75 78, daily 8 a.m.- midnight.

Lubitsch, Bleibtreustr. 47, tel. 882 37 56, daily 10-1 a.m.

Mövenpick in the Europa Center, tel. 264 76 30, daily 8 a.m.-midnight; Fri, Sat till 1 a.m.

Paris Bar, Kantstr. 152, tel. 313 80 52, daily noon-2 a.m.

Cinemas around the Ku'damm

Book your movie tickets well in advance or make sure you line up an hour or so before the screening. Special rates are frequently on offer on Tuesdays and Wednesdays (discounted ticket prices of DM 6 to 8 for any film; the usual ticket price ranges from DM 9 to 15).

Astor, Kurfürstendamm 217, tel. 881 11 08.

Broadway, Tauentzienstr. 8 (in the Minicity), tel. 26 55 02 76.

Cinéma Paris, Ku'damm 211, tel. 881 31 19.

Delphi, Kantstr. 12a, tel. 312 10 26.

Europa-Studio in Europa Center, tel. 261 79 07.

Filmbühne Wien, Kurfürstendamm 26, tel. 881 48 88.

Filmkunst 66 + 66 1/2, Bleibtreustr. 12, tel. 882 17 53.

Film-Palast Berlin, Kurfürstendamm 225, tel. 883 85 51 (one of the most beautiful and comfortable movie houses in Berlin; features a unique sound system in the Art Deco hall).

Gloria Palast/Gloriette, Kurfürstendamm 12, tel. 885 43 19.

Hollywood, Kurfürstendamm 65, tel. 883 50 77.

Marmorhaus, Ku'damm 236, tel. 881 15 22.

Royal Palast in the Europa Center, tel. 230 91 60.

Zoo-Palast, Hardenbergstr. 29a, tel. 25 41 47 77.

Theaters on the Ku'damm

Schaubühne am Lehniner Platz, Kurfürstendamm 153, tel. 89 00 23.

Theater and **Komödie am Kurfürstendamm**, Kurfürstendamm 206, tel. 883 10 03 or 47 02 10 10.

Vaganten-Bühne, Kantstr. 12a, tel. 312 45 29.

Sights, Museums

Amerika Haus, Hardenbergstr. 22-24, tel. 310 00 10, Mon-Fri 11 a.m.-5 p.m..

British Council, Hardenbergstr. 20, tel. 31 109 90, lectures, exhibitions.

Europa Center with **Tourist Information** (entrance on Budapester Str., tel. 25 00 25), cabaret and revue show (see p. 215).

Jüdisches Gemeindehaus Berlin (Jewish Community Center), Charlottenburg, Fasanenstr. 79, tel. 88 02 80, lectures, readings, and exhibitions.

Kaiser-Wilhelm-Gedächtniskirche, Breitscheidplatz, tel. 218 50 23, Memorial Hall in the old tower: Mon-Sat 10 a.m.-4:30 p.m.; New Church (Neue Kirche): daily 9 a.m.-7 p.m.

Käthe-Kollwitz-Museum, Fasanenstr. 24, tel. 882 52 10, Wed-Mon 11 a.m.-6 p.m.

Königliche Porzellan-Manufaktur (Royal Porcelain Manufactory), Charlottenburg, Kurfürstendamm 27 (in Hotel Kempinski Bristol Berlin; Fasanenstrasse entrance), tel. 886 72 10, Mon-Fri 10 a.m.-7 p.m., Sat 10 a.m.-4 p.m. Exhibition and sale of all wares from the manufactory.

Kunstforum der Grundkreditbank (Art Forum of the Grundkredit Bank), Budapester Str. 35, tel. 20 90 58 30, daily 10 a.m.-6 p.m.

Literaturhaus Berlin, Fasanenstr. 23, tel. 882 65 52 (with a bookstore and the Café Wintergarten, readings and changing exhibitions).

Maison de France, Kurfürstendamm 211, tel. 885 90 20, lectures, exhibitions.

Villa Grisebach, former city mansion, now the Pels-Leusden art gallery, Fasanenstr. 25; Mon-Fri 10 a.m.-6:30 p.m., Sat 10 a.m.-2 p.m.

AROUND THE BRANDENBURG GATE

"When you come into Berlin, it's just to your right," is how painter Max Liebermann gave directions to his studio in his typically cocky Berlin manner. As one of the leading representatives of Impressionism in Germany, this famous artist and honorary citizen of Berlin lived for nearly 40 years on **Pariser Platz**, in house number seven, directly on the northern side of the Brandenburg Gate.

It is extremely hard to imagine that the barren square on the eastern side of the Brandenburg Gate was once among Berlin's choicest pieces of real estate. Historical pictures show it decked out in its finest attire, with the stately palaces of the nobility which bordered the square as a closed architectural ensemble extending from north to south. "Berlin's reception room" played a prominent role in international politics. The French, American and Dutch embassies stood here at the entrance to the government quarter. Redern Palace, at the corner of Wilhelmstrasse, which was expanded by architect Karl Friedrich Schinkel, was replaced by the legendary luxury hotel Adlon in 1905. However, it will all shine again with its former glory in coming years: the **Hotel Adlon** reopened in 1997, and the embassies of France, Great Britain, and the US may move back to the Brandenburg Gate. Pariser Platz is a huge construction site at present, but in a few years it will be Berlin's most beautiful plaza.

From 1907 on, the Royal – later Prussian – Academy of Arts, which Max Liebermann presided over from 1920 to 1932, was located in the former Arnim Palace. It was regarded as one of the most beautiful exhibition halls in Berlin. As a meager token of the original construction, one of the side wings still remains

Left: "Golden Elsa," as the Berliners call the Victoria atop the Victory Column.

standing at Pariser Platz number four. The East Berlin Academy still uses it as a workshop and gallery.

The Brandenburg Gate

The **Brandenburg Gate** was inaugurated without pomp or bathos on August 6, 1791, as one of Berlin's 14 city gates. The record states "that the same military guard took up watch at the newly built station at this gate." Adjacent Pariser Platz received its name in 1814 to commemorate the return of the Prussian troops from Paris. They staged a traditional victory march here, casting a patriotic glow on the Brandenburg Gate. Prussia's glory was already long a thing of the past when, on the night of October 3/4, 1990, hundreds of thousands of people from East and West celebrated the unification of Germany around the illuminated monument.

At the end of the 18th century Berlin numbered a good 150,000 inhabitants. As late as 1866/67, the so-called *Akzisemauer* (Excise Wall) still ran all around the residence. Whoever wanted to enter or leave the city was required to pass through one of the designated customs gates for the purpose of a "visitation" by the state treasury. Some of these gates' names, for example, Hallesches Tor, Oranienburger Tor and Schlesisches Tor, are still on the map of the city; but only the most splendid of these, the Brandenburg Gate, can still be seen at its traditional location.

Frederick the Great (1740-1786) had the Unter den Linden promenade expanded into an avenue. His nephew and successor, Friedrich Wilhelm II (1786-1797), added the Brandenburg Gate as a dignified conclusion to the western end of the street. A plain gate consisting of posts had stood at that spot from 1737 until it was torn down in 1788. Carl Gotthard Langhans (1732-1808) was responsible for the architectural renewal, and he

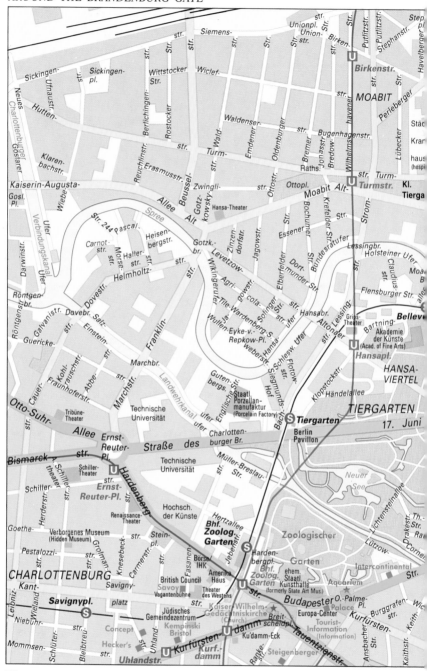

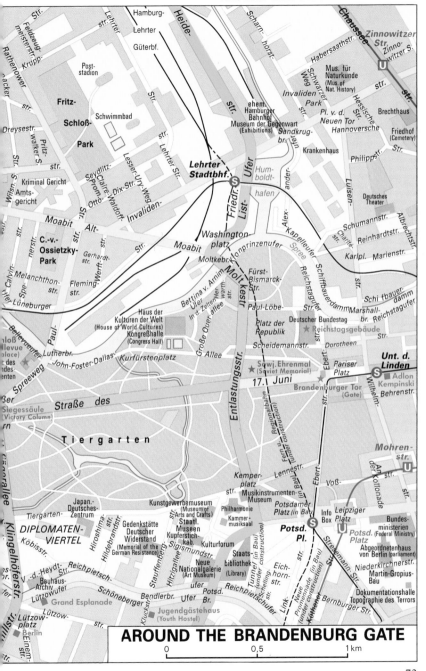

AROUND THE BRANDENBURG GATE

0   0,5   1 km

no longer followed the rules of Baroque, the prevailing style until then. In accordance with the new bourgeois pulse of the times, the chief building director, who had been invited to Berlin from Silesia, was inspired by the spirit and aesthetics of classical antiquity, specifically by the porticos of Greek temple courtyards.

Even if the design's general arrangement was based on the propylaea of the Acropolis in Athens, the Brandenburg Gate was "no mere imitation, but an intelligent new creation of significant monumental effect," as Richard Borrmann emphasized in 1893 in his seminal work on Berlin's monuments. Langhans crowned the portal with a victory chariot carrying as a symbolic figure the Goddess of Peace, Eirene. "The quadriga standing on the attic represents the triumph of peace," he wrote. The idea of a peace gate corresponded with the

Above: The grand old Hotel Adlon after renovations. Right: The Brandenburg Gate illuminated at night.

"owner's" intentions; "Fat Willy," as the Berliners called their corpulent monarch, wasn't interested in military conquests. The state treasury's 110,000 talers for the Brandenburg Gate were a durable investment. Construction of the 65-foot (20-meter) high sandstone monument lasted two years. It is 215 feet wide and 36 feet deep (65.5 by 11 meters). Of the five openings, the middle one was reserved for members of the ruling house.

To crown the monument, sculptor Gottfried Schadow (1764-1850) created the copper **Quadriga**. The 19-foot (6-meter) high statue was put into place in 1793. The Potsdam coppersmith Emanuel Jury executed the design. His uncle in Berlin, Heinrich Jury, who operated a smithy at the Spittelmarkt, had twelve daughters. One of them, the well-shaped Rieke, modelled for the chariot rider, thus becoming anonymously famous throughout the country.

The Brandenburg Gate was conceived as the entryway to the capital. In contradiction to some apocryphal stories, the

quadriga was never turned around from west to east. "The good woman has also had her destiny...", mused German writer Heinrich Heine. In 1806 Emperor Napoleon had her kidnapped and took her to his capital. Following his defeat, Prussian soldiers brought the statue back to Berlin from Paris.

The insult had been repaired, and the Brandenburg Gate became a national symbol. Patriotic enthusiasm reached new heights when Friedrich Wilhelm III re-inaugurated the Quadriga at its accustomed place on August 7, 1814. To commemorate this victory, court architect Schinkel had the goddess modified to a Victoria. On her victory staff she now carried a military medal he designed himself, the Iron Cross. The Prussian eagle was enthroned on the oakleaf wreath.

The Prussian monarchy adopted "the most beautiful gate in all of Europe," according to the Berlin newspapers, as a backdrop for pompous parades. But the gate was also witness to the revolution of March 1848, when rebellious Berlin took

to the streets to fight for democratic rights.

Since the founding of the Reich in 1871, Berlin, as Germany's most important metropolis, had grown far beyond the boundaries of the former Prussian seat of government. The Brandenburg Gate now sat at the middle of everything. There is hardly an event in the tides of recent history that is not reflected in the image of the heavily symbolic construction.

The quadriga also gazed over the revolution of 1918, which paved the way for the election of a constitutional assembly; later it was misappropriated by the Nazis as a stage prop for their propaganda and self-glorifying shenanigans. At the end of World War Two it served as a tank barrier. In 1948, when the Cold War haunted the four-sector city, the portal became the symbol and site of the East-West conflict. Located on East Berlin territory in the district Mitte, it marked the demarcation line between the Soviet and British sectors. "To beautify democratic Berlin," the city council in the East rebuilt it from

1956 to 1958. As owner of the only mold, the Western Senate made a new quadriga. Before it was re-erected in the East, Victoria again lost her Iron Cross. After fresh renovation in 1992, the cross was replaced – another act in this Berlin farce.

Traumatic memories are associated with the events of August 13, 1961; the order to close the border to West Berlin, signed by SED-party head Ulbricht, became effective an hour before midnight, and the Brandenburg Gate was the first crossing point to be sealed. A symbol of the divided capital and of a divided country, it dozed in the heavily-defended border strip for 28 years. Millions of tourists, as well as the high and mighty of the world, saw it there from one side or the other: John F. Kennedy and Ronald Reagan from the western side, Nikita S. Khrushchev and a thoughtful Mikhail Gorbatchev from the eastern side.

Above: The "Reichstag" will become the seat of the German Parliament, the Bundestag, in 1999.

On November 9, 1989, the division of the nation came to a peaceful end. The incredible news of the opening of the Wall had hardly been announced when the area around the Brandenburg Gate began crawling with people. Berliners from both parts of the city met at the 13-foot (four-meter) wide concrete obstacle.

Unfortunately, the damage to the Brandenburg Gate was expensive in the wake of the all-Berlin party-of-the-century that took place on the following New Year's Eve. A group of young climbers made it all the way up to the attic and, after plenty of champagne and beer, gave their vandalism free reign. The chariot was once again dismantled, lowered on ropes, and carried off to the Museum of Transportation and Technology for a thorough restoration. Since August 6, 1991, the bicentennial of its opening, the Brandenburg Gate, so charged with destiny, has once again been basking in its old glory. For months, however, Berlin's politicians were unable to decide whether to open it to vehicular traffic. Now, regular private traffic is deviated around the gate, whereas state visitors, taxis, public buses and cyclists are allowed through.

The Reichstag

The **Reichstag Building**, crowned with four corner towers, stands at the eastern edge of the Tiergarten. Built to plans by Paul Wallot and dedicated in 1894, the magnificent building served as the German Empire's parliament for its first 24 years. On November 9, 1918, a new era began at today's **Platz der Republik** when Philipp Scheidemann, leader of the Social Democratic Party, proclaimed the German Republic from the railing of the Reichstag balcony.

On the night of February 27, 1933, the glow of fire over the 114-foot (35-meter) high iron-and-glass cupola signalled the growing grip of dictatorship. The Nazi rulers used the Reichstag fire as an excuse to neutralize their political opponents with emergency laws and police terror. The photo of a Red Army soldier raising the Soviet flag above the destroyed Reichstag on April 30, 1945, went around the world. About 20,000 Russian soldiers died in the battle for Berlin. In 1946 the Red Army erected the **Soviet Memorial** in their memory.

The Reichstag was rebuilt by resolution of the German Bundestag as a symbol of national unity on the political dividing line through Berlin, and the interior was designed as a modern parliament building. A public exhibit in the western wing displays political ideas and decisions of the last 200 years of German history. On October 4, 1990, one day after the official reunification, a freely-elected representative assembly of all of Germany, with delegates from the West German Bundestag and the last GDR Volkskammer, met in the plenary hall. In the summer of 1995 the artist Christo, famous for wrapping famous monuments, also wrapped the Reichstag building.

After the Bundestag's decision to make Berlin the national capital and seat of the federal government, followed by a long planning phase, the Reichstag is being rebuilt on a model by Sir Norman Foster, albeit not in its original form. It will once again receive a glass cupola, which will be accessible to the public.

The area in front of the Reichstag extending down to the Spree river has become important since reunification. The new **Government Quarter** is to be built here. The cornerstone for the new chancellery has already been laid beside the Reichstag, directly on the Spree. Offices for the elected parties, the members of parliament, and the federal administration will be built in the Dorotheen blocks, in the Alsen and Luisen buildings located in the meander of the Spree (*Spreebogen*).

In 1937/38, as part of the monumental revamping of the capital of the Third Reich, General Building Inspector Speer had the east-west artery known today as **Strasse des 17. Juni** widened to 167 feet (51 meters). The **Siegessäule** (Victory Column) and the **Bismarck Group** by court sculptor R. Begas, two typical symbols of imperial Germany of the 19th century, were moved from the Reichstag to the **Grosser Stern** (Great Star).

The Victory Column was inaugurated with patriotic decorum in 1873 to celebrate the campaigns against Denmark, Austria and France. Thanks to the *Goldelse* (Golden Elsa) as Berliners call the 26-foot (8-meter) high **Victoria** at the top of the column, the Victory Pillar has become a popular "trademark" of the Tiergarten. A 285-step climb to the viewing platform at 220 feet (67 meters) is recommended for its magnificent view.

The Tiergarten

The area over which the bronze lady now gazes, the **Grosser Tiergarten** (Big Zoo), was originally graced by a jewel of

the Baroque era. The 555-acre (225 ha) common stretches from the Brandenburg Gate to Charlottenburg. It served originally as a game preserve for the electoral princes. In the 19th century Peter Joseph Lenné turned the Tiergarten into a landscaped park. Information plaques point to quiet areas and historical sights.

The way northward ends at the **Spreebogen**, a bend in the Spree. The **Kongresshalle** (Congress Hall) which stands there, an American contribution to the international architectural exhibit of 1957, has been given the nickname "Pregnant Oyster" due to its daring shell-shaped roof. Too daring, perhaps: it has already collapsed once. Artists from non-European countries come regularly to discuss North-South issues in the **House of the Cultures of the World**. A former noble palace on Spreeweg, **Schloss Bellevue**, has been used by federal presidents as an official residence in Berlin since 1959.

Above: The Congress building – known by Berliners as the "pregnant oyster."

Former president Richard von Weizsäcker suggested the future of things when, in 1993, he made Berlin the official residence of the president. Flags hoisted on the roof signal the that someone is home. A side-trip leads to Hanseatenweg, where the **Academy of Arts** at the Bellevue city train station offers exhibits and other events.

In the mid-19th century, westward migration began with the transformation of **Tiergarten-Süd** (the southern section) into an affluent residential neighborhood. This noble quarter was destroyed in World War Two. Shambles of some of the former embassies lead a shadowy existence in the former **Diplomatic Quarter**. Since the decision to make Berlin the capital of Germany again, several nations have declared their willingness to reopen the offices they had here once upon a time. That is the case, for example, with the **German-Japanese Center**, an exact copy of the former Japanese embassy, which houses economic and cultural exchange programs with the Far East.

Stauffenbergstrasse 13-14, once the seat of the German Army High Command, is the site of the failed officers' putsch against Hitler on July 20, 1944. Four main conspirators were executed on the evening of the assassination attempt. In the offices of the former Bendler-Block, the **Gedenkstätte Deutscher Widerstand** (Memorial to German Resistance) has an exhibit on the topic, with over 5000 photos and documents.

Kulturforum and Potsdamer Platz

At the **Landwehrkanal**, on the southern edge of the Tiergarten a short way from the **Herkules-Brücke** (Hercules Bridge), stand some of the projects from the international architectural exhibit of 1987, such as the **IBA-City Villas** on Stülerstrasse. The **Bauhaus Archives** building, opened in 1979, is a late work of Bauhaus founder Walter Gropius. Hans Scharoun bequeathed a document of contemporary architecture in the **Philharmonie**. This concert house was built in 1960-62 as an overture to the **Kulturforum**, which unites various institutions of the State Museums of Berlin – Foundation for Prussian Cultural Heritage under one roof on the northeastern edge of the Tiergarten: the **Kunstgewerbe Museum** (Museum of Arts and Crafts), the **Kunstbibliothek** (Art Library), the **Kupferstichkabinett** (Copperplate Engraving Cabinet), the **Musikinstrumenten Museum** (Musical Instrument Museum) and, in a new building since June 1998, the **Gemäldegalerie** (Picture Gallery). The **Neue Nationalgalerie** (New National Gallery) is also located on the confines of the Kulturforum, as is house No. 2 of the Berlin State Library, the **Staatsbibliothek zu Berlin**.

Not far from the Kulturforum, Berlin's new center is shaping up on **Potsdamer Platz**. On the formerly barren acreage cut in two by the Wall, the number of construction cranes now standing has no rival anywhere else in Europe. The futuristic **Info-Box** on Potsdamer Platz gives a good picture of what the city will look like in the future. The terrace on its roof offers a panoramic view of the mighty building site.

The service center planned by Daimler-Benz forms the core of this new city center. The gigantic project of *debis*, a Daimler-Benz subsidiary, was completed at the end of 1998. A cool three billion DM was spent on the building. This commercial space, spread over 720,000 square feet (67,000 sq meters), houses shops, apartments, restaurants, a musical theater, the Berlin Casino and two Imax movie theaters, as well as a five-star hotel of the Hyatt group. The builders and the government officials responsible are hoping by this to prevent Potsdamer Platz from becoming a lifeless office and dormitory city.

Next door, Sony is building its European headquarters, as well as an entertainment and residential center and, towards the south, Asea Brown Boveri is also erecting new headquarters. Planners and engineers are still struggling with the traffic problem: vehicles and trains are to be routed on a north-south axis through a new Tiergarten tunnel. This structure will be a technical masterpiece as the concrete foundations must be built right on the water table. And lest we forget: a new train station is being built on Potsdamer Platz with capacity for the ICE, Germany's ultra-fast train.

Located at the intersection of five busy avenues, Potsdamer Platz was awash in the traffic in the 1920s and 1930s. After the war it was a gold mine for black marketeers, since the Soviet, American and British zones met here. In the Wall years, Potsdamer Platz "enjoyed" dubious fame as a viewing platform for pilgrims to the Wall. Nowhere was the Wall so photogenically spray painted, nowhere was the view into the "Far East" more depressing. This is all history now.

FROM UNTER DEN LINDEN TO ALEXANDERPLATZ

Once upon a time Marlene Dietrich sang: "*Solang noch untern Linden die alten Bäume blühn, bleibt Berlin Berlin.*" ("As long as the old trees on Unter den Linden bloom, Berlin will remain Berlin.") The song is quite right of course: **Unter den Linden** has long exerted a powerful attraction on people – even today when it is slowly turning into a genuine boulevard once more.

The history of Unter den Linden is the history of the Hohenzollern dynasty. In 1573 a riding path for the electorate was laid out so that the upper ranks of the nobility could ride to the hunt in the Tiergarten. In 1647 Elector Friedrich Wilhelm had this promenade planted with walnut and linden trees. Friedrich II enlarged the *Lindenallee* so that it became showpiece boulevard. The architectonic history of this avenue began when he gave Wenzeslaus von Knobelsdorff initial instructions to make plans for its expansion.

After twelve years under National Socialism and the destruction wrought by the Second World War, much of Unter den Linden's flair was lost. After the war, the government of the German Democratic Republic expanded this 4550-foot (1390-meter) avenue into a lifeless parade ground that came to an abrupt end at the Brandenburg Gate.

Just beyond Pariser Platz, where the rebuilt **Hotel Adlon** now stands, Unter den Linden will be flanked by a host of embassies.

Albert Speer, Hitler's chief architect, considered this area very significant: in 1939, he built the New Chancellery on **Wilhelmstrasse** at the corner of **Vossstrasse**. In 1945 the building was reduced to ashes by the Allies.

Left: History in a nutshell – the cathedral, the arsenal and the TV tower.

Side Trip to the Old Gendarmenmarkt

Having arrived at the intersection with Friedrichstrasse, it's worth making a side trip to the **Gendarmenmarkt**.

The **Westin Grand Hotel** stands in ccontrast – so to speak – to the **Haus der Demokratie**, once the meeting place for the various political initiatives that formed the basis of the political parties in the East after the revolution of 1989. At this point, take a look at the **Komische Oper** (Comic Opera), where Walter Felsenstein acted his way to supra-regional renown. Another emporium of music is located on Gendarmenmarkt: the old **Schauspielhaus** (Playhouse), now called the **Konzerthaus Berlin**, constructed by Schinkel in classical style and restored in 1984. The **German** and **French Cathedrals** border Gendarmenmarkt. The French Cathedral houses the **Huguenot Museum** on the ground floor, and an exclusive wine tavern in its cupola. Restoration work on the German Cathedral after a fire in 1994 has been completed.

Friedrichstrasse, once the haunt of elegant strollers, was one vast and grandiose construction site until 1998. Some billions of marks are being invested here in projects which include the **Lindencorso** and the **Hofgarten**, right on the corner of the Linden, and the gigantic new **Friedrichstadtpassagen**, into which the upmarket French store **Galeries Lafayette** has already moved. At the end of Friedrichstrasse, almost in Kreuzberg, the **American Business Center** is also being built. Whether all of these businesses will make any money is debatable, considering the enduring lack of the right caliber of consumers in Berlin.

Around Bebelplatz

If you walk along **Behrenstrasse**, you will eventually arrive at Unter den Linden again, specifically at **Bebelplatz**,

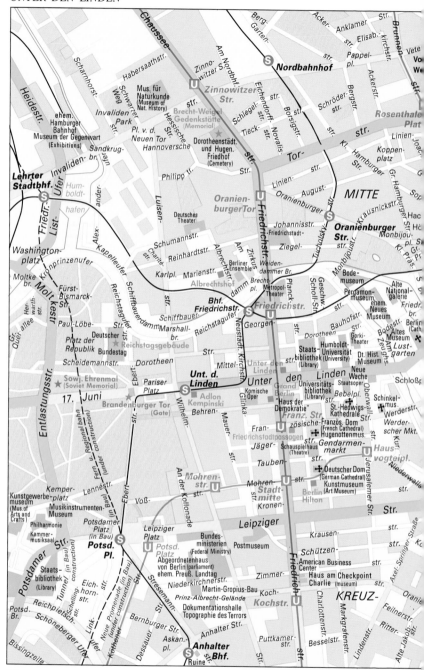

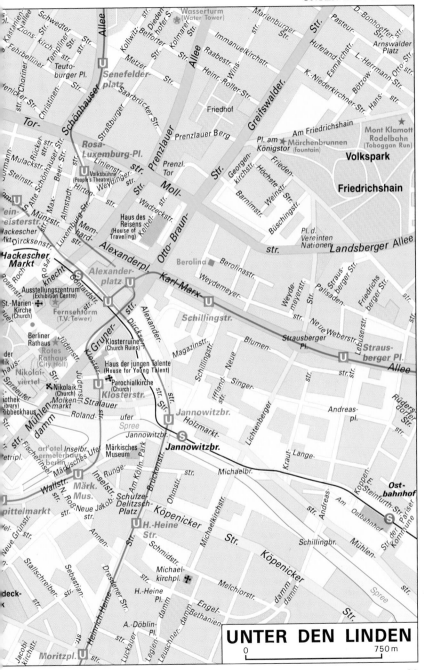

UNTER DEN LINDEN

0   750 m

Cathedral, modelled after the Pantheon in Rome. Friedrich II had this church – a cathedral since 1929 – built for the approximately 10,000 Catholics who lived in Berlin at the time. Philanthropy can certainly be ruled out on the part of the king; with the construction of the church, Friedrich II was attempting to pacify the Catholics in his own country after his annexation of Catholic Silesia.

You can see an **equestrian statue of Frederick the Great** just before Bebelplatz on the Linden: on May 31, 1851, the wraps were taken off this work. Sculptures portraying his contemporaries decorate the monument's pedestal. The former GDR had problems with this part of its national heritage and banished "Old Fritz" to Sanssouci. It was not until 1980 that the equestrian statue was restored to its old spot. From here, the statue has a view of the **Lindenforum**, the set of buildings surrounding Bebelplatz. St. Hedwig's Cathedral, the Palace and the Opera are all portions of the *Forum Fridericianum*, which Friedrich had constructed as the ostentatious core of the Prussian royal seat. To this day it has lost but little of its splendor.

There are two additional sculptures diagonally across the street, albeit not on horseback, but rather sitting in poses of deep thought: **Wilhelm** and **Alexander von Humboldt**. In 1810, on the initiative of the older of the scholarly brothers (Wilhelm), a university was founded in the former palace of Prince Heinrich. It has consistently attracted and produced scientists of world repute. Over the course of time the **Humboldt University** has employed 27 Nobel Prize winners alone. Directly opposite stands the **Alte Bibliothek** (Old Library), which today houses seminar rooms for the university. Because of its convex façade the Berliners refer to it simply as the *Kommode* (chest of drawers).

Right next to the college, the former **Deutsche Staatsbibliothek der DDR**

which is usually full of parked cars. As so frequently in Berlin, it also recalls some of Germany's less savory past. On May 10, 1933, Joseph Goebbels ceremoniously had 20,000 books publically burned here that had been declared un-German. These included the works of Heinrich Heine, Kurt Tucholsky, Heinrich and Thomas Mann, and Bertolt Brecht. It's a striking bit of cynicism that Goebbels should have sought out the plaza in front of the State Opera, a glorification of the mind and the muse. When it was reconstructed in the 1950s, the architects went to great lengths to imitate the original style of Knobelsdorff, who completed the first building in 1743 as the first free-standing theater. Knobelsdorff's special design is best reflected today in the six-columned gabled portico.

Towering over the southeast end of Bebelplatz is the dome of **St. Hedwig's**

Above: Equestrian statue of Frederick the Great. Right: The Gendarmenmarkt with the theater and the French cathedral.

(State Library of the GDR, nowadays House 1 of the State Library of Berlin, Prussian Cultural Heritage) contributes to the atmosphere of science and learning. Since merging with the State Library in the west the library houses over six million books, 600,000 manuscripts, maps and incunabula.

Further east on Unter den Linden is the **Neue Wache** (New Guard), designed by Karl Friedrich Schinkel. It was employed by the former GDR as a monument dedicated to the victims of fascism and militarism. A changing of the guard – marching in Prussian goosestep no less – took place hourly; every week there was a full-blown military parade. This spectacle continued until reunification and the demise of the GDR people's army.

A sculpture by Käthe Kollwitz, *Mourning Mother with a Dead Son*, was placed as a memorial in the Neue Wache in November 1993. The 800-pound bronze statue bears the following controversial inscription: "To the victims of war and tyranny." Two bronze plates at

the right and left of the entrance carry the names of the various groups who suffered from these avoidable plagues. The Jewish community in Berlin criticized the concept of the Neue Wache, making a special point of the fact that the memorial fails to properly differentiate between the criminals and their victims.

The **Altes Zeughaus** (Old Armory) adjacent to the Neue Wache previously served as a war museum and was converted in 1952 into a museum of German history, displaying the history of humanity from primitive man up to the latest "socialist achievements," with everything seen from a Marxist viewpoint of course. After the Wall fell, there was an exhibition here of the great variety of vehicles used in escapes from East to West Germany. After reunification the **Deutsches Historisches Museum** relocated here. The building is closed for enlargement and renovations until 2002.

Close by is the **Kronprinzenpalais** (Palace of the Crown Prince), a pompous construction originally built for Crown

Prince Friedrich, later used by the Berlin city authorities to accommodate important guests.

Schlossplatz

Going over the **Schlossbrücke** (Castle Bridge) takes you directly to **Schlossplatz** (Castle Square), site of the **Palace of the Republic** and the former **Staatsrat** (Council of State) building of the GDR. The former Foreign Ministry of the GDR has been torn down, opening the view to the **Forum Fridericianum**.

The Palace of the Republic, from whose façade the SED party emblems were removed in March 1990, served as the seat of the elected parliament until the day before its dissolution. Shortly before reunification the "Palazzo del Prozzo" was closed because of its high asbestos levels. (This nickname is a play on the meaningless Italian word *prozzo,* which sounds like the verb *protzen* in German, meaning to show off). What will happen to the building is unclear. Some argue for tearing it down, others would like to see it protected.

Gate IV, the last remnant of the **Berliner Stadtschloss** (City Castle), was integrated into the façade of the Council of State building. This certainly wasn't done to honor the Hohenzollerns, but rather in memory of Karl Liebknecht, who proclaimed the Socialist Republic from the balcony of the castle in November 1918. The castle was heavily damaged in the Second World War and the remnants were dynamited in 1950, when it still could have been saved. Wilhelm von Boddien, a businessman from Hamburg, had the castle façade rebuilt in 1993 as a structure of steel and plastic sheeting. A real rebuilding of the castle is still a distant dream, on financial as well as on city planning grounds.

Right: The Red City Hall has become the administrative nerve center of the city.

Today Rathausstrasse extends along where the Hohenzollerns once resided. Since 1986 the "victorious battle of the proletariat against exploitation" has been displayed between the Spree and Spandauer Strasse. In the center stands a bronze sculpture by Ludwig Engelhardt which depicts Marx and Engels in their habitual brooding poses. It took the work and skill of many master builders before the **Berliner Dom** (cathedral) achieved its current appearance. The original Dominican church dating from 1297 was torn down in 1747 and replaced three years later by the cathedral conceived by Knobelsdorff and Boumann. Between 1817 and 1822 Schinkel gave the building its classical grandeur, before a new building replaced the old. This one was realized by Julius Karl Raschendorf between 1894 and 1905. Heavy damage during the bombings of World War Two made extensive restoration necessary. This job has meanwhile been completed. The main room, the **Predigtkirche**, is now accessible, and that is where the six sarcophagi of the Hohenzollerns are located, representing one of Germany's most important historical treasures.

Museum Island

Adjacent to the castle, a triumphal arch leads into the **Lustgarten** (Pleasure Garden), which is bordered on its north side by the **Altes** (Old) **Museum**. A part of the antiquities collection found a new home here in the spring of 1998. This building, completed in 1830 by Schinkel, is considered to be Germany's oldest museum. The Altes Museum is part of the **Museum Island** (*Museumsinsel*), which is surrounded by the Spree and one of its tributaries, the Kupfergraben.

In addition to the **Neues** (New) **Museum** and the **Alte National Galerie**, the **Pergamon** and **Bode Museums** are part of this renowned complex. The reunification of Berlin will also have conse-

quences on the museum scene on Museum Island. Unification of the archeological and 19th-century art collections on the island is being scheduled for the next decade. In the interim, visitors will have to put up with certain limitations, such as the shutting down of the Bode Museum until 2004.

The Television Tower and its Surrounding Area

The "little GDR" derived a lot of pride from its huge **television tower**. At a height of 1197 feet (365 meters) it looms over the entire city center and is visible from a great distance in good weather. The 26,000-ton colossus, with a diameter of 138 feet (42 meters), attracts some 1.3 million visitors annually. From the tower's sphere, at an altitude of 650 feet (203 meters), visibility extends over a radius of about 25 miles (40 km), covering the entire area of Greater Berlin.

Built between 1965 and 1969, at the same time as the television tower, were the flanking two-storied pavilions with restaurants, cafés and the **Alexanderplatz Exhibition Center**. Next door, the **Marienkirche** today is the only remaining stone witness of the time of the city's foundation. The **Neptunbrunnen** (Neptune Fountain) is another point of interest for passers-by on the plaza between the Marienkirche and the **Rotes Rathaus** (Red Town Hall). The fountain, designed in 1886 by Reinhold Begas, portrays the god of the sea with his royal retinue, cherubs and marine beasts. The acting mayor of Berlin has already moved back into the Rotes Rathaus. The building received its name from the red brick used in the building, which was completed in 1869, and not from its administrative role during the Communist years.

Excursion into the Past

All that is left of the medieval town hall of Berlin is the **Gerichtslaube**, a yard where the court adjourned, which was reconstructed in the Nikolaiviertel

using the original one as a model. It is just one of several historical rediscoveries that were built up around the **Nikolaikirche** from 1981 to 1987. The church itself, dedicated to the patron saint of seafarers and merchants, was Berlin's first stone church (1264). It was destroyed many times, and was only finally completed in the 19th century.

A little haven of traditional Berlin exists in the surrounding **Nikolaiviertel** (Nikolai Quarter) between the Spree river and Spandauer Strasse. Love of detail, however, stopped with the style of construction. The standard Communist concrete slabs were used in the 1980s to build old-fashioned Berlin cafés, bars and museums. In addition to the Gerichtslaube, also worth seeing in the **pedestrian zone** of the Nikolaiviertel the **relief frieze** by Gerhard Thieme depicting Berlin's history and the **Foundation**

Above: In the restored Nikolaiviertel. Right: Market stalls enliven the huge expanse of Alexanderplatz.

Fountain. The **Ephraim Palais**, built in 1764, was literally removed in 1935: the blocks of stone were all numbered and stored, which meant that it would be possible to rebuild the edifice.

Alexanderplatz

The passages under the town hall lead, in a westerly direction, to **Alexanderplatz**. During the Socialist era something undefinably stuffy seemed to pervade Alexanderplatz due to the sterility of its buildings and its vast emptiness. It is hard to believe today that in the 1920s the Berlin doctor and writer Alfred Döblin, author of the novel *Berlin Alexanderplatz* (filmed as a 15-part TV series by Fassbinder), which immortalized the square, could have felt it to be "the pulsating heart of a world city."

A lot has changed since reunification, however: no sooner have you emerged from the S-Bahn underpass at Alexanderplatz station, than you will find life on the square coming alive with a bevy of color-

ful street peddlers. The stalls have already smothered two artistic remnants of the Cold War era: the **Weltzeituhr** (World Time Clock) by Erich John, a symbol of the internationalism of the GDR, and the **Brunnen der Völkerfreundschaft** (People's Friendship Fountain), by Walter Womacka, both dating from 1969. The symbolic content has gone, and the surroundings give off the unmistakable aroma of pure, unadulterated capitalism.

The 39-story **Forum Hotel Berlin** dominates the entire square. Its exclusive restaurant on the top floor boasts a spectacular view of the city center. The rebuilding of Alexanderplatz, which ultimately led it to becoming a pedestrian zone, began in 1961 with the construction of the **Haus des Lehrers** (Teacher's House, recognizable from its "belly wrap") and the neighboring **Kongresshalle**. In the following years the **Haus des Reisens** (House of Travel) appeared, a cynical title considering the travel restrictions for East Germans. Further-

more, the headquarters of the Stasi, East Germany's secret police, on **Keibelstrasse**, abutted the back of the building.

A surviving section of the 13th-century town wall graces Klosterstrasse, not far from Alexanderplatz. The impressive ruin of the **Klosterkirche** (Monastery Church) is followed by the former Haus der jungen Talente (House of Young Talent). The house is a favorite meeting place for the younger generation. It was originally built in 1700 by Jean de Bodt and was restored in 1954. This little nook of traditional Berlin architectonic design around the Klosterkirche is rounded off by the Parochial Church and the **Traufenhäuser**. One of the latter houses the inn "Zur letzten Instanz" (Court of Last Appeal; Waisenhausstrasse 16).

Friedrichstrasse and Scheunenviertel

Diagonally opposite the church, when looking towards Alexanderplatz, is a bus stop. From here, you can walk to Friedrichstrasse. On the way there you pass

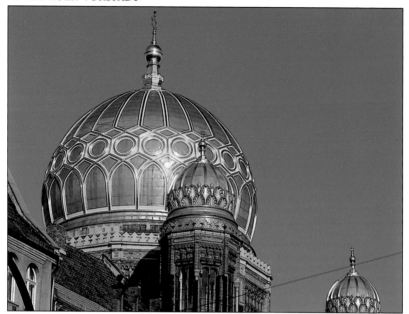

by the **Molkenmarkt** (once Berlin's main marketplace), cross the Spree river and turn onto Breite Strasse. Continue to the **Stadtbibliothek** (City Library) and the **Ribbeckhaus**, ending up at the old Gendarmenmarkt. A stroll along Friedrichstrasse on the other side of Unter den Linden makes sense at this point.

The **International Trade Center**, opened in 1978, stands a short distance before the Friedrichstrasse S-Bahn station. Service industries and restaurants, trade associations and representatives of various firms have set up shop in this skyscraper, which was constructed by a Japanese firm.

On the other side of the Friedrichstrasse station, the entertainment district of downtown Berlin's 300 year-old north-south axis begins. On one side are the **Metropol Theater** (currently closed due to bankruptcy), the **Distel** cabaret, and the **Friedrichstadtpalast**; on the

Above: The restored dome of the New Synagogue on Oranienburger Strasse.

90

other side is Brecht's **Berliner Ensemble** and Max Reinhardt's renowned **Deutsches Theater**. The area around the **Oranienburg Gate** was once the so-called *Scheunenviertel* (literally "barns quarter" or slums), Berlin's Jewish residential neighborhood. The Nazis used this name for the entire **Spandauer Vorstadt** (Spandau Suburb), as this part of the city is called, in order to defame the Jews. The **Neue Synagoge** (New Synagogue) on **Oranienburger Strasse**, destroyed in 1938 on *Reichskristallnacht* (Night of Broken Glass) and now rebuilt, recalls the 150,000 Jews who lived in Berlin before World War Two.

The **Scheunenviertel** was once one of Berlin's poorest districts, albeit full of liveliness and crazy bars. Efforts were made to salvage the old buildings, and the government of the Mitte district decided to place the entire Scheunenviertel under protection order. A lively scene with restaurants and *Kneipen* (pubs) is spreading here in and around the **Hackesche Höfe**, with its typical courtyards.

THE MAKING OF A CAPITAL

On June 20, 1991, the German Bundestag reached its decision to move the seat of Parliament and the bulk of the governmental offices from Bonn to Berlin. Ever since then, plans for the move have been in the making, and construction work has long since started. Most of the effort regarding this construction has been centered in the districts of Tiergarten and Mitte.

The inauguration of the new **Reichstag** is scheduled for the Spring of 1999. Restoration and design of the new building, under the guidance of the English architect Sir Norman Foster, are going to cost a whopping DM 600 million. The new glass cupola can already be seen from afar today. It will be accessible to the public when it is completely finished. A lookout platform standing at a height of 164 feet (50 meters) will allow the curious a view of the Government Quarter, in addition, there will also be a cafeteria here to provide rest and sustenance for weary sightseers.

On the other hand, the schedule for the future **Lehrter Bahnhof** (train station), which won't open until 2003, is way off track, so to speak. Only Lady Luck will allow the tunnel diggers to close the huge hole yawning in front of the Reichstag by May 1999.

Many other government buildings, too, will not be completed on time for the opening of the Reichstag, so that deputies will have to work their way along palisades while going about their job.

Government Quarter in the Tiergarten

The first one to move his residence to the Tiergarten was the President, who took over **Schloss Bellevue** in February 1994. To the south of the castle, a new building has been erected to house the **Bundespräsidialamt** (President's Of-

fice). The **Spreebogen**, a meander in the Spree to the north of the Reichstag, will play a major role in the design of the capital. The **Kanzleramt** (Chancellery), designed by architects Charlotte Frank and Axel Schultes, will stand in the western section, dwarfed by the immense **Office of the Federal Chancellor**. Attached will be a five-story administrative wing. Behind the building, beyond the Spree, is the **Chancellor's Garden**. The popular **Tempodrom**, a tent where concerts and other events are held, is to be moved to a solid home at the Anhalter Train Station in 1999.

The future residence for deputies and administration employees will be in the eastern Spreebogen. In the **Alsen** and **Luisen Blocks**, which are being built on both banks of the river, 1700 rooms will open for deputies and committees, whereby the jump over the Spree is supposed to symbolize the growing together of the two halves of the city. 2000 more offices are to open in the **Dorotheen Blocks** on the east side of the Reichstag. Planning is modeled after the historic Dorotheen City: older buildings under protection order (such as the Palace of the Reichstag President and the Technology Chamber) will be worked into the new construction. In addition, there will be cafés and shops in the buildings to guarantee an urbane lifestyle.

Ministries in Mitte

The ministries will have their primary or secondary seats in various locations around the district of Mitte. For this purpose, most of the buildings will be renovated and in part enlarged.

The **Auswertiges Amt** (Foreign Office), for example, will be moving into the former Reichsbank building, which was erected on the Spree from 1934 to 1938. After 1945 the Finance Ministry of the GDR used it, until the Central Committee of the SED moved into it in 1959.

91

The building of the **Bundesministerium der Finanzen** (Ministry of Finance) in the Detlev Rohwedder House on Wilhelmstrasse and Leipziger Strasse has a similar past. It was built in 1936-38 to house the Reich's Air Force Ministry. The constitution of the GDR was designed here in 1949, and in 1950 it became the GDR's "House of Ministries."

The oldest part of the future **Bundesministerium für Wirtschaft** (Ministry of the Economy) on Invalidenstrasse dates to the time of Friedrich II. The U-shaped complex of the Invalidenhaus was originally built in 1748-49 and is now to be incorporated into the new ministry. The **Verkehrsministerium** (Ministry of Transportation) is nearby. Other ministry locations in Mitte include Hausvogteiplatz, Mauerstrasse and Jägerstrasse.

The **Bundesrat** (Federal Council) also found itself a classy address in Berlin: the façade of the former mansion of the Prus-

sian *Landtag* (Parliament) on Leipziger Strasse is by and large in mint condition. The Berlin deputies meet opposite in the former Prussian Landtag. The **Verteidigungsministerium** (Ministry of Defense) will spread out in the so-called **Bendlerblock**. The Ministry of Defense of the Weimar Republic had already made itself at home in this building after World War One. During World War Two the core of the military's resistance to Hitler was formed here. After the failed attempt to assassinate Hitler on July 20, 1944, the freedom fighters gathered around Count Claus Schenk von Stauffenberg were executed in the honor yard of the east wing. The **Memorial to German Resistance** is located here.

The **Informationszentrum zur Hauptstadtplanung in Berlin** (Information Center for the Planning of the Capital in Berlin) has all the material a visitor might need to find out more. It is located in the former GDR State Council building on Schlossplatz, and is open daily from 9 a.m. to 7:30 p.m. (tel. 20620-0).

Above: The new silhouette of the Reichstag slowly emerges.

BRANDENBURG GATE
BERLIN MITTE

Using Berlin's public transportation is the best way of visiting the Tiergarten and Berlin's historic center. Bus No. 100 goes from the Zoo to Prenzlauer Berg and passes by most of the important sights. A ride with the S-Bahn from the Zoo to Alexanderplatz is also a good bet (Lines No. 3, 5, 7, 9).

Cafés and Restaurants

Borchardt, Französische Str. 47, tel. 203 97 10, daily 11:30 a.m.-2 a.m., food served till midnight.
Brauhaus GeorgBräu, Spreeufer 4, tel. 242 42 44, daily noon-2 a.m., in Summer from 11 a.m.
Café Einstein, Unter den Linden 42, tel. 204 36 32. There's a second Einstein on Kurfürstenstrasse.
Fofi's, Rathausstr. 25, tel. 242 34 35, daily from 11:30 a.m.
Grand Café in the Westin Grand Hotel, Unter den Linden, tel. 232 32 03, daily noon-6 p.m.
Lutter & Wegner, Charlottenstr. 56, tel. 202 95 40, daily from 11 a.m. Restaurant with wine bar and retail wine sales.
Opernpalais, Unter den Linden 5, tel. 20 26 83, daily 9 a.m.-midnight: with Berlin's most beautiful café, the Operncafé and several restaurants.
Reinhard's, Poststr. 28, tel. 242 52 05, daily 9 a.m.-1 a.m.
Ristorante Porta Brandenburgo, Wilhelmstrasse 87-88, tel. 229 95 87, daily 11:30 a.m.-midnight. Classical Italian cuisine, which the Japanese cook enhances with French refinements.
Spreeblick, Mitte, Probststr. 9, tel. 242 52 47, daily from 11 a.m.
Turmstuben in the Französischer Dom, Mitte, Französische Str. 5, tel. 204 48088, daily noon-1 a.m. Pubs and cafés in the Nikolaiviertel are grouped mainly around the church square.

Sights

Berliner Antique and Flea Market, S-Bahn arches/Georgenstrasse, on Friedrichstrasse, Wed-Mon 11 a.m.-6 p.m. Furniture, jewelry, clothes from the 1920s.
Berliner Dom, Mitte, Lustgarten, tel. 20 26 91 11, Predigtkirche, imperial stairway, Hohenzollern crypt, baptismal and nuptial church; Mon-Sat 9 a.m.-7:30 p.m., Sun 11:30 a.m.-7:30 p.m.
Berliner Rathaus, Mitte, Rathausstr., tel. 240 10.
Berliner Stadtbibliothek (Municipal Library), Mitte, Breitestr. 32-34, tel. 20 28 64 01, Mon-Fri 10 a.m.-7 p.m., Sat 10 a.m.-6 p.m.
Brecht-Weigel Memorial, Mitte, Chausseestr. 125, tel. 282 99 16, Tue-Fri 10 a.m.-noon, Thu 5-7 p.m., Sat 9:30 a.m.-2 p.m. (only with guided tours).

Deutscher Dom, Mitte, Gendarmenmarkt 1, Tue-Sun 10 a.m.-7 p.m.; exhibition: "Questions of German History."
Deutsches Historisches Museum (History), Unter den Linden 2, tel. 21 50 20, Thu-Tue 10 a.m.-6 p.m., exhibitions in the former Zeughaus, closed until 2002.
Dorotheen and Friedrichswerder Municipal Cemetery, Mitte, Chausseestr. 126, daily 8 a.m.-8 p.m.; adjacent is the **Huguenot Cemetery**. B. Brecht, J. G. Fichte, K. F. Schinkel, H. Mann and A. Zweig are among these cemeteries "residents."
Ephraim-Palais, Mitte, Poststr. 16, tel. 24 00 20, Tue-Sun 10 a.m.-6 p.m.
Fernsehturm am Alex (TV tower), Mitte, Panoramastr. 1a, tel. 242 33 33, daily 9 a.m.-1 a.m.
Französischer Dom (French Cathedral), Mitte, Gendarmenmarkt, tel. 204 15 06, visits Tue-Sat noon-5 p.m., Sun 11 a.m.-5 p.m.
Gedenkstätte Deutscher Widerstand (Memorial to German Resistance), Tiergarten, Stauffenbergstr. 13/14, tel. 26 54 22 02, exhibition on German resistance during the Nazi years, Mon-Fri 9 a.m.-6 p.m., Sat, Sun 9 a.m.-1 p.m.
Hackesche Höfe, Mitte, Rosenthaler Str. 40/41. Residential and commercial center in Art-Nouveau style built in 1905, with backyards.
Haus der Kulturen der Welt (House of World Cultures), Tiergarten, John-Foster-Dulles-Allee 10, tel. 39 78 70.
Huguenot Museum in the Friedrichstadt Church, Mitte, Gendarmenmarkt 6, tel. 229 17 60, Wed-Sat noon-5 p.m., Sun 11 a.m.-5 p.m.
Marienkirche (St. Mary's Church), Mitte, Karl-Liebknecht-Str. 8, tel. 242 44 67, Mon-Thu 10 a.m.-noon and 1-5 p.m., Sat, Sun noon-5 p.m., organ vespers: Sat 4:30 p.m. (May-Oct).
Nikolaikirche, Mitte, Nikolaikirchplatz, tel. 24 00 20, exhibition on city history: Tue-Sun 10 a.m.-6 p.m. Glockenspiel daily 10 a.m., noon and 4 p.m.
Reichstag Building, German Bundestag, Tiergarten, Platz der Republik, tel. 22 73 21 31; closed till 1999 for renovations.
Schinkel Museum, Friedrichswerder Church, Mitte, Werderstr., tel. 208 13 23, Tue-Sun 9 a.m.-5 p.m.
Siegessäule (Victory Column), Tiergarten, Strasse d. 17. Juni, at the Grosser Stern, tel. 391 29 61, Mon 1-6 p.m., Tue-Sun and holidays 9 a.m.-6 p.m.
St. Hedwig's Cathedral, Mitte, Unter den Linden, tel. 203 48 10, first Sun of the month 4:30 p.m. organ vespers, Wed 3-3:30 p.m. organ music.
State Library of Berlin – Prussian Cultural Heritage, House 1: Mitte, Unter den Linden 8, tel. 2015-0, Mon-Fri 9 a.m.-9 p.m., Sat till 5 p.m. House 2: Tiergarten, Potsdamer Str. 33, tel. 26 61, Mon-Fri 9 a.m.-21 p.m., Sat till 5 p.m. Call for tour info.

BERLIN DISTRICTS

KREUZBERG
From Rags to Riches

Every big city has its anti-city district, a mark of shame lovingly cultivated by friends, subjected to the abusive tirades of self-professed arbitrators of law and order, proudly trotted out as being so very different from the run-of-the-mill, yet at the same time so typical. Where else but in the middle of Berlin could Kreuzberg ever be found? A granite paving stone in the park on Alexandrinenstrasse marks the middle of the city.

The Kreuzbergers have a lot more ideas than money. Kreuzberg means poetry, music and painting in some dismal courtyard in a romantically dilapidated ambience. The loud cry of myth rang in our ears and myths are not so fond of having their feet put back on the ground: but that's what Kreuzberg can expect now that Berlin itself has rejoined the world at large.

Kreuzberg: A Mixture

Modern Kreuzberg is a social ghetto in an overcrowded space: a total of 153,000

Preceding pages: Ornate façades recall Kreuzberg's prosperous past. Left: An artist bearing the typical Kreuzberg look.

Kreuzbergers live together in a space of only 4.1 square miles (10.4 sq km), a greater density than anywhere else in all of Berlin. The inhabitants' average age is 30, making it by far the youngest district of Berlin, and the greatest number of singles lives here, too; half of all the residents live alone. But Kreuzberg is also poor – 20,000 Kreuzbergers are on welfare, and the jobless rate is 20 percent.

Through the tinted windows of tour buses, visitors can study punks and bums from a safe distance and can experience society's contradictions in full collision, live and in color. Particularly the *Wessis*, as non-locals from West Germany are called, glorify Kreuzberg as a Mecca and El Dorado for drop-outs, as a promised district for the so-called "scene," which sometimes behaves like a Gallic village, continuously squabbling within itself but united against the "enemy": the inhabitants of Zehlendorf's villas, Ku'damm's chi-chi crowd and Christian Democratic senators.

Kreuzberg has a unique atmosphere, a colorful blend of opposites. Originally, the term conjured up the vision of working in the back courtyard and living in the front building. Today it means cohabitation with pensioners who have lived here for decades, West German Kreuzbergers-by-choice and Turkish families: the beer-

97

drinking Berliner in the same boat as the social outsider and the Kreuzberg yuppie. The Kreuzberg mixture is also a feeling for life, for letting the imagination soar to utopian heights, in spite of the district's unfavorable living conditions.

But almost everything that has been written about Kreuzberg up until now is no longer true: Kreuzberg was roughly pushed from the edge back into the middle in both geographic and socio-economic terms. The Wall had pressed the district onto the margin, so that in some nooks the world seemed to have come to an end. Suddenly the district is in the middle of Berlin and has become attractive for real estate companies. Business rents have in some cases increased tenfold. Many a *döner kebab* stand has had to close its business overnight. And artists' studios, alternative businesses and fringe theaters are also being threat-

ened by the fall of the Wall. Of the 28.5 miles (46 km) of Wall between East and West Berlin, nearly six miles (nine km) were in Kreuzberg. "Thorn in the flesh of the city and time-barrier between two velocities," is what GDR dramatist Heiner Müller called the Wall.

Kreuzberg is a product of the administrative reform of 1920, when Greater Berlin was created. At the time, the district was patched together from the historical districts Südliche Friedrichstadt, Tempelhofer Vorstadt and Luisenstadt. These were mostly poor suburbs for workers toiling in Berlin's factories. Thus, Kreuzberg was long the classical Berlin working class quarter. Today, inofficially, there are even two Kreuzbergs: Kreuzberg 61 and SO 36, the latter being an old, prewar postal designation standing for southeast.

The wounds the Wall inflicted on the city are nowhere more visible than in the former **Südliche Friedrichstadt**, the part of Kreuzberg that borders today on the old, once elegant center of the city, which

Right: The ruins of the Anhalter Railway Station. Above: The rare Mohawk can still be spotted in Kreuzberg, even nowadays.

was destroyed in World War Two and later split down the middle by the Wall. Today it is a sad sight, a concrete desert with shoddy suburban character, disrupted and lifeless.

At the **Hallesches Tor** subway station an exit leads directly onto **Mehringplatz**. The former Belle-Alliance-Platz was a public marketplace in the days of the Kaiser. Today it is a concrete circle of apartments standing in closed ranks. **Friedrichstrasse**, the only street in the axis of the square, has been preserved as a pedestrian zone. The western segment of the street is an ugly site today, though once upon a time it was the heart of the business and entertainment quarter.

Running almost at a right angle to it is **Stresemannstrasse**, whose name has been changed to conform to new political situations at least six times. Once it boasted the residences of such famous literary figures as Theodor Fontane, Günther Eich and Joachim Ringelnatz. But, above all, it was an important access street to the **Anhalter** train station, which

was built in 1874 and destroyed by bombings in 1943. Only the portal still stands, seemingly lost in the middle of **Askanischer Platz**, the sad remains of what was once an unusually large terminus station: after all, the still-young German capital needed an impressive train station! They called it the "Gateway to the Blue Distance." Trains left for Anhalt, Dresden, Halle, Munich and Frankfurt from here. In 1936, at the zenith of the travel boom, 1000 taxis waited here for the approximately 180 trains arriving and departing daily.

In 1999 the barren land around the old ruin will make way to athletic grounds and green lawns, and the **Tempodrom** will find a new home here, which will include an open-air stage.

Terror and the Wall

Where Stresemannstrasse crosses the Anhalterstrasse stands the **Martin Gropius Building**, the former Berlin Museum of Handicrafts, built in 1877 in the style of a bombastic Italian palazzo. The building was destroyed in World War Two and is now one of Berlin's most beautiful exhibition halls (also closed for renovations at present). The Wall used to run along Niederkirchnerstrasse, but today on the east side of the street, opposite the Gropius building, you can see the former Prussian Landtag (Parliament). The Berlin deputies moved into it in 1993 after a costly – and therefore controversial – renovation, The parliament's former location, in the old Schöneberg city hall, had become too small.

In front of the Gropius building is a large, empty, rough piece of land, such as are found here and there in Berlin. This expanse between **Niederkirchnerstrasse** (named after Katja Niederkirchner, who was a member of the anti-Nazi resistance), **Stresemannstrasse**, **Wilhelmstrasse** and **Anhalterstrasse** is called **Prinz-Albert-Gelände** (grounds). After the Second World War the city planners forgot it – perhaps intentionally. During the National Socialist period, the Gestapo, the SS and the *Sicherheitsdienst* (SD) terrorized the country and occupied Europe from this seemingly harmless lot.

On an elevation in the middle of the grounds is an overview map tracing the course of the old streets and the buildings lining them. The hill is all that remains of the Gestapo cellar, where prisoners from the so-called "house prison" were interrogated and tortured. In 1987 the remnants of this cellar were discovered and excavated. Just in time for Berlin's 750th anniversary, the Senate decided to erect a monument to the victims of the Nazi regime. Today, visitors to the documentation hall **Topography of Terror**, and to the now accessible cellars, can get a very strong sense of what happened back then in the middle of Berlin.

Nothing at the intersection of **Friedrichstrasse** and **Kochstrasse** recalls the once famous **Checkpoint Charlie**, the old border crossing for allied personnel,

diplomats and foreigners. That capitalism has been victorious is clearer here than anywhere else: a major American investor is having an **American Business Center** built here for DM 600 million.

Zimmerstrasse, **Jerusalemerstrasse** and **Kochstrasse** are part of the old Berlin newspaper district. At the end of the 1920s the newspaper boom reached its peak with 114 newspapers published daily; in 1945 the quarter was bombed out. Nothing is left of that former variety. Axel Springer, whose publishing house still dominates Berlin's media landscape, built his company highrise as a "bulwark against Socialism" directly in front of the Wall and on the exact spot where the right-wing Scherl publishing company,

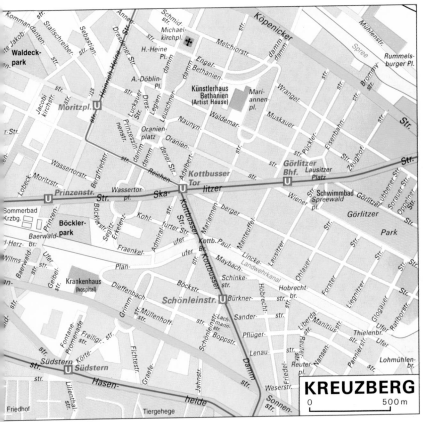

KREUZBERG

0   500 m

bought out from Hugenberg, had had its offices before World War Two. Springer, for many years a solitary figure in this deserted landscape, received company in 1989 when the alternative **Tageszeitung** moved from the Wedding district to Kochstrasse, where it now sits right in the middle of everything.

The Ullstein publishing house, a subsidiary of Springer, is located on **Lindenstrasse**, which marks the border between the Südliche Friedrichstadt and Luisenstadt. Here stands the **Berlin Museum**, the only construction in western Berlin still remaining from the time of Friedrich Wilhelm I. It is currently closed for renovations, but will probably open in 1999. The Prussian Court held sessions within

its walls well into the 19th century; in 1969 a citizens' initiative gathered enough interest and support to found this city museum. Today, a piece of the Wall with original graffiti graces its entrance.

During the early 19th century **Luisenstadt** was a prime business address. Some of today's industrial moguls, Siemens for example, started out as a mini-business in one of its backyards.

The End of the World?

Behind Moritzplatz begins the section of **Oranienstrasse** that is SO 36's main drag. The average number of black leather jackets, bandanas, Turkish vegetable shops and *döner kebab* stands is

101

much higher than elsewhere in Berlin. Oranienstrasse is the street where the most leaflets and posters have been posted in the display windows and with the most slogans sprayed on house walls. It is a street that, despite its colorfulness, always wears a veil of gray. In the snack bar "Brooklyn" – its name is its agenda – on the corner of **Adalbertstrasse**, one can sometimes hear "We Gotta Get Out of This Place," and everyone nods in time to the music. Or, between coffee and Eric Burdon, someone may scream out his or her nightmares. This may be the street with the greatest number of social outcasts. The punks at **Kottbusser Tor** around the corner make no bones about their no-future attitude. The multi-storey concrete complex in whose shadow they sit or lie seems to be the solidified confirmation that one can only feel awful here.

Bethaniendamm, which ends at **Mariannenplatz**, leads to one of Kreuz-

berg's idyllic spots: the first square in Berlin that was planned to be decorative, and it has remained quite a jewel, if hard-won. Originally, the Senate wanted to tear down the buildings in the Bethanien quarter, but the residents raised a ruckus and were just able to prevent a radical "renewal" of the area.

At the center of Mariannenplatz is the **Künstlerhaus Bethanien**, a former deaconesses' hospital. Twenty-one studios for Turkish and German artists are located here, as well as the Turkish district library, workshops and rooms for exhibits and theatrical and musical performances. While there are a few German-Turkish meeting places in Kreuzberg, everyday life goes on mostly in benign indifference to each others' culture at best, even though one-third of all Kreuzbergers have Turkish passports. Unluckily, the German inhabitants' contact is usually restricted to shopping at the Turkish vegetable vendors' or to eating a *döner kebab*. One minor exception is the *Hammam*, a Turkish steam bath in the

Above: View of Kreuzberg at the Görlitzer station.

women's center **Schokofabrik** (Chocolate Factory), where young Turkish and German women enjoy relaxation and body care together.

Only one stop on the elevated train separates the **Görlitzer Bahnhof** station at the end of Oranienstrasse from the **Schlesisches Tor** station. Until November 1989 this was the terminal station in every sense of the word. Hardly anyone strayed onto the **Oberbaumbrücke**. Since then, the red brick bridge has been reopened to pedestrian and vehicular traffic to the district of Friedrichshain, and even the U-Bahn lines No. 1 and 15 roll through until **Warschauer Strasse**.

The **Landwehrkanal** was built in the middle of the 19th century to connect the Upper Spree at Schlesisches Tor with the Lower Spree in Charlottenburg. Freight barges transported coal, gravel, limestone, fruit and potatoes. Today, only excursion steamers chug past.

Savoir-vivre in Kreuzberg

Regal buildings, some of them with ivy-covered Art-Nouveau façades and small front gardens, line the **Paul-Lincke-Ufer** (*Ufer* = river bank). It is a chic place even label-conscious yuppies need not be ashamed of. In the summer it's a gorgeous spot to enjoy the sunshine in one of the cafés on the bank of the river, or to cast a glance across to the **Maybachufer**, with its colorful Turkish open-air market.

Distinguished buildings from the age of the Industrial Revolution can also be seen diagonally across the canal on the **Planufer** and around the **Südstern**, an exclusive area of Kreuzberg. The Südstern also marks the beginning of **Bergmannstrasse**, which runs between Schleiermacherstrasse and Mehringdamm, and has strings of inviting little shops. The quarter's "shopping center" is the **Marheineke-Markthalle**, one of three market halls remaining from the 14

that the Magistrate had built in the 19th century to improve hygienic conditions of the weekly markets.

Although the slope is quite steep behind Bergmannstrasse, this part of Kreuzberg is completely built-up, so that there is not a single free spot. In the middle of the concrete wilderness is **Chamissoplatz**, a beautiful, quiet, nostalgic little square. A piece of Kreuzberg as it once was: dignified, but not genteel. Straight ahead on Bergmannstrasse, here named Kreuzbergstrasse, is **Viktoria-park**, in which the **Kreuzberg mountain**, indeed the "Cross Mountain," as the district name translates, rises. This hill also used to be called Goetzscher Vineyard, for wine was in fact cultivated here. It is worth climbing the mere 216 feet (66 meters) – after all, the district adopted the mountain's name, though only after long and tedious arguments.

From the top, one sees almost all of Kreuzberg and, of course, the little waterfall which seems to babble off to **Grossbeerenstrasse**. On this street, a mighty gateway leads into **Riehmers Hofgarten**, a small idyllic garden courtyard with 24 apartment buildings of upper-crust lineage. Master mason and building contractor Wilhelm Riehmer built this unusual complex in 1881. Buying the grounds at a bargain price, he showed true speculator's sense, for the Hofgarten became the address of the upper class. Officers from the nearby dragoons' barracks and important treasury officials rented the five- and six-room apartments, which are divided into smaller ones today. Illustrious tenants still live here: doctors, gallery owners and Kreuzberger artists. The complex includes the **Yorck/ New Yorck** double cinema, the **Riehmers Hofgarten** hotel, the **Bar Centrale** and the **Restaurant Riehmers**.

If you continue walking along to the end of Grossbeerenstrasse, the Hallesches Tor, the outset of this walk, will soon come into sight again.

PRENZLAUER BERG: URBAN COOL IN THE OLD NEIGHBORHOOD

Long before the Wall came down and the city was reunified, **Prenzlauer Berg** was one of the liveliest districts in East Berlin. Not because it became a showcase community while the Socialists were in power – quite the contrary: except for one little area where new apartment buildings went up alongside narrow streets, Prenzlauer Berg has been consistently seedy for four decades.

It was the GDR's avant-garde crowd that chose the grey, dilapidated buildings for their residences: artists, dissidents, grass roots pressure groups and squatters moved in. Since reunification in 1989 this mixture has become flashier and has received new stimuli from the now much larger outside world. Yet this district still numbers among those parts of the city

Above: Taking a rest on Husemannstrasse.
Right: Children at play in a typical courtyard.

with the lowest real incomes. Gradually the houses are being repainted and stuccoed; many apartments have been luxuriously refurbished. For the younger generation, these days, Prenzlauer Berg is the second most coveted district after Mitte. Bars, cafés, clubs and galleries have opened in "Prenzelberg," so the district does have alure for the socially active.

The feeling here is somewhere between working-class neighborhood and hotspot, on the one hand typically Berlin and on the other hand experimental and vivacious. Nowhere else in the city's east are there so many small shops where one can buy anything from postage stamps to groceries – and increasingly health foods.

The Tenement District

Anyone who has heard of Berlin as being the biggest tenement city in the world will find this prejudice confirmed: four- and five-story buildings embrace up to five tiny courtyards. These complexes were built at the end of the 19th

century in accordance with a particular architectural concept: James Hobrecht at that time defended the idea of having poor and rich families jammed together in the front and rear buildings of these complexes as constituting a social revolution. On his way to school a child from a basement apartment in the fourth building in the rear would have to pass through the same front gate as the child who lived in the luxurious second floor of the first building. His critics thought his idea was "socio-political quackery."

But the small apartments with their common toilet in the hallway have attracted young people in recent decades. They moved into apartments that had been cleared by socialist housing policies. Their predecessors were usually families with small children who had moved – not always happily – to the huge ghetto-like new housing projects on the northeastern edge of Berlin. The elderly were the only ones who stayed. The people who move in now are from France, the US and often from West Ger-

many. Some squatters have even managed to legalize their status, as they once did in the western part of the city. They receive grants from the Federal Government with which to renovate the houses.

Schönhauser Allee

If you would like to get an idea of what this district, with its many small neighborhoods, is like, start at the Schönhauser Tor. You might notice that most of the linden trees are gone. They have been dying off since the 1980s and had to be felled due to permanent overdoses of exhaust fumes or gas from defective pipes. This is an evil which has cost this densely populated area more than 400 trees, many of which were a hundred years old or more. Still, this street, with its typical Berlin charm, is a good place for a stroll. Right behind Senefelderplatz the subway emerges from underground and continues until just before Pankow. The elevated viaduct, nicknamed "The City Council's Umbrella," is quite a sight. In

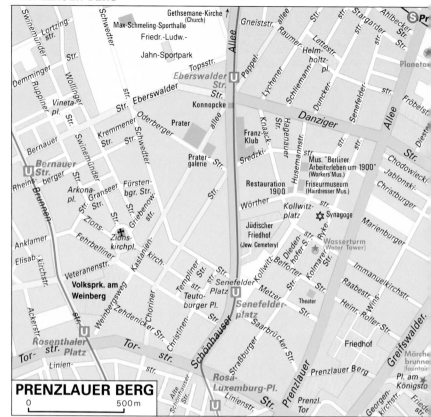

PRENZLAUER BERG

0   500m

1990, **Schönhauser Allee** became an urban renewal project, with the renovation, excavation, closing of gaps and the restoration of the beautiful buildings from the founding years of the German Empire. The color grey, formerly the characteristic of the East, is disappearing.

Senefelderplatz is typical of this rapidly-built district – but it will hardly be possible to guess its original appearance once the garden architects have implemented their plans over the next few years. A monument was erected here in 1892 to commemorate the inventor of lithography, Alois Senefelder. A few steps further along the Allee is number 22, a large brick building which is now a police station.

This **police station** was built in 1880 by the Jewish financier Manheimer as an additional old people's home for the then large Jewish community of Berlin. In 1944 the community was removed as owner from the land register and the building became one of the notorious "assembly points" for the Nazi death camps. Until recently there was not even a plaque to commemorate the fact that Jewish citizens were sent from here on their last journey to the death camps. Adjoining the former old people's home is the **Jewish Cemetery**, with its 5000 graves the largest cemetery in Berlin. It was consecrated in 1827. The Manheimers are buried here, as are famous Berliners such as the painters Max

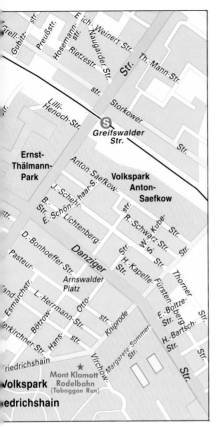

district. Here and in the side streets there is a plethora of restaurants, bars and trendy cafés. **Husemannstrasse** begins at Kollwitzplatz. For the 750th anniversary celebrations the GDR government revamped the street and made it look like the backdrop for a movie about life in the late 19th century. It then was the only restored part of the district amongst all that melancholic grey, but the other streets have caught up in the meantime. However, it remains a good stretch, with its old-fashioned stores, craftsmen's shops, cafés and bars, which somewhat bring back to life the late 19th century.

Not far from here is another special natural treat of Prenzlauer Berg: the area around the waterworks, which is delineated by Kolmarerstrasse, Diedenhoferstrasse, and Rykestrasse. The graceful **water tower** at Knaackstrasse 23 was the first one in Berlin, built in 1856. The second, fat tower dates back to 1876 and has been lived in since the 1950s. Its machine room was used as a torture chamber by the SA during the 1930s, as a memorial stone to their victims relates. Debates still rage over this unusual bit of property, as to whether it should become a public facility or be renovated to house expensive apartments. It is presently used for concerts and exhibitions.

Around the fat tower, bars and numerous little restaurants have clustered, including a Russian one, **Pasternak** (Knaakstr. 24). At Rykestrasse 53 a small **synagogue** is hidden, which was one of the few Jewish temple buildings in Berlin to survive the twelve years of Nazi terror. Since its restoration at the end of the 1970s, it has once again become a meeting-place for the the Jewish community.

Liebermann and David Friedländer, and the composer Giacomo Meyerbeer. Along the main paths, monumental family memorials reflect the rise of many Jewish families in the years after 1850.

Kollwitzplatz and its Environs

Wörther Strasse turns right off Schönhauser Allee and continues to **Kollwitzplatz**, named after the artist Käthe Kollwitz (1867-1945), who lived here (in house no. 25) and replicated the social misery of her neighborhood in her paintings and sculptures. Two monuments on the square commemorate her work.

The plaza, surrounded by high residential buildings, is one of the centers of the

Gethsemane Church

We continue on to Stargader Strasse, which leads to **Gethsemane Church**. This building is more than 100 years old and since 1989 has symbolized passive resistance in the GDR. When the regime started its decline in the autumn of that year, the church and its silent vigils suddenly became the center of opposition. On the night of October 7 the predominantly young people who had gathered here were suddenly faced by the forces of law and order. Equipped as if for a civil war, they attacked the demonstrators with unprecedented brutality. There were random arrests of those holding candles and calling for political change. Only six months later were the judgments that were passed out that night quashed.

From Stargader Strasse we continue on to **Schliemannstrasse 23**, site of the publishing house of grass roots groups, Basis Druck, and of the Robert Havemann Foundation and its archives. The writings of the former dissident Havemann, who is generally considered the intellectual mentor of East German opposition, and documents pertaining to the *Wende* (the "turning point," as the 1989 revolution is always rather gently referred to) are kept here. Right next door are the Matthias Domaschk Archives – named after a young civil rights activist who died while being detained by the Stasi, and whose death has still not been cleared up to this day – and the Environment Library, another nucleus of East German opposition. Until 1990 it was part of the Zion Temple located at the square of the same name and which, during the GDR period, was the only library in East Berlin stocking Western publications.

The cemetery on Lychener Strasse – you can't miss it as it is surrounded by a red wall – is called the **Friedhof der freien Geister** (Cemetery of Free Thinkers). Heinrich Roller, the inventor of stenography, is buried here, as is Wilhelm Hasenclever, a publisher and the first chairman of the SPD. The cemetery has now been restored and is a kind of a

Right: The old water tower in Prenzlauer Berg, a local landmark.

green oasis in the midst of this district of stone, concrete and brick.

Kastanienallee

If you continue on along Pappelallee and cross Schönhauser Allee, you will hit Kastanienallee (Chestnut Avenue). The chestnut trees used to cover the street like a green cathedral but, unfortunately, most of them have succumbed to leaks from the city's gas pipes. The street isn't very appealing at first glance, but in a way it still represents the character of Prenzlauer Berg best: if you pass through the front courtyards, you end up in a maze of backyards.

A lot of the traditional workshops are still located in these courtyards – the old Berlin mixture: people live in front and work in back; sometimes this arrangement gets a little mixed up, too. In addition to all kinds of restaurants and cafés, you will find a slew of little grocer's shops. At the beginning of the street is the famous **Prater**, one of the oldest beer gardens in Berlin. It hosts all sorts of events, from afternoons of tango to house parties. Number 77 is the district's oldest surviving house.

Oderberger Strasse, a street with avant-garde galleries turns right and left off Kastanienallee. Worth seeing is the **Stadtbad** (pool) designed by Ludwig Hoffmann and built in 1902. Unfortunately, it is closed at present. You can try to talk the custodian into letting you have a look at the pool area: reminiscent of a cathedral, promenade floors several stories high surround the old public pool.

Thälmann Park

Behind Prenzlauer Allee, near the S-Bahn station, is the new residential area, **Thälmannpark**, which extends as far as Greifswalder Strasse. It was one of the last prestigious projects of the old GDR, built in extreme haste to commemorate

the birth of Thälmann, a Communist leader murdered at Buchenwald. The residential area went up on a piece of former gasworks land without prior decontamination of the ground. The old gasometers , a precious monument of the Industrial Revolution, were dynamited in 1984. Next to the projects, on the northern edge of Thälmann Park, is the **Zeiss Planetarium**, which covers astronomy, and boasts a cinema and an exhibition of the venerable Zeiss Works in Jena, specializing in optical instruments.

Between Fröbelstrasse and Dimitroffstrasse is the district office, which used to be a hospital for the poor. It starts at Prenzlauer Allee 75 and has a little chapel where the dead were once laid out. Today, the **Prenzlauer Berg Museum für Heimatgeschichte und Stadtkultur** (Museum of Local History and Urban Culture) puts on exhibitions of contemporary history here. In 1945 the first Soviet Commandant lived here; the basement was used as a prison, which the Stasi later took over.

At the end of a wretched little park lies the district's number one bone of contention: the massive **Thälmann Monument**. Some people are fighting bitterly to have this 40-foot (12-meter) colossus torn down, while others insist it remain. For a while there was a plan for an unusual park that would demote the gigantic statue without destroying it. It was to be hidden behind a maze of green poplars.

This heroic statue with raised fist illustrates the GDR well. The people were invited to parade on the square before it, and had to crane their necks to look at their Leader! The statue was built by the Soviet monumentalist artist Lev Kerbler, hence the ressemblence to Lenin. The local populace came up with the portmanteau name "Le-Mann" for the monument, combining the names of the two Communist leaders.

All plans to tear down the statue or hide it behind greenery have been foiled because of lack of funds. In the meantime, the district has learned to live with its old friend from the GDR.

THE NORTH

In the North of Berlin lie the districts of Reinickendorf, Wedding and Pankow. In contrast to Wedding, which is a densely built-up district, the outlying districts of Reinickendorf and Pankow boast a fair acreage of natural landscape.

Reinickendorf

Reinickendorf's district coat-of-arms shows a fox next to six ears of wheat, symbolic of the six villages that once lay among forests and fields and which, together with two manors and a garden city, were incorporated into Greater Berlin's 20th administrative district in the municipal reform of 1920. With an area of about 34 square miles (89 sq km), Reinickendorf is, after Köpenick, the second largest district in Berlin, with over 250,000 inhabitants. This northernmost district in the Greater Berlin area still has a lot of woods and a great deal of water. Reinickendorf's nickname, the "Green North," is certainly well deserved. The old villages and settlements have, for the most part, managed to maintain their individuality, since the separate communities never really grew together.

The old village of **Tegel** has always been popular with Berliners as a goal for outings. A new center for innovation and founding businesses is being built on the grounds of the former Borsig works, as is a shopping center as well. Architecturally interesting is the modern residential settlement **Am Tegeler Hafen**, which was built in 1987 under the aegis of the **Internationale Bauaustellung**, the architectural exhibition. The most imposing building by far is the **Humboldt Library** on **Karolinenstrasse**. The carefully planned combination of living, culture and leisure has been achieved only partially so far.

Right: The skyline of high-rise blocks in the Märkisches Viertel.

In April 1997 a bronze monument to the brothers **Wilhelm and Alexander von Humboldt** – who are buried in their family's tomb at Tegel Castle – was erected nearby.

The architectural exhibit also spawned another project, namely construction of a special plant to remove phosphates from **Tegeler See** (Lake Tegel). Right next to the old harbor basin, the **Tegeler Fliess** flows into the lake. Hiking paths lead through charming natural surroundings, a unique swamp landscape of the March, that stretches from Tegel to Lübars.

The **Tegeler Forst** (forest) separates the village of **Heiligensee** from the other Reinickendorf communities. Far afield of the high-rise blocks and industry complexes, Heiligensee lies on a narrow spit of land between the Havel river and the Heiligensee lake. In this fishing village, first documented in 1308, time seems to have stood still. Fishermen smoke their own fish as they have been doing for ages. The old village common is among the largest and prettiest in Berlin. Farmhouses, smithies, a pub and a schoolhouse from the 19th century are grouped around the village church.

Nearly as idyllic, but more modern, is the garden city **Frohnau**, located all the way in the north of Reinickendorf. This is an affluent neighborhood with villas and country houses from the beginning of the 20th century clustered around **Zeltinger Platz** and neighboring Ludolfinger Platz. Evidence of this posh past is the polo field on **Gollanczstrasse**, opened in 1913, where tournaments are still held.

The **Edelhoffdamm** is the site of a Far Eastern refuge for meditation: in the 1920s Berlin doctor and linguist Paul Dahlke, a convert to Buddhism, established a **Buddhist House** in Frohnau. You enter the grounds through a portal in the shape of an elephant. This is followed by a climb up 73 steps to reach the temple, which stands on an elevation. This institution in Frohnau is open to the

general public and serves as the center of the Buddhist community in Berlin, which is permanently supervised and instructed by three monks from Sri Lanka.

A true jewel on the edge of the metropolis is the former village of **Lübars**. It was first mentioned in 1247, and duly celebrated its 750th anniversary in 1997. The old village core is tucked away in the fields and moor meadows of the Tegeler Fliess valley.

Within sight of this idyll towers the silhouette of the **Märkisches Viertel**, the most infamous satellite city of the 1960s. Since then, however, the Märkisches Viertel has earned global kudos as an example of excellent design of a 1960s project, thanks to an extensive renovation project which put new façades on the buildings and improved outdoor spaces.

Last but not least, no visitor should omit a side trip to the most industrial section of Reinickendorf, Reinickendorf-Ost (East), with the **Schäfersee** (Shepherd's Lake), an idyllic spot in spite of the dense surrounding buildings.

Wedding: Industry and Neighborhood

Around the turn of the century, **Wedding** developed into the most important industrial district in the north of Berlin, and soon gained notoriety as a radical, even "red," working-class district. Schering, Schwarzkopf, AEG and other major companies were founded here. Today a population of 160,000 is crowded into the relatively small district. Wedding lost its character as a purely proletarian district a long time ago; a colorful mixture of nationalities now lives here, and resident bohemians value the old factory halls which provide cheap studio space.

The district's history can be traced back to the year 1251. The name is derived from the nobleman Rudolf de Weddinge, who had an estate established here around 1200. The district's second historic root lies in the **Gesundbrunnen** section. The name means "Fountain of Health," and according to an old legend, the Prussian King Friedrich I discovered a spring here whose water was rich in

iron. This later became a spa named "Friedrich-Gesundbrunnen." In the 19th century the surrounding area developed into an entertainment quarter. On the Art-Nouveau façade of the building at **Badstrasse 38/39**, a relief of the former well house still recalls the old spring. This quarter has retained the name Gesundbrunnen, but the Berlin dialect simply refers to it as the *Plumpe*. Wedding's diversity is best revealed in the old buildings of the **Arnheim'sche Tresorfabrik** (safe factory) on Badstrasse, which house the largest sculptors' studio in Europe, and by the **Innovation Centers BIG** and **TIP** in the **AEG Building**, where small companies test out new technologies. A glimpse at the old **AEG gate** is a good yardstick of change.

The most famous street in Wedding is without doubt **Bernauer Strasse**. In 1961, when the Wall was being built, tragic scenes took place here when the

Above: The simple village church of Lübars in the light of sunset.

entire length of the street was divided down the middle. In desperation, East Berliners jumped from windows onto West Berlin territory. Until November 1989 the street attracted plenty of visitors wanting to have a look at the Communist border facilities.

On November 9, 1989, the first crossing for East Berliners was set up here. Since then there has been vehement discussion as to whether a **Berlin Wall Memorial** should be set up here. Many local residents who had been forced to live cheek-by-jowl with the concrete border for so many years do not want any reminder of the horrors of the Cold War. But the city fathers intend to have their way. The memorial was officially dedicated in the fall of 1998, even though it had not yet been completed.

One of Berlin's best-known hospitals, the **Rudolf-Virchow University Clinic**, still stands on **Amrumer Strasse**, where it was built between 1889 and 1906 by the famous Berlin architect Ludwig Hoffmann. Unfortunately, some of the buildings had to make way for the modern clinic, which is being expanded into a university clinic. The world-famous **Berlin Heart Center** also stands on the clinic grounds. The **Freie Universität** (Free University) also opened the **Zahnklinik Nord** (dental clinic) here in 1983. And the **Technische Fachhochschule Berlin** (Technical College of Berlin) has its main offices across from the hospital.

Historic buildings are rare in Wedding. Between 1832 and 1835 Berlin's most famous architect, Karl Friedrich Schinkel, built the **Alte Nazarethkirche** on **Leopoldplatz** in the style of a basilica. In the future, the church will provide room for cultural projects. Schinkel also designed a second church in Wedding, **St. Paul's**, at the corner of Pankestrasse and Badstrasse. The **Wedding District Court** on **Brunnenplatz** was designed in quite a strange way. Erected at the beginning of the 20th century, this court building, with its decorative portal and pompous vaulted ceilings, is a reproduction of the Albrechtsburg in Meissen.

A brand new, large-scale shopping complex, the **Gesundbrunnen Center**, opened at the Gesundbrunnen train station in 1997, serving the north of Berlin. Every Summer from now on, too, the open-air stage in the **Volkspark Rehberge** will host a theater festival, and in the **Max Beckmann Auditorium** on Luxemburger Strasse you can even hear the Berlin Philharmonic occasionally.

Pankow: Northern Berlin's Spot of Nature

The little **Panke** stream, which rises north of Bernau, gave this district its name. Today, about 100,000 people live in **Pankow**, which, together with Köpenick, is considered to be one of the better residential areas in the former territory of East Berlin. During the Cold War, Pankow earned dubious fame thanks to the so-called "Pankow Regime." **Schloss**

Niederschönhausen, in the heart of Pankow, was the office of Wilhelm Pieck, the first and only president of the former GDR, and later became the temporary seat of the State Council. A wall now separates the inconspicuous construction and its auxiliary buildings from the public **Schlosspark**, which was designed by Lenné and is open to the public from May to October.

Nearby **Majakowskiring**, colloquially known as "the town," was off-limits until the 1970s. This government quarter was where many GDR bigwigs lived. The Senate originally intended to house all the officials expected from Bonn in the former diplomat villas, but their representatives refused out of hand after inspecting the concrete-and-gravel blocks.

Pankow also attracted a considerable number of artists: writer Arnold Zweig, brother of the better known Stefan Zweig, lived at Hehmeyerstrasse 13, singer Ernst Busch at Leonhard-Frank-Strasse 11, and Ossietzky's family at what is now Ossietzkystrasse 24-26. A slew of galleries testify to the busy creative life of Pankow today.

Two of a total of 69 Pankow buildings declared national monuments are located on **Breite Strasse**: the **Altes Rathaus** (Old Town Hall), with its impressive tower, and the **Parish Church** on the **Village Green**. The church, built of fieldstone, is the district's oldest building, probably dating back to the 15th century. For over 130 years the **Pankower Wochenmarkt** (a weekly open-air market) has thrived behind the church.

The communities of **Rosenthal**, **Buchholz** and **Buch**, which are surrounded by forest and meadows, exude a pastoral atmosphere more typical of the March of Brandenburg than of the city of Berlin. The **Max Delbrück Center for Molecular Medicine** in Buch is internationally known for its research work. Scientists and doctors work together here on the development of new therapies.

THE WEST

Once upon a time **Schöneberg**, **Charlottenburg** and **Wilmersdorf** were independent communities located outside the gates of Berlin. The three districts, which were incorporated into Greater Berlin in the famous reform of 1920, developed into residential districts for the well-to-do.

The Schöneberg Neighborhood

Schöneberg, a relatively small district with 154,000 residents in an area of 4.7 square miles (12.3 sq km), is known primarily for its **Rathaus** (Town Hall). Between 1949 and 1990 West Berlin's political decisions were made here. This stately edifice was built between 1911 and 1914 at a cost of eight million gold marks, a very palpable manifestation of

Above: An angel – symbol of peace in a Schöneberg yard. Right: An almost rural scene – the Grunewald hunting lodge.

Schöneberg's wealth. High above the town hall stands the 230-foot (70-meter) tower where the *Freiheitsglocke*, a copy of the famous Liberty Bell in Philadelphia, has been rung every day since 1950. In June 1963 hundreds of thousands of Berliners cheered President John F. Kennedy on the Rathaus square when he proclaimed, "Ich bin ein Berliner"("I am a Berliner"), a statement of solidarity with the beleaguered city. In the same year, the Berliners renamed the square **John-F.-Kennedy-Platz**.

The original town hall was on **Kaiser-Wilhelm-Platz**, the former center of Schöneberg. This square crowns a small elevation, called "Schöner Berg" (Beautiful Mountain), which gave the district its name. Few traces remain of the village that once was here. The **Landkirche** (Rural Parish Church) rising above **Hauptstrasse** was built in 1766. Its exterior was renovated in 1955.

Next to the church, an old cemetery harbors the mausoleums of Schöneberg's *Millionenbauern* – the 19th century mil-

lionaire real estate sharks. These Berlin citizens made fortunes by speculating on the land. Their former villas on Hauptstrasse recall the district's past splendor.

Heinrich-von-Kleist Park, situated on **Potsdamer Strasse**, is the successor to the botanical garden which was located in Schöneberg until 1908. The **Königskolonnaden** (Royal Colonnades) designed in 1780 by Carl von Gontard, line Potsdamer Strasse. They originally adorned the Königsbrücke at Alexanderplatz, but the expansion of the inner city displaced them in 1910. The **Preussische Kammergericht** (Prussian Superior Court), built between 1909 and 1913, is located in the rear of the park. During the Nazi period the notorious *Volksgerichtshof* (People's Court), under the infamous Roland Freisler, held its sessions here. After the war, the Allied Control Council took up quarters in it for three years, and in 1972 the Four Powers Treaty for Berlin was signed here. Until 1991 the Center for Allied Air Security worked here. A year later, the Allies gave the building

back to the city, and the Superior Court moved back into its old quarters. Not far from Kleistpark, on the corner of **Pallasstrasse** and **Potsdamer Strasse**, the Berliners once cheered the six-day bicycle races in the Sportpalast. But they also cheered Joseph Goebbels when he called for "total war" here in 1943.

In the course of its turbulent history **Potsdamer Strasse** has been completely transformed. During the days of the Kaiser and the Weimar Republic it was one of Berlin's best business addresses, but after the construction of the Wall it deteriorated into a seamy district, with gambling and prostitution accounting for much of its financial turnover. The street has since become attractive once again; numerous publishers and public relations agencies have opened offices here.

Berliners meet around **Winterfeldtplatz** at night; during the day they can be found buying fresh fruit at the market. Pubs, cafés, small shops, and used-book dealers complete the picture on the way to **Nollendorfplatz**.

The "**Schöneberg Island**" between **Torgauer Strasse** and **Sachsendamm** is a densely built-up part of the city. It is a typical workers' neighborhood, and is completely surrounded by railroad tracks. Berlin's oldest **gasometer**, still in operation, towers above the roofs, visible from far and wide. The "island" also contains the historic **St. Matthäus Cemetery** at Grossgorschenstrasse 12/14, where the Brothers Grimm and Berlin doctor Rudolf Virchow rest in peace.

The town of **Friedenau** developed very differently: well-heeled officials and retirees preferred the quiet of this settlement of country houses on the **Bundesallee** to the noise of the city. Later, numerous artists followed suit, including writers Max Frisch, Erich Kästner, Günter Grass, Hans Magnus Enzensberger and Uwe Johnson. Children in Berlin captured the area's atmosphere in a rhyme that goes: "In Friedenau, the sky is blue, the goat and his wife are dancing, too."

Charlottenburg Beyond the Ku'damm

This district's traditional neighborhood lies around **Gierkeplatz**, where the **Luisenkirche** church, built in 1716, stands. Pubs, shops and old apartment buildings embody traditional Berlin *Gemütlichkeit* here. The oldest buildings are the former **Ackerbürgerhaus** at Schustehrusstrasse 13 and the one-time **schoolhouse** in the Gierkezeile, built in 1786.

Charlottenburg's highest building provides Berlin with one of its great symbols: the **Funkturm** (radio tower) on the fair grounds. The 452-foot (138-meter) construction was inaugurated in 1926 for the third German Radio Exhibition.

The first trade fair buildings went up in 1936. Between 1973 and 1979, when the old halls became too small for modern demands, the **Internationales Congress Centrum (ICC)** was added to the complex. A bridge crosses the Autobahn, joining the two complexes. Over 20,000 people fit into the colossal building, which looks a little like a spaceship.

The **Gedenkstätte** (Memorial) **Plötzensee** was established in 1952 by Berlin's Senat in the prison where 1800 members of the anti-Nazi resistance were executed between 1933 and 1945.

Wilmersdorf: Churches and Government Offices

Wilmersdorf shows two contrasting faces. The district consists of densely built-up metropolitan sections as well as Grunewald, an exclusive settlement with almost perfectly rural quality, most of whose 146,000 residents are government officials or white-collar workers. The famous – and infamous – "Wilmersdorfer widows," beneficiary heirs of the aforementioned, live here as well.

Little remains of the old farming community of Wilmersdorf. The core of the village once stood on the **Wilhelmsaue** meadow and, parallel to it, **Berliner Strasse**, which today is a lively business street. A granite block near Mehlitzstrasse marks the spot where the old village green once sprawled. The **Schoeler-Schlösschen**, Wilmersdorf's oldest residential building, stands as a last relic of times past. Built in 1752, it was later converted into a rococo palace and, at the end of the 19th century, was purchased by a Berlin doctor named Heinrich Schoeler. It now houses a day-care center. Behind it lie the **Schoelerpark** and the neo-Gothic **Auenkirche** (Meadow Church).

Berlin's largest administrative center, with over 30,000 employees, sprawls all around **Fehrbelliner Platz**. The buildings on the square are in monumental National Socialist style. The Wilmersdorf town hall, the local gallery, the Berlin

Right: The 1926 radio tower in Charlottenburg. Far right: Celebrating summer in a Kreuzberg yard.

Senate's administration for Interior Affairs and for Housing and Construction, have offices here, as does the Federal Insurance Agency.

In contrast to Wilmersdorf's densely laid-out inner city, the section called **Schmargendorf** seems like a small town. The old village church, Berlin's smallest, on **Breite Strasse**, makes it plain that Schmargendorf once subsisted on farming. The fieldstone foundation and the bell date from the 14th century. The most beautiful building is certainly the brick town hall on **Berkaer Platz**, built between 1900 and 1902 in the neo-Gothic style typical of the March. Architect Otto Kerwien designed the façade imaginatively, with crenelations, small towers and decorative coats-of-arms.

Koenigsallee in the Grunewald quarter took its name from banker Felix Koenigs, who participated in the laying out of the surrounding garden suburb. Established in 1889, it forms the genteel conclusion of the Kurfürstendamm, which had just been expanded to a boulevard celebrating imperial pomp. 538 acres (234 ha) of forest fell victim to the elegant quarter, and the swamp had to be drained. During the Weimar Republic well-known artists and politicians moved into the magnificent villas. On the corner of **Koenigsallee** and **Wallotstrasse** a stone memorializes Walter Rathenau, the Weimar Republic's statesman who was murdered on this spot by right-wing radicals in 1922. Rathenau lived at Koenigsallee 65.

Wilmersdorf enjoys a reputation for religious tolerance. The houses of worship of the most varied religions coexist peacefully here. The architecture of the **mosque** on the corner of **Berliner Strasse** and **Brienner Strasse** lends the area an unmistakably exotic flair. This Muslim prayer center, with its round cupola and minarets, constructed between 1924 and 1927, took exotic Indian chapels as its models. Not far away, light green onion domes indicate the path to the Russian-Orthodox **Christi-Auferstehungs-Kathedrale** on Konstanzer Strasse. It was built in 1938.

117

THE SOUTH

Berlin's south exhibits a heterogenous appearance to say the very least. **Zehlendorf** is a popular goal for excursions, and it boasts an expensive residential quarter. **Steglitz** and **Tempelhof** are similarly quiet but more middle-class, whereas **Neukölln** and **Treptow** still bear the typical characteristics of a genuine working-class district.

Green Zehlendorf

Zehlendorf is one of Berlin's most exclusive residential quarters and a paradise for affluent retirees. And this is little wonder, since the district is a true haven from Berlin's hectic big-city bustle. The Zehlendorfers live amidst vegetation: forest, water and green areas cover more than half of the dictrict's total area. Al-

Above: The Glienicke Bridge spanning the Havel. Right: Summer attracts myriad Berliners to the long Wannsee beach.

though Zehlendorf, with its 27.2 square miles (70.6 sq km), is more spacious than most of Berlin's districts, only 100,800 people live here. That makes Zehlendorf a favorite destination for outings from the hustling, bustling city. In the summer months, when Berlin becomes intolerably hot, people escape for a swim or sunbath at the **Strandbad Wannsee** (Wannsee Beach), which is within comfortable walking distance from the S-Bahn station Nikolasee. Every season over 500,000 day-trippers stream to the long, sandy beach of Europe's largest artificial swimming area.

Alexander von Humboldt praised the magnificent view of the Havel from the **Glienicker Brücke** in the south of Zehlendorf when it was still only a wooden bridge. The present iron construction, built between 1908 and 1909, made headlines several times while Germany was divided. East and West used to make spectacular trades of captured spies on this bridge, whose middle constituted the border to the GDR. Now, the most beautiful route from Berlin to Potsdam once againcrosses the bridge, which had been close to normal traffic since 1961.

Not far from the Glienicker Bridge, **Blockhaus Nikolskoe** lies on an elevation in the middle of the forest. The Prussian King Friedrich Wilhelm III had this Russian-style log cabin built in 1819 for his daughter Charlotte, who had been married to Prince Nicholas, who later became Czar Nicholas I of Russia. The caretaker of the log cabin operated a tavern, a sideline that became a tradition handed down to the present. Arson almost completely destroyed the restaurant in 1984, but the building has been reconstructed to match the original perfectly. Next to it, a nice onion-shaped Russian dome crowns the **St.-Peter-und-Paul-Kirche**. Marrying couples frequently use this sweet venue for their nuptials, and Berliners, in general, love to attend Christmas Mass within its romantic surroundings.

Steglitz: The Downtown of the South

In contrast to Zehlendorf, Steglitz is an inner-city district with an above average population density: 187,000 people live here in an area of only twelve square miles (32 sq km). More than half of all Steglitzers now live in newer housing complexes, but the neighborhoods of **Lichterfelde** and **Lankwitz** have managed to retain their suburban character and their old 19th-century villas and, by extension, their human dimensions.

Schlossstrasse makes a good side trip into the district. In the postwar years it developed into one of the most popular shopping streets in Berlin's south. A six-story shopping center, the **Forum Steglitz**, was added to **Walther-Schreiber-Platz**. The inconspicuous building next door cherishes memories of a glorious past. In 1928 the **Titania-Palast** opened as Berlin's largest cinema house, with 1900 seats. After the war the Berlin Philharmonic gave its first concert here, which contributed to raising the spirits of the bombed out Berliners. And, in 1951, the Titania-Palast hosted the renowned Berlin Film Festival for the first time. It has been beautifully restored.

The **Tower Restaurant**, opened in 1976 beside the Autobahn overpass, is the modern landmark on Schlossstrasse. Berliners nicknamed it the *Bierpinsel* (Beer Brush). Old and new Steglitz meets at **Hermann-Ehlers-Platz**. On one side of the square the 426-foot (130-meter) high **Steglitzer Kreisel** stretches into the sky. This highest of Berlin's highrises became a write-off ruin in the 1970s. Today it houses a hotel and part of Steglitz' district administration.

Diagonally across from the Steglitzer Kreisel stands the **Altes Rathaus** (Old Town Hall), built between 1896 and 1898 in Gothic style characteristic of the March. In 1901 young people founded the *Wandervögel* (Wandering Birds) youth movement in the building's cellar restaurant, which no longer exists today.

The popular field marshal Graf von Wrangel once lived in the **Wrangel-Schlösschen** on the corner of Schlossstrasse and Wrangelstrasse, in the heart of the former village of Steglitz. The quaint building has since become a restaurant. In the manor's former annex, the world famous **Schlosspark Theater** has found a permanent home.

The pioneer aviator Otto Lilienthal also lived in Steglitz, where he did some of his daring flying. In **Lilienthal Park** on Lichterfelde's **Schütte-Lanz-Strasse**, where he conducted some of his aeronautic experiments, a monument to him was erected in 1932.

One little curiosity in Berlin is the animal cemetery next to the Lankwitz home for abandoned animals on Dessauer Strasse. It is the final resting place for over 3000 animals, and a touching testimony to the love people have for their pets. It is slated to be closed in 1999.

Above: The harness-racing track in Mariendorf – a "good bet" for an outing.

Tempelhof

190,000 Tempelhofers live in near isolation in their residential district and enjoy a reputation for being quiet, lawabiding citizens. The quarter is primarily known for its airport, but, with its areas of **Mariendorf**, **Marienfelde** and **Lichtenrade**, it has more to offer than just the sound of jet engines and the smell of kerosene. Horse racing fans gather on Wednesdays and Saturdays at the **Trabrennbahn Mariendorf** (harness-racing track). The racetrack, built in 1913, attracts half a million visitors annually.

Activity is much calmer on the former **UFA Studio Grounds** on Oberlandstrasse, the second largest UFA studio complex. Today Germany's second television channel, ZDF, produces films here. Another "dream factory" of the past has its offices on **Viktoriastrasse**, where the **ufafabrik** now operates a movie theater, a stage for performances and other events, and a café. The former **Ullsteinhaus** at the Stubenrauch Bridge, with its 236-foot (72-meter) tower, is by far Tempelhof's most conspicuous building. Professor Eugen Schmohl erected this publishing house in 1925-26. It was Berlin's first reinforced concrete highrise.

Neukölln:
The Workers' District in the South

300,000 people live in **Neukölln** in Berlin's southwest, making it the city's most populous district. Formed in 1920 from the city of Neukölln and the villages of **Britz**, **Buckow** and **Rudow**, Neukölln is still a typical Berlin workers' neighborhood, but it also has some pleasant green areas. **Richardplatz** shows traces of Neukölln's rural past. It served as the core of the ancient Richardsdorp, first mentioned in a document in 1360. A 14th-century village church on the edge of the former village green merits a visit. The village smithy on Richardplatz dates from the 18th century and has been considered a national monument since 1949. Its fires still burn for the traditional craft.

Not far from Richardplatz, the **Böhmisches Dorf** (Bohemian Village) stretches along **Kirchgasse**. The monument for Friedrich Wilhelm I, dedicated in 1912, reminds us that the king granted asylum to religious refugees from Bohemia in 1737. Directly behind the monument is the former schoolhouse of the **Bohemian Brothers Community**, one of Neukölln's oldest buildings. Workers felled the first tree for its construction on March 2, 1753. A chalice is visible in the gable, which is also reminiscent of the Bohemian immigrants. To this day, the Bohemian Village's old colonists' farmsteads still exhibit a rural flair and a touch of Slavic tradition in the middle of the city.

The area between the Neukölln town hall and Karl-Marx-Platz forms the center of Neukölln. **Karl-Marx-Strasse**, which runs through it, is both traffic artery and main commercial drag. The

same applies to Sonnenallee and Hermannstrasse, which run parallel to it. The **ESTREL Residence Congress Hotel**, opened in 1994, whose 2200 beds make it the biggest hotel in Germany, rises on Sonnenallee like the bow of a ship.

From the early 1960s to the mid-1970s the precincts of **Buckow** and **Rudow** witnessed the building of the huge **Gropiusstadt** housing project. Architect Walter Gropius designed this fine example of social housing, with 17,000 apartments for up to 60,000 people. The **Hufeisensiedlung** (Horseshoe Settlement) in Neukölln's **Britz** precinct is considered one of the most beautiful projects to emerge from the wave of urban construction in the 1920s in Germany.

Schloss Britz (Britz Castle), built in 1706, is a neat little gem and a contemplative place to take in a concert or exhibition. Finally, Britz also boasts the restored **Stechan'sche Mühle** (built in 1865), which stands a short distance from **Britzer Garten**, where the Federal Garden Show was held in 1985. The mill is still operational (tours are provided), and there is a café and restaurant for visitors.

Nature and Industry in Treptow

Originally a fishing village and now an odd mixture of expansive parks and large industrial complexes, Treptow stretches along the banks of the Spree. Its 102,000 residents live in the areas of **Adlershof**, **Baumschulenweg** and **Niederschönweide**. **Bohnsdorf** and **Alt-Glienicke**, on the other hand, have preserved a largely rural character. Treptow's garden and country taverns once attracted flocks of visitors especially from the city, though their former flair has all but vanished today. Only the largest and best-known of the restaurants from the old days still exists, the **Eierschale Zenner**, which offers a view of the Spree. The neoclassical building was designed in 1822 by C. F. Langhans the Younger.

THE EAST

The color gray still dominates Berlin's eastern half and the streets still lack the dizzying dazzle of the western half. The streets in the center of this part of the city are often dilapidated and deserted, but the outlying areas are worst of all.

Marzahn, Hohenschönhausen, Hellersdorf

In these districts, anonymous, uniform, pre-fabricated houses weigh heavily upon residents and visitors alike. The buildings and the neighboring playgrounds are equally devoid of imaginative design. The shops here couldn't lure anyone to a shopping spree, nor do the restaurants or pubs, so much a part of Berlin life, seem to place any value on at-

Above: Berlin's East is dotted with anonymous high-rise blocks. Right: The renovated Schloss Friedrichsfelde shines with new splendor.

tracting guests. Marzahn and Hellersdorf were created as recently as 1986 by appropriating acreage from Lichtenberg.

Lichtenberg

Lichtenberg renounced two-thirds of its area, but its remaining ten square miles (26 sq km) show greater contrasts than any other district in the eastern part of Berlin. Its remaining 172,000 inhabitants live mostly in tenements built in the second half of the 19th century. These stand next to ostentatiously expensive villas from the turn of the century. Lichtenberg may not have the most, but it does have the highest chimneys in East Berlin. They belong to the **Rummelsburg Heating Plant**, formerly the Klingenburg Power Plant, on Hauptstrasse, which was constructed between 1926 and 1927. The first European attempt to fire a power plant with coal dust was made here. But the black clouds of smoke badly polluted the environment – only now are filters being installed in the smokestacks.

Lichtenberg's treasures are the **Tierpark** (zoo) in **Friedrichsfelde** and **Schloss Friedrichsfelde**. This palace, built at the end of the 17th century and completely renovated in 1981, hosts excellent concerts. **Karlshorst**, which became known for its **Trabrennbahn** (harness-racing track), also belongs to Lichtenberg. Horse races have been held since 1893 on the grounds, which extend over about 192 acres (80 ha) of land.

One of Lichtenberg's landmarks is the **Rathaus**. The foundation stone for the March-style brick building with its three little towers was laid in 1897. Now exiled to the western edge of the district, it is still an essential Berlin sight, although its fame is not as great as that of the Red, Köpenicker or Pankower town halls.

Friedrichshain

Friedrichshain is one of the smallest districts in Berlin's east, with 109,000 residents. It seems repellent at first glance, dominated as it is by ugly apartment buildings, factories, the central stockyard and the Ostkreuz. **Karl-Marx-Allee** is the axis of the district. The street was originally named Frankfurter Allee, but was dubbed Stalinallee in 1950, and has borne its current name since 1961. During World War Two, bombs flattened the buildings along this avenue, which is why pompous buildings in the elaborate Stalinist style flank this great east-west thoroughfare.

Most tourists see nothing of **Friedrichshain** but Karl-Marx-Allee, yet the district has more to offer. Another well-known and frequented site is the **Volkspark** (People's Park) **Friedrichshain**. The Friedrichshainers built it in 1840 in answer to the expansion of the Tiergarten behind the Brandenburg Gate.

Everyone turns up in the Volkspark for some air: in winter, people seeking solitude, in summer, sun-worshippers. Lovers and those in need of inspiration come year-round. The peaks of the two **Hainberge** can be climbed. The larger one rises about 256 feet (78 meters). Berliners call it simply **Mont Klamott**. This "mountain" and its 98-foot (30-meter) smaller brother are artificial elevations, constructed after 1945 from Berlin's rubble. In the meantime, stately trees and tangled bushes have grown on Mount Klamott. The plateau topping it offers a view of Berlin's east.

Directly below the hill is the former **Leninplatz**, which until early 1992 was dominated by a monumental sculpture of Lenin. The controversy over whether to leave it or tear it down raged for weeks, until finally the Senate prevailed and had the stone monstrosity demolished. Entries are currently being sought in a competition to redesign the square.

The path from the smaller rubble mountain toward the western tip of the park leads to the **Märchenbrunnen** (Fairy Tale Fountain). In 1913 the city architect, Ludwig Hoffmann, designed the fanciful sculptures for this neo-Baroque fountain. In summer, water rolls down terrace by terrace to the **Königstor** (King's Gate). Near the swan pond, the curved roof of a **Japanese pavilion** rests on lathe-turned beams of bright vermilion. A bell hangs from the eaves as a symbol of peace, donated for this purpose by the World Peace Bell Association. Over 123 acres (50 ha) in size, the park grounds also contain sports facilities, exciting playgrounds and an open-air stage seating 3000.

At the intersection of Dimitroffstrasse and Landsberger Allee, the **Sport- und Erholungszentrum** offers something for everyone: indoor and outdoor swimming pools, saunas, ice-skating and roller-skating rinks, a restaurant, ice cream parlor and café.

The **Ostbahnhof** (until recently called the Hauptbahnhof) was built in 1842 and is the only one of the four Berlin long-distance train stations actually located in the core of the city. It has been remodeled, expanded and even renamed several times.

Weissensee

Originally only a quiet village on the March, **Weissensee** first awoke from its age-long slumber during Berlin's 19th-century industrial boom. The "prince" who kissed this Sleeping Beauty awake was a Hamburg businessman. He bought the Weissensee estates and, in gratitude, the people of Weissensee named two streets after him, Schönstrasse and **Gustav-Adolf-Strasse**. Like Lichtenberg, this district was truncated in 1986; today 52,000 people live here on a mere one-half square mile (1.5 sq km), making Weissensee the smallest of all Berlin's districts. It has managed to preserve its nearly pristine suburban character in the midst of the big city: the district is replete with single-family houses, gardens and plenty of idyllic verdant spots.

Weissensee owes its reputation as a site for relaxation primarily to four connected lakes: **Fauler See**, **Obersee**, **Orankesee** and **Weisser See**. Fauler See and its surroundings are a small and concise nature reserve. Thirty different species of birds have been spotted here in the middle of the metropolis. On a hot day, people go for a swim in the Orankesee or the Weisser See. Rowboats also ply the Weisser See, which is relatively sheltered from the noise from **Klement-Gottwald-Allee**. The latter leads cityward to **Antonplatz**. There, directly across from the **Toni** movie theater, the sculpture of a mischievously smiling gardener, who commemorates the *Schusterjungen*, Berlin's shoemaker apprentices of the 19th century, greets passers-by .

Weissensee's fame extends far beyond Berlin's borders, thanks primarily to the **Jewish Cemetery**, whose gate opens onto **Herbert-Baum-Strasse**. This largest of all European Jewish cemeteries

Right: A bird's eye view of the Jewish cemetery in Weissensee.

contains 150,000 grave sites. Before World War Two a high percentage of Jewish Germans lived in Weissensee and many kept small stores here.

Inaugurated in 1880, the cemetery grounds seem almost consoling nowadays, with their abandoned, wild vegetation bursting with life. But the inscription "Auschwitz" on many of the gravestones serves as a stark reminder of the horrors wrought by the National Socialists. Simple and elaborate graves lie close to each other; the graveyard contains the remains of unknown people, as well as famous personalities from the cultural and political spheres: Rudolf Mosse (1843-1920), one of Berlin's great publishers, once owner of the newspaper *Berliner Tageblatt,* lies here, as does his chief editor, Theodor Wolff (1866-1907). The founder of the publishing house *S.-Fischer Verlag,* Samuel Fischer (1859-1934), has found his final resting place here beside Hermann Tietz (1837-1907), one of Berlin's most famous businessmen and founder of the *Hertie* chain of department stores. And, finally, a plaque honors the parents of writer Kurt Tucholsky; his father Alex (1855-1905), who lies buried here, and his mother Doris (1869-1943), who died in the Theresienstadt concentration camp. The Weissensee Jewish Cemetery not only silently witnessed the violence of Germany's past, but also people's efforts to save themselves: during the period of Nazi rule Jews repeatedly hid in the mausoleum of the singer Josef Schwarz (1881-1926).

Köpenick: Suburb on Müggelsee

Köpenick is the largest and least densely populated district of Berlin: 111,000 people on 49 square miles (127 sq km). It is most famous as a recreation area for Berliners, as one of the city's great green areas: cruises on the **Grosser Müggelsee** lake and visiting **Schloss Köpenicker** are especially popular, especially in summer (More on these in the chapter "Oases of Nature: Palaces, Parks and Lakes" on page 168).

SPANDAU

The Spandauers probably display the most local patriotism of any Berliners. In the eyes of the over 200,000 people who live here, their district is still located *next to* Berlin. When they go shopping "in the city," they mean in Spandau's old town, but if they drive to the Kurfürstendamm, they say that they are going "to Berlin."

Spandau was first mentioned in a document in 1197. By 1232 it had already been granted civic rights – five years earlier than Berlin. Work to turn it into a fortress with a citadel began in 1626.

Spandau's Old Town

Spandau's old town is the only one in Berlin proper that still has a genuinely original look. Its oval form recalls the shape of the erstwhile fortress.

Above: The Spandau lock. Right: Enjoying food and drink in the cozy atmosphere of the Spandau Citadel's cellar.

Rathaus Spandau, the town hall at the U-Bahn station of the same name, is a good starting place for a stroll through the old town. One special trait of the town hall (designed by architects Reinhardt and Süssengruth and built between 1910 and 1913) is the 236-foot (72-meter) tower, which was erected in the yard and not atop the main building because the ground was so shaky. This government building, which cost nearly 3.5 million gold marks, was the expression of the town's independence. In 1920 the citizens lost their independence – by law, not by attitude – when Spandau, together with five other rural communities and three large estates, was integrated into Greater Berlin as the eighth district.

The **Gotisches Haus** (Gothic House) at Breite Strasse 32, in the pedestrian zone of the old town, is a special place. It was built around 1500 and is the oldest residential house in Berlin. You'll find information on Spandau here, a department of the **Stadtgesichtles Museum** (city history) and changing exhibitions.

A farmer's market is held regularly on the large rectangular square, and Germany's largest advent market settles into the entire pedestrian zone before Christmas.

The massive silhouette of the **St.-Nicolai-Kirche** on **Reformationsplatz** dominates the townscape in the center of the old town. It was built in the middle of the 15th century and is among the oldest Gothic city churches in the March of Brandenburg. Its predecessor was mentioned in documents as early as 1240. Among its most valuable furnishings are a bronze baptismal font from the year 1398, a Baroque wooden pulpit and a Renaissance altar donated in 1582 by the master builder of the Spandau fortress, Count Lynar.

In front of the main portal of St. Nicolai's stands the monument to **Elector Joachim II**, which was dedicated in 1889. It recalls the Elector's 1539 conversion to Lutheranism, which took place in this church. This event made Spandau the starting point for the Reformation in the March of Brandenburg.

The cellar of **house No. 3/4** on Reformationsplatz contains another relic from days gone by, the left-over wall of a 13th-century Dominican monastery, kept behind a protective glass pane.

The most romantic part of Spandau's old town is undoubtedly **Behnitz**. Picturesque townhouses, modest half-timbered houses and narrow cobbled alleys make up the dreamy tableau. **Behnitz No. 3**, built in 1868, once housed Spandau's Office for Military Construction and the arsenal. **Behnitz No. 4** is a restored half-timbered house from the 18th century. Next to it stands the **Heinemannsches Haus**, built in the 1770s in late-Baroque style and named after its original resident, the composer Wilhelm Heinemann.

St.-Marien-Kirche, which opened its doors in 1848, was the second Catholic church in the March of Brandenburg since the Reformation, the first having been completed in 1723 near Spandau.

Behnitz is the oldest settled part of the old town. The finds here go as far back as the Stone Age. People often refer to the part of town just behind the busy **Strasse Am Juliusturm** as **Kolk**, but in fact, Kolk is only a street in Behnitz.

A 164-foot (50-meter) section of the old city wall rises to its original height on the **Hoher Steinweg**. Remains of a 14th-century defensive tower have come to light on its rear side.

The **Spandau Lock** is clearly visible from the intersection of Möllentordamm and Behnitz. It started operating in 1910, but evidence of a lock on this location dates back to 1723.

The Spandau Citadel

The **Spandau Citadel**, an outstanding example of Italian Renaissance fortress-building skill, stands at the point where the Havel and Spree rivers meet a few steps from the old town. In the 12th century the Askanians built a castle surrounded by water on this spot. The citadel itself was completed in 1560 on order from Elector Joachim II as a means to protect Berlin. It continued to serve military aims until after World War Two. Restoration work on it began in 1977.

The **Kommandantenhaus**, where an exhibition on the citadel can be seen, and the **Palas**, originally a Gothic construction from the first half of the 15th century, have already been restored. Changing exhibits are shown in the Palas' authentic **Gothic Hall**.

Spandau's hallmark, and oldest section of the citadel, is the 105-foot (36-meter) **Juliusturm** (Julius Tower). This formerly defensive and residential tower was built around 1200. Its lookout platform offers a grandiose view over Spandau and its surroundings.

Spandau's Precincts

For centuries the fortress reigned in Spandau's development. Not until its "de-fortressing" in 1903 did the city ex-

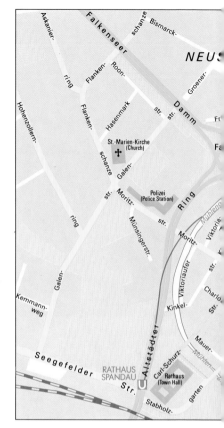

pand into the surrounding countryside. **Neustadt** (New City), formerly called Oranienburger Vorstadt (suburb), grew to the north of the old town. To the east of it, a new Spandau precinct is being built for 50,000 people.

In Spandau's south lie the former villages of Pichelsdorf, Gatow and Kladow. They were not incorporated into Spandau until 1920, and even today farmers still raise crops and livestock in what could be considered rural communities, as amazing as that might seem so close to Berlin.

The earliest record of the fishing village of **Pichelsdorf** is in a document from the year 1375. In 1816 the first German steamship, the *Prinzessin Charlotte von Preussen,* was built here.

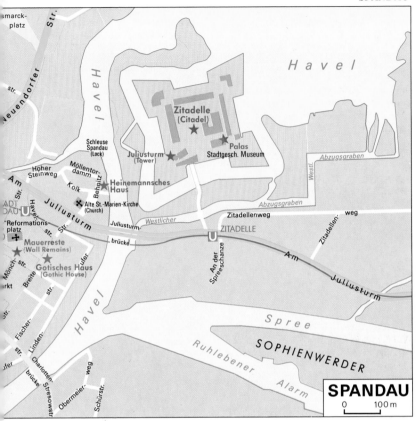

H a v e l

Zitadelle
(Citadel)
★

Schleuse
Spandau
(Lock)
Juliusturm ★
(Tower)

Palas ★
Stadtgesch. Museum

Abzugsgraben

Höher
Steinweg

Möllentor-
damm

Kolk

Behnitz

Heinemannsches
Haus

Alte St.-Marien-Kirche
(Church)

Reformations-
platz

Juliusturm str.

Juliusturm-
brücke

Westlicher

Zitadellenweg

ZITADELLE

weg

Zitadellen-

Am

Juliusturm

Mauerreste
(Wall Remains)

Gotisches Haus
(Gothic House)

An der Spreeschanze

S p r e e

SOPHIENWERDER

Ruhlebener

Alarm

SPANDAU

0   100 m

The centerpiece of old **Gatow**, first documented in 1258, is the 14th-century village church, built of fieldstones. The airport used by the Allies for the purpose of supplying the Berliners during the blockade lay between the villages of Gatow and Kladow.

The earliest kown document mentioning **Kladow** dates back to the year 1267. The village church in **Alt-Kladow** dates from the year 1818, but it had a much older predecessor. Next to the churchyard, a **300-year-old linden tree** casts its shadow on the plaque recounting its history. Several old farmhouses surround the village green.

The industrial and residential buildings of **Siemens AG** dominate the **Siemens-stadt** to the east of Spandau. Siemens, is the largest corporation in Spandau, and is hence revered as a major job provider. In 1897 the budding electrical company Siemens & Halske bought its first plot of land on **Nonnendammallee** and erected a cable and dynamo plant.

In the following years the number of production plants increased and the first apartments for employees were built. In the 1920s, architect Hans Hertlein created the Siemensstadt's typical architecture using red brick. He also designed the landmark of this part of Spandau, the **Siemensturm**, a 230-foot (70-meter) tower with a mighty tower clock, which still overshadows the part of the factory complex located on **Wernerwerkdamm**.

BERLIN DISTRICTS

Kreuzberg

The best way to reach Kreuzberg is with the U-Bahn lines No. 1 and 15, or with the 129 bus.

Two covered markets worth seeing, be it for the architecture alone, have survived here: At Eisenbahnstrasse and Marheinekeplatz. On Oranienstrasse and Bergmannstrasse you'll find trendy boutiques for clothes, jewelry and second-hand clothing.

Art to see and buy, readings:
Galerie am Chamissoplatz, Chamissoplatz 6.
Grober Unfug, Zossener Str. 32/33. Besides the **Comic-Galerie,** you'll also find one of Berlin's largest comics shops here.

If in Kreuzberg, do not fail to eat Turkish food, preferably at one of the ubiquitous **kebab snack stands.**

Middle Eastern fast food is also very popular: there are **falafel stands** on Spreewaldplatz, Gneisenaustrasse (corner of Zossener Strasse) and Yorckstrasse (between Riehmers Hofgarten and Grossbeerenstasse). Kebab and falafel snack bars are open till late in the night.

Cafés on Paul-Lincke-Ufer: **Café am Ufer** (No. 42), **Café Übersee** (No. 44).
Restaurants: Barcomi's (Bergmannstr. 21), **Zur Kleinen Markthalle** (Legiendamm 32) is the restaurant to go for roast chicken. The **Van Loon** is a restaurant ship in the Urban harbor. Fine cuisine in a beautiful ambiance can be had at the **Altes Zollhaus** (Old Arsenal, Carl-Herz-Ufer 30).
Cultural Centers and Museums:
Künstlerhaus Bethanien, Mariannenplatz 2, tel. 25 88 41 51.
German Museum of Technology in Berlin, Kreuzberg, Trebbiner Str. 9, tel. 25 48 40.
Martin Gropius Building, Stresemannstr. 110, tel. 25 48 60 (closed until mid-1999 for renovations).
Topography of Terror, covers the dark years of Nazism in Berlin, Stresemannstr. 110, tel. 25 48 67 03, daily 10 a.m.-6 p.m.

Prenzlauer Berg

All sights of this district can be seen on foot from Schönhauser Allee: **Jewish Cemetery,** Schönhauser Allee 22, Mon-Thu 8 a.m.-4 p.m., Fri 8 a.m.-1 p.m.; before Jewish holidays 1 p.m., closed on Jewish holidays.

Pubs, Cafés, Restaurants:
The spectrum ranges from **Café Anita Wronski** (Knaackstr. 26-28) to the trendy bar **Kommandantur** (Knaackstr./Rykestr.), the old-fashioned Berlin *Kneipe* **Metzer Eck** (Metzer Str. 33), the **Res-** tauration 1900 (Husemannstr. 1), the Russian inn **Pasternak** (Knaackstr. 24) or the wine bar **Alea lacta** (Lychener Str. 39), all the way to high class Italian cuisine in the **Trattoria Lappeggi** (Kollwitzstr. 56) or **Il Pane e le Rose** (Am Friedrichshain 6).

The **Prater,** an old-fashioned Berlin restaurant at Kastanienallee 7-9 (tel. 247 67 72), has one of the city's largest beer gardens.

Theater-goers should check out the menu of the **Volksbühne** on Rosa-Luxemburg-Platz.

In the **Kulturbrauerei,** a cultural center neatly located in a former brewery (Knaackstr. 97, tel. 441 92 69/-70), there are concerts, exhibitions and debating evenings. In the northern wing: **Collection of Industrial Design,** artifacts from product culture and everyday life.

Pfefferberg (Schönhauser Allee 176, tel. 449 65 34), a giant warehouse dating from the 19th century, has concerts, exhibitions, events. The big beer garden is especially beautiful.

Zeiss Gross Planetarium, (Prenzlauer Allee 80, tel. 42 18 45 12).

Reinickendorf, Wedding and Pankow

The **Heimatmuseum** tells about the history of **Reinickendorf,** Alt-Hermsdorf 35, tel. 404 40 62, Wed-Sun 10 a.m.-6 p.m., closed holidays. If on an excursion to **Lübars,** you can enjoy coffee or robust Berlin food in the **Alter Dorfkrug,** Alt-Lübars 8, tel. 402 71 74. For finer cuisine, try **Rockendorf's**. This restaurant, which is located in the precinct of Waidmannslust (Düsterhauptstrasse 1, tel. 402 90 35) is one of the best – and most expensive – in town. Open to the public, too, are: the **Borsig-Werke,** the **Russian Cemetery** (in the precinct of Borsigwalde, Wittestr. 37) and the **Buddhist House** in **Frohnau.**

A walking tour of **Tegel,** beginning at the Alt-Tegel subway station (U 6), is recommendable. It leads through Berlin's oldest pedestrian zone to the former Tegel meadows, the **Greenwich Promenade,** and **Tegel Lake.**

Wedding: Subway line No. 9, exit at Leopoldplatz oder Nauener Platz. This is where the neighborhood life of the district unravels.

Heimat (local) **Museum,** Pankstr. 47, tel.45 75 41 58, Tue, Wed 10 a.m.-4 p.m., Thu noon-6 p.m., Sun 11 a.m.-5 p.m.

The sights described in **Pankow** can all be seen on a walking tour beginning at the S-Bahn station Pankow (line No. 8 or 10). The old heart of the village is in the proximity, and the **Schlosspark** (Castle Park) next to **Majakowskiring,** with the **literatur-**

WERKstatt berlin (No. 46/48, tel. 482 47 65), has readings, festivals and discussions. Next to it is the local museum, the **Panke Museum**, (Heynstr. 8, tel. 481 40 47, Tue, Thu 10 a.m.-6 p.m., Sun 10 a.m.-5:30 p.m., closed holidays.
Restaurant: Kartoffelhaus No. 1 (Mühlenstr. 30, tel. 478 4640, daily from 11 a.m.) good place to round off a stroll through Pankow.

The West –
from Spandau to Schöneberg

Spandau is connected to Berlin's inner city via **Heerstrasse** and the U-Bahn line No. 7. Buses drive to all precincts in Spandau from the city hall, the **Spandauer Rathaus**.
The **Spandau Citadel** and the **Museum of Spandau History** are open Tue-Fri 9 a.m.-5 p.m., Sat, Sun and holidays 10 a.m.-5 p.m. Guided tours Sat, Sun and holidays, from May to Oct 1 p.m., 2:15 p.m. and 3:30 p.m., Nov-Apr 1:30 and 2:15 p.m., for groups please book in advance (tel. 334 62 70). In the **Zitadellenschänke** you can eat solid, home-style food (Tue-Sun from 6 p.m., tel. 334 21 06).
Gotisches Haus (Gothic House, Breite Str. 32) with the **Spandau Information Office**, museum section and changing exhibitions (tel. 333 93 88).
Charlottenburg, local color off the Ku'damm and its environs unfolds to the north near Kaiserdamm and Bismarckstrasse. Bits of old Charlottenburg can be discovered now and then on both sides of **Schlossstrasse**.
The **Funkturm (Radio Tower)** is an excellent place to get a terrific view, daily 10 a.m.-11 p.m.; by the way, the restaurant up at 180 feet (55 meters) is better known for its view than its cuisine, tel. 30 38 29 96, daily 11:30 a.m.-11 p.m.
The **Gedenkstätte Plötzensee** (memorial) is quite a distance from the other former centers of Nazi terror, Hüttigpfad, daily 8:30 a.m.-6 p.m., tel. 344 32 26. Around 1800 opponents of the Nazi regime were put to death in this Nazi penitentiary, whose very name sent shivers down many a back.
In **Wilmersdorf**, do not forego a visit to the **Wilmersdorf Museum** and the **Communal Gallery**, which is right next door and holds changing exhibitions, Hohenzollerndamm 174-177, Mon-Fri 10 a.m.-6 p.m., also Sun 11 a.m.-5 p.m. For special exhibitions, tel. 86 41 25 39.
A pretty area to stroll around in and do some window shopping extends between Olivaer Platz and Fasanenplatz, with row upon row of exclusive boutiques, galleries, cafés and restaurants.
Schöneberger Rathaus (Town Hall), John-F.-Kennedy-Platz, tel. 78 76-0, has the "Liberty Bell" and an exhibition on the history of the city hall.

Tours for groups: Kultur Büro Berlin (tel. 440 09 36). A market is held on the square in front of the city hall, Tue and Fri 8 a.m.-1 p.m.
Otherwise, a must is a walk over to **Nollendorfplatz** and **Winterfeldplatz**. On Winterfeldtplatz a real insider market is held Wed, Sat 8 a.m.-2 p.m. Also interesting, albeit somewhat tough, is the area around **Potsdamer Strasse**.
Also in Schöneberg is the **Insulaner**, a mountain made of rubble culled from the bombed out city after the war, with the **Wilhelm Foerster Observatory** and the **Planetarium**, Munsterdamm 90, tel. 790 09 30, star-gazing with telescope: Tue, Thu, Fri 9 p.m., Sat 6 p.m. and 9 p.m., Sun 4:30 p.m. and 6 p.m.

Districts in the South
and in the East

Zehlendorf and **Steglitz** are best visited by taking the 148 bus. From the terminus of the No. 1 U-Bahn line, Krumme Lanke, you can take a rewarding walk on **Mexikoplatz** to **Potsdamer Chaussee**. S-Bahn station Mexikoplatz is the only Art-Nouveau station to have survived the war.
Zehlendorf: Dahlem Museums.
Steglitz: residence of the architect Gustav Lilienthal (Marthastr. 5).
Tempelhof: ufaFabrik Viktoriastr. 13, tel. 75 50 30.
Neukölln, best investigated from the U-Bahn stations of the No. 7 line, is centered on **Hermannplatz** and **Karl-Marx-Platz**, the major shopping streets are **Karl-Marx-Strasse** and **Hermannstrasse**.
Schloss Britz (Britz Castle) in the south of Neukölln is open to the public, Alt-Britz 73, tel. 606 60 51, guided tours are Wed 2-6 p.m.
A market is held on the Maybachufer, the **Türkenmarkt**, Tue and Fri, noon-6:30 p.m.
In adjacent Treptow, the broad **Stralauer Allee** and **Am Treptower Park** are worth seeing; the **Archenhold Observatory** stands in the park. Alt-Treptow 1, telescope viewings, Wed 6 p.m., weekends 2-5 p.m., tel. 534 80 80. Close to the park: **Haus Zenner** (Alt-Treptow 14-17, tel. 533 73 70; Sun-Thu 9a.m.-2a.m., Fri-Sat till 4 a.m.).
Lichtenberg and **Friedrichshain** straddle **Karl-Marx/Frankfurter Allee** and the S-Bahn stations of the No. 3 line.
Neighborhood life in Friedrichshain is particularly lively on **Petersburger Strasse** and around **Boxhagener** and **Bersarinplatz**.
The Jewish Cemetery in **Weissensee**, is located at Herbert-Baum-Str. 45, Sun-Thu 8 a.m.-5 p.m., Fri 8 a.m.-3:30 p.m. (before Jewish holidays only till 1 p.m.), closed on Jewish holidays. tel. 925 33 30.

AROUND BERLIN

POTSDAM
LANDSCAPES OF THE MARCH

POTSDAM

Potsdam lies immediately to the southwest of Berlin, surrounded by a string of Marchland lakes. "Prussia was built up from Potsdam and illuminated from Sanssouci. The Havel river can assume its place among German cultural waterways," wrote Theodor Fontane in his *Wanderings Through the March of Brandenburg.* Thanks to its palaces and historical buildings, the city has indeed become one of Europe's most important cultural sites. About 25,000 buildings and parks in Potsdam have been declared national monuments. Some of the greatest minds of Europe worked in Potsdam: Voltaire lived here between 1750 and 1753, and Lessing completed his *Miss Sara Sampson* in 1755 in Potsdam. Heinrich Heine, Ludwig Tieck and Theodor Fontane found a favorable climate for their work in this city as well.

The City of Potsdam

In the year 993 the written history of Potsdam began in a document signed by Otto III granting the town civic rights.

Preceding pages: Adolph von Menzel's "Friedrich the Great's Flute Concerto." Left: The terraces of Sanssouci Palace.

But the community remained insignificant until the 17th century, when Elector Friedrich Wilhelm had the *Stadtschloss* (City Palace) built by his court architect Memhardt from 1664 to 1670, and used it as his official residence. In the 18th century, Friedrich Wilhelm I, the austere "Soldier King," turned Potsdam into a kind of garrison town, bequeathing to it the strict architectural lines that it still bears today to a certain extent. His son, Friedrich II, later began to reconstruct Potsdam as a showcase for visiting dignitaries. The city also owes him **Sanssouci Palace**, the "Prussian Versailles" as it became known. After World War Two the city of Potsdam was rebuilt, albeit in rather slipshod fashion, in its shadow.

Now that Potsdam has regained its status as capital of the state of Brandenburg, which it had lost in 1952, it will win back some of its former glamor.

Potsdam's almost 140,000 residents will continue to be faced with a great deal of work in the next few years. The architectural wounds inflicted during the Second World War and during the subsequent decades of neglect will heal only gradually. The city itself and the state of Brandenburg lack the financial means for the rapid restoration of the historic buildings. The *Preussische Schlösser und Gärten Berlin-Brandenburg* foundation,

135

which cares for the regional palaces and parks, will be financed primarily by the federal government to do the restoration and upkeep work. The city's millenial celebrations in 1993 provided a good incentive for Brandenburg and its capital to rebuild some of its old luster. Potsdam's cultural landscape, by the way, was already placed on the UNESCO World Heritage list in 1991. A threat to this historic gem is the planned **Potsdam Center**, a gigantic mall, which would definitely alter the unity of the ensemble.

The inner city area is framed on the west by the **Brandenburg Gate**, in the north by the **Jägertor** (Hunters' Gate) and the **Nauener Tor**, and in the east by **Bassinplatz**, with the **French Church**. Architect Knobelsdorff designed this round Baroque church, which was completed in 1753; Schinkel planned the 1833 refurbishing of the interior. The en-

semble around the **St.-Nikolaikirche** (1830-1837), with the **Altes Rathaus** (Old City Hall, 1753) and the **Marstall** on the **Alter Markt** (Old Market), makes up the southern edge of Bassinplatz. The neoclassical Nikolaikirche presides over the center of Potsdam. Schinkel designed it and supervised its construction from 1830 to 1837, using the ideas of Crown Prince Friedrich Wilhelm.

Potsdam's **Stadtschloss**, the city palace which the Great Elector ordered built in the 17th century, used to stand on the Old Market. His successor transformed the modest building into a splendid piece of architectural extravaganza. Unfortunately, bombardments during World War Two caused irreperable damage to the palace and the garrison church, and what was left standing was finally torn down in the 1960s, a purely political decision, and rather a painful mistake that destroyed the harmony of the Baroque inner city. From a technical point of view it would have been possible to repair and maintain these two buildings.

Above: Potsdam's pleasant pedestrian zone.
Right: Decorative 18th-century façades in the Dutch Quarter.

The makeshift **Hans-Otto Theater** was irreverently erected in front of the Nikolaikirche. This was to be the GDR's first new theater building. At the time of unification only the foundation had been laid, and a provisional theater building was quickly erected. A new theater is planned for this site by the year 2001.

The **Film Museum** (Breite Strasse, near the Marstall) documents the history of Babelsberg Studios with costumes, photos, posters, special effects demonstrations and special exhibitions. Cinematic treats are offered in the museum's movie theater.

A pedestrian zone leads from Potsdam's Brandenburg Gate to the **Kirche St. Peter und Paul**. Schinkel's pupil W. Salzenberg built this church between 1867 and 1870, imitating Istanbul's Hagia Sophia. The cross streets leading to the shopping avenue are the site of intense construction work now. The same applies to the **Holländisches Viertel** (Dutch Quarter), north of the Church of Peter and Paul. Special efforts are now

being made to rescue the 134 brick buildings of this 18th century settlement. The houses were built in typical Dutch style under the direction of Johann Boumann to accomodate the Dutch craftsmen Frederick the Great had invited to Potsdam to work on Sanssouci. The expected influx of workers did not materialize and so it was predominantly local soldiers and their families who moved in. The plan now is to restore the entire quarter, but only part of the work is finished. A variegated mix of cafés, restaurants, bars, galeries, art and antique dealerships have settled here in the meantime. A visit to the pottery market in September is worth a side trip to the *Holländisches Viertel*.

A tour of Potsdam should also include the **Russian colony Alexandrowska** near the **Nauener Tor**. In 1812 a contingent of 62 Russian prisoners-of-war arrived in Potsdam. King Friedrich Wilhelm III enlisted them in his men's choir. After Czar Alexander I signed an alliance with the King of Prussia, he didn't demand their return but gave them to the

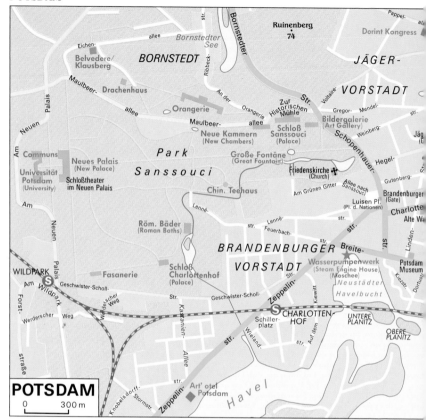

POTSDAM

0   300 m

Prussian monarch as a present instead. In 1826 the King built 14 log cabins for them as well as the **Alexander-Newski-Kirche**, modelled on Kiev's Desiatin Church. West of the Russian colony, the **Neuer Garten** (New Garden) spreads on the western banks of the Heiligensee.

Schloss Cecilienhof stands in the midst of this park. In 1945 the victorious powers of World War Two negotiated the Potsdam Treaty, which divided Germany into four zones of occupation, here. The famous round table and the rooms where the delegates did their work can be visited. The rest of the palace houses the luxurious **Schlosshotel Cecilienhof**, with its elegant restaurant. A stroll around the *Neuer Garten* reveals the **Marmorpalais**

(Marble Palace) on the lake shore. It was designed by Carl von Gontard and built between 1787 and 1792. And, after many years of restoration, this museum palace is once again open to the public.

An unusual monument to technology graces the Neustadt's Havel cove, an old-fashioned **waterworks**. From the outside, the building looks like a Moorish mosque with a minaret. Inside, the steam engine driving the water works is still functional. The facility, built in 1841-42 according to plans by L. Pesius, pumped water from the Havel up to the **Ruinenberg** (Ruin Mountain), an artificial collection of Roman and Greek ruins above Sanssouci Palace, and supplied all of the park's fountains.

Potsdam-Babelsberg

Northeast of the inner city, in **Potsdam-Babelsberg**, Schinkel built the neo-Gothic **Schloss Babelsberg** in the shape of a fort. Prince von Pückler-Muskau had the park laid out according to designs by Lenné. Babelsberg is Germany's film city: Bioscop was already making movies here between 1912 and 1924, and UFA-Films was founded here in 1945. Between 1946 and 1990 DEFA made some films that were so controversial the public only saw them after 1990. Today the studios belong to a French media corporation, and TV series, talk shows and films are produced here. In **Filmpark Babelsberg**, half a million visitors a year attend rehearsals, watch stunt shows and costume-makers at work, or inspect the world's largest props collection. The **Hochschule für Film und Fernsehen**, where some of Germany's finest actors and directors are trained, is next door. It is a relatively new institution with a fine reputation. Students from German-speaking countries compete fiercely for a place to study acting, camera, editing or screenwriting.

Lining **Karl-Marx-Strasse**, the former villas of once famous movie stars Marika Rökk, Brigitte Horney, Heinrich George and many others recall the old UFA period. Some of the buildings where prominent personalities lived once belonged to Jewish owners who had to sell them at absurdly low prices during the Nazi era. In the southern part of Babelsberg, behind Heinrich-Mann-Allee, the cupolas of the **Sternwarte Babelsberg** rise from the **Telegrafenberg**. Astronomers have used this observatory since 1876. The architect Mendelsohn drew up the unusual plans for the **Einsteinturm** at one end of the park. Built in 1920, it is now a solar observatory.

Sanssouci

Friedrich II (Frederick the Great), provided his own plans for **Schloss Sanssouci**, which was constructed in rococo style from 1745 to 1747 above terraced vineyards near Potsdam. The palace's name means "without worry," a fact reflected in the entire complex – most of the buildings and the gardens, with their pleasant symmetry and overgrown trellises, seem light and carefree.

Sanssouci Park is best explored along the **Hauptallee**. This path traverses the grounds from west to east, connecting the main entrance, the **Obelisk Portal**, with the **Great Fountain** directly at the foot of the palace terraces, and with the **New Palace** at the western end of the park. The **Art Gallery** standing to the right of

the palace has gone down in museum history as the first building expressly built to exhibit paintings (1755-1757). On the left rise the **New Chambers**, built in 1747. Originally conceived as an orangery between 1771 and 1774, the building was converted into a guest house and thus received its present name. At the beginning of the 19th century King Friedrich Wilhelm IV sketched ideas for a park and palace. The result, executed by Schinkel and Lenné, lies further to the south: **Charlottenhof**. The palace, the **Fasanerie** and the **Roman Baths** exhibit neoclassical and Florentine features.

The Hauptallee leads to the **New Palace**, an elaborate showcase built between 1763 and 1769 as the home of the royal family after the end of the Seven Years' War. The palace is in the process of intensive restoration; 55 rooms, some of them authentically reproduced, a theater,

Above: Gold-plated sun symbol in the park of Sanssouci Palace. Right: Between Pfaueninsel and Nikolskoe.

reopened in May 1991, and an enchanting café, set up in original rooms, all await visitors here. Another grandiose building stands in the north of the park: the **Orangery**, which Friedrich Wilhelm IV ordered built in 1840. Italian Renaissance palaces provided the models for this over 950-foot (300-meter) long, monumental building. The panoramic view of the entire park and Potsdam from the Orangery's towers is magnificent. Friedrich Wilhelm IV's unusual collection of copies of Raphael paintings hangs in a gallery that has been arranged in several of the rooms.

Villages around Potsdam

The **Heilandskirche**, built from 1841 to 1844, stands a few miles north of Potsdam in **Sacrow**, on a spit of land between the Havel river and the **Jungfernsee** (Virgin's Lake). Only since the opening of the GDR borders has it been possible to visit the church.

In May and June the blossoms of orchards and strawberry fields lay a beautiful blanket of "snow" on the **Havelland**, the region surrounding Potsdam as far as Werder. Early summer lures campers and water sports fans into the woodlands along the Havel river. The area between Potsdam, Rathenow and Genthin used to be a large flood plain. The incline of the Havel's bed was too gentle, causing backwash whenever there was high water in the Elbe river. During the middle ages, fishermen and farmers instituted flood control measures by building levies around the water-driven mills. They diked the Havel, allowing lakes and bogs to form around *Werders*, the name given to the settlements. The **Havelland-Hauptkanal** (main canal) has drained the area between **Fehrbellin** and **Nauen** since 1718.

The **Ketziner Wetlands** conservation area offers a particularly romantic hike. Today grebes and swans breed here,

water lilies blossom and colonies of herons nest in the lakes northwest of the city of **Kienitz**; just over 100 years ago, these bodies of water were clay quarries for the brick industry booming with the rapid construction of apartment buildings for workers in Berlin. Ships on the Havel canals transported the bricks into the city.

If you take a boat southwest from Potsdam, you will cross the **Templiner See** and arrive in **Caputh**, a town on a spit of land between Templin and Schwielow lakes. A Baroque palace, built in 1662, with unusual stucco decoration, graces Caputh. A room in the cellar has been decorated with original Delft tiles. Friedrich I loved to have himself rowed out here from the city palace on a magnificent gondola. Another illustrious resident, Albert Einstein, had a country house in Caputh at Waldstrasse 7 until 1933, when he was forced into exile by the Nazis, going then to the US.

From here, it's a short trip overland or with the car-ferry to **Werder**, the center of the Havelland's fruit-growing region.

The little city developed from an old-Slavic castle mound on a Havel islet, the *Werder*. Until the 18th century no bridge connected it with the western shore of the Havel, which is as wide as a lake at this point. Werder's favorable climate has enabled the cultivation of fruit and grapes since the Middle Ages, and by the mid-19th century fruit-growing had become the most important source of income. The **Baumblütenfest** (Tree Blossom Festival; April/May) is one of the great favorites with Berliners, who come in droves to the banks of the Havel.

Werder, on its little island and with its old fishermen's houses, is well worth the time for an excursion. Not to be missed is the **Heilig-Geist-Kirche** (Church of the Holy Spirit), which has an interesting painting called *Christ as Pharmacist*, no doubt an unusual role for the great prophet. The **Hoher Weg** looks out over the city and the Havel landscape, where sailing regattas enliven the river in the summertime. On clear days the view stretches all the way to Potsdam.

LANDSCAPES OF THE MARCH

Oranienburg and Sachsenhausen

The S-Bahn line No. 1 takes just about an hour to reach the terminus station **Oranienburg**. This land and water traffic hub at the gates of Berlin was first mentioned in documents in 1216 (at the time it was a small Slav settlement named Bochzowe, or Bötzow in German). The Ascanian princes kept a castle here that stood guard over the Havel.

When Elector Friedrich Wilhelm made a gift of the "Bötzow province" to his spouse Luise Henriette von Oranien for the purpose of building a castle, the name of the town was changed to Oranienburg. The castle itself was completed in 1652 in the place of the old castle surrounded by water. In 1814 a chemical factory was established in Oranienburg castle, where chemist Friedlieb F. Runge isolated aniline, caffeine, atropine and carbolic acid. The castle is currently being restored, but still hosts musical evenings. The former **Baroque Lustgarten** (Pleasure Garden) has a few special nuggets, besides being a pleasant place to stroll, namely the **Garden Portal** (I. A. Nerung, 1690) and the **Orangery** (G. C. Berger, 1759), which reward the effort of a walk. The **Stadtmuseum** (City Museum) and **Nikolaikirche** should also be included on the itinerary.

The northeastern part of the town, **Sachsenhausen**, is of sadder fame: in 1933, on the grounds of a former brewery, the first concentration camp on German soil was established. It held more than 7000 permanent prisoners. From 1936 onwards the concentration camp served the Nazis as a full-fledged extermination camp, and subsequently claimed the lives of more than 100,000 people.

Right: Wall surrounding the concentration camp at Sachsenhausen, north of Berlin.

Between 1945 and 1950 the Soviet occupation forces turned the existing camp into their own "Special Camp No. 7." Without rhyme, reason or due process of law, they condemned young people, women and men to forced labor, or deported them to the Soviet Union.

Hiking Trails around Oranienburg

The diversity of the surrounding landscape makes Oranienburg a favorite recreational area for Berliners. Starting from **Lake Lehnitzsee**, some excursion steamers cruise as far as Niederfinow. A hike around Lehnitzsee, beginning at the S-Bahn station Lehnitz, especially enjoyable in the summer, offers broad views over the lake. Swimming is also a possibility.

A good hiker with a whole day at his or her disposal can set off from the S-Bahn station **Birkenwerder**. This trail extends for a good eight miles (13 km) from Birkenwerder through the very charming **Briesetal** valley and **Oranienburger Heide** (heath) as far as Lehnitzsee. The Briese, a small stream, leaves Wandlitzsee to feed into the Havel at Hohenneuendorf. The trail follows the stream through the valley past the **Elsenquelle** and **Helenenquellen** springs, and then crosses over the **Hubertusbrücke**.

On the **Schlagbrücke**, a left turn onto the **Mühlenbecker Gestell** puts you on a nearly empty road connecting Summt and Lehnitz and leading directly back to the S-Bahn station Lehnitz.

From the eastern shore of Lehnitzsee, a round-trip hike wends past the **locks** on the northern tip of the lake. From here it is only a few meters to the Sachsenhausen concentration camp memorial.

Bernau

20,000 people live in the city of **Bernau**, about 19 miles (30 km) away from downtown Berlin in the direction of

Stralsund. The wall surrounding Bernau's old town core is about 300 feet (100 meters) from the S-Bahn station where the Berlin trains stop. This quaint little district town so typical of the March merits a quiet stroll. The path to follow runs along the old town wall, which has been completely preserved and is gradually being restored.

The imposing **Steintor** (Stone Gate), overshadowed by the **Hungerturm** (Hunger Tower) is all that's left of the three original gates into town. The Steintor, which is in very good condition, has housed a museum of local history and culture since 1882, although it is only open during the warm months.

The city proudly shows off such old, restored buildings as the **Kantorhaus**, the **Adlerapotheke** (pharmacy), the hotel **Schwarzer Adler** and the **Rathaus** at the marketplace, as well as its modern apartment buildings, none of which is over five stories high and whose open inner courtyards fit in well with the small-town ambience.

A beautiful, four-aisled, late-Gothic hall church from 1519 is the main attraction on the **Bernau Market Square**. The **Pfarrkirche St. Marien** (St. Mary's Parish Church) displays a surprisingly rich interior. Art historians attribute the six-winged main altar, which can be transformed twice by opening flaps, to the workshop of Lukas Cranach the Elder (around 1520). Experts have restored the *Madonna under the Canopy*, the nearly life-sized *Triumphal Cross Ensemble*, the *Sacramental Tabernacle* and other artworks. Concerts on the 29-stop organ are among the cultural highlights of Bernau.

Hikes around Bernau

Hiking out of the city in a northeasterly direction, you pass through the former city gate at the **Pulverturm** (Powder Tower). Immediately to the left, right up against the city wall, stands the **Henkerhaus** (Hangman's House) **Museum**, with a display of the medieval instruments of torture used by Bernau's executioner.

AROUND BERLIN

0   15 km

A special hiking area beckons beyond the city's cobblestones: the **Liepnitzsee**, a lake with what some consider the purest water in Germany. The water of the Liepnitzsee is of drinking quality, for its only feeder is a vigorous, cold, deep spring. To keep the lake and its shore clean, motorboats have been forbidden and cars prohibited from parking nearby. Only fishermen are permitted to try their luck at certain times.

Another charming hike, and one particularly rewarding for amateur botanists, leads from Bernau through **Ladeburg**, whose marketplace boasts two ancient trees, to **Lobetal**. Many different species of conifers from various climatic zones thrive in the forest park planted in 1930 a little way south of the village.

The path continues onward, first to **Biesental**, then to **Lanke**. More than ten lakes still provide swimmers and nature

Left: Shipbuilding, the only game in town in Eberswalde-Finow. Right: Musicians in front of the Strausberg town hall.

lovers with water clean enough to pass the most fastidious muster. In Lanke, people also swim in the **Krumme Lanke**, the lake that perhaps best illustrates the typical Berlin expression *j.w.d. – janz weit draussen* (out in the boondocks). Old, shadowy forests with perfect stands of silvery beech trees frame the crystalline lake and offer trails for long, meditative walks.

The idyllic **nature preserve area** between Barnim and the Eberswalder glacial valley is full of contrasts, and radiates a very special primordial quality. To fully enjoy and explore it, you should bring along a bicycle and perhaps a few days' time.

Hikers in the **Prenden lake area** will be rewarded with unbridled, romantic beauty. A longer tour by car or bike (about 25 miles/40 km) leads from Bernau through Briesetal to Eberswalde-Finow and to the ship elevator in Niederfinow. Like so many other towns of the March, neighboring **Eberswalde** also has a **Heimatmuseum**, with abundant documentation of local history and culture and of the industrial trials and tribulations of the valley of the Finow. The tourist office is located in the same building.

The itinerary then proceeds to **Niederfinow** (six miles/nine km on the F 167, and then north for another mile or so). The **ship elevator** is located here. This imposing technical construction received its present form between 1927 and 1934. A 502-foot (157-meter) canal bridge connects it with the Oder-Havel Canal. The elevator raises the ships into a huge, water-filled trough, bridging differences in height of up to 115 feet (36 meters).

Northeast of Eberswalde stands **Chorin Monastery**. This Cistercian monastery, which was built between 1273 and 1334, is one of the oldest constructions illustrating the North German Gothic architectural style using bricks. Friends of music should not miss the concerts of the **Chorin Music Summer**.

Strausberg

Berlin's easternmost advance guard, the county seat of **Strausberg** (at the end of the S-Bahn line No. 5, Charlottenburg-Strausberg), stands on the southern edge of the recreational area known as the **Märkische Schweiz**, which translates as the "Switzerland of the March."

As early as 1200 the margraves of Brandenburg entertained an estate here, later developing it into a town. The name "Strutzberch" appears for the first time in the 1240 chronicle that was written by the bishop of Magdeburg. The name derives from the ancient Sorbian and originally meant "pod" or "hull," referring to the form of the **Straussee**, on whose eastern shore the city spread. Originally, the city's name had nothing to do with the *Strauss* (ostrich), depicted on Strausberg's coat-of-arms.

Strausberg has an interesting and fairly well-known military history. The army, under the Weimar Republic, was stationed here. The sober and unadorned of-ficers' quarters in the proximity of the barracks grounds have seen several generations of army people already, including the Soviet military high command in the former GDR.

The ferry crossing the Straussee every thirty minutes is unique in the whole of Europe: it moves on electrical overhead wires supplying the power.

During a walk through Strausberg you will inevitably come across remnants of the town's medieval fieldstone city walls, including a few guard houses and the remains of the two gates to the city.

The **Pfarrkirche St. Marien**, an early Gothic fieldstone church, underwent a number of changes but still exhibits late-Gothic characteristics, particularly in the interior. Figure paintings from the 15th century, including a *Christ as Judge of the World* and a *Coronation of Mary*, decorate the vaults, and the precious late-Gothic winged altar with Mary on the moon's crescent and the carved altar depicting the Madonna with a radiant halo are treats for art-lovers.

147

In the Switzerland of the March

Strausberg lies on the periphery of the **Barnim**, an extensive ground moraine plate. Idyllic forest lakes have formed in deep-cut watercourses which provide wonderful places for swimming or fishing.

The *Märkische Schweiz* (Switzerland of the March) is a prime hiking area, especially in autumn or winter. The "Switzerland" epithet is an association with the beauties of the Swiss countryside. In the fall, extensive deciduous and mixed forests adorn its beautiful hills and dales in colorful dress. It's the favorite season for long hikes through this paradise.

The 96 square miles (250 sq km) of the **Naturpark Märkische Schweiz** is a natural gem with a starkly structured relief.

Mixed forests and lakes, the largest of which is the **Scharmützelsee**, provide the backdrop for the pretty little town of **Buckow**, famous as the one-time home of Bertolt Brecht and the actress Helene Weigel. The bus covers the nine miles (15 km) from Strausberg to Buckow. Brecht's and Weigel's former home, where such plays as *Coriolan* and *Turandot* were written after 1952, is now open to the public.

Beech groves abound in the forests around Buckow, in fact, the town's name derives directly from the Slavic word for beech, *buk.*

There are further natural wonders on the **Wildbach Sophienfliess** stream. A small parking lot opens up just beyond the turnoff from the Strausberger Chaussee toward Buckow.

If you come by bus, ask for the **Wurzelfichte** (literally, the "root fir") stop, starting point for a one-mile (1.6 km) stroll to the town. A few steps lead down into a small valley. A 64-foot (20-meter) tall, approximately 150-year-old fir tree grows on the other bank of the stream. Twenty people can crowd into the confusion of its washed out roots. The hiking trail, called the **Poetensteig** (Poets' Path) for good reason, enchants every hiker with the romance of its wild, natural beauty. The Poetensteig climbs steeply past the **Gasthaus Tirol** restaurant up to the stately **Jenas-Höhe** (355 feet/111 meters). From here, the path leads through the **Finkenherd** and the **Wolfsschlucht** ravine, circumnavigates the little **Tornowsee** lake, bypasses the **Günterquelle**, a spring with high iron-content, and finally goes back to the town. The path ends near the city park, which was designed by landscape architect Peter Joseph Lenné.

Königs Wusterhausen

Southeast of Berlin, directly where the Dahme and the Notte canals flow together, is **Königs Wusterhausen** – or "KW," as Berliners call this recreational town. From where S-Bahn line No. 46 ends (Westkreuz/Königs Wusterhausen) an extensive system of bus lines and passenger trains offers connections to the near and more distant surroundings of KW, the so-called **Dahmeland**, with extensive forests and lakes all the way to the Spreewald. The Autobahn will also take you to the town, but if you're going by car, the country roads through the posh suburbs of **Grünau**, **Schmöckwitz**, **Eichwalde** and **Zeuthen** might be worth your while. **Wildau**, an industrial park, was built according to an exceptional architectural plan. In 1898 the Wildau locomotive factory and the workers' housing project were both integrated architecturally into the ensemble.

Königs Wusterhausen itself is a fairly small town. The consumer attractions offered along the pedestrian zone in its center are modest. For the last 40 years most residents of this satellite city have

Right: The Spreewald in summer is a pleasant recreational place to be.

worked and done their shopping in Berlin. Königs Wusterhausen was important and well-known not only as a Prussian garrison town, but also for its coal harbor and the radio broadcasting facilities on the **Funkerberg** (Broadcaster's Mountain). In 1913 the army erected its wireless transmitter on the hill, and the first radio broadcast in Germany was aired from here on December 22, 1920. Interestingly, the broadcasting towers also figure in the town's coat-of-arms.

The story of KW's founding is quickly told. In 1690 the two-year-old son of the King of Prussia was made owner of "palace and people." Then, after he was enthroned as Friedrich Wilhelm I in 1713, he ordered the hunting palace built as we know it today. For 20 years the "Soldier King" regularly used the palace as his lodge during the autumn hunting season. He made Wusterhausen into Königs Wusterhausen. A particular attraction is the weekly market held each Saturday. KW has been trying to rid itself of the suburban image and achieve independence as a local capital. In this way it will become a center of business where new industrial and commercial zones will be set up.

Numerous campsites, most with facilities for trailers, provide accommodation for visitors to the lakes and hiking trails of the region.

The **Schlosshotel** in the little town (pop. 2000) of **Teupitz** makes a good vacation home for those preferring more comfort. Located on a peninsula extending into the **Teupitzsee** (accessible from the marketplace), the medieval water-surrounded castle of the Schenken von Landsberg dynasty was converted into a hotel with a good restaurant. Its private beach provides a magnificent panoramic view of the lake. Parts of Teupitz still vaguely recall its past as a fishing village.

From Teupitz to Bad Saarow

Hikers starting out from Teupitz to explore the lakes of the March encounter hardly any limits to their *Wanderlust*.

From Teupitz, waterways lead into the **Spreewald** or, by way of Storkow, to the **Scharmützelsee**.

Of course, you don't have to paddle the whole way. The regional train RB 36 toward Frankfurt-on-the-Oder from KW stops in **Wendisch-Rietz** on the southern shore of the March's "sea" in about 20 minutes (Scharmützelsee station). At the train station, one can first gaze at the lake stretching northward for seven miles (eleven km). It's two-thirds of a mile (one km) to the dock of the passenger steamer for **Bad Saarow**, and about 1.3 miles (two km) to the vacation village in **Wendisch-Rietz**. Sails spangle the huge lake, especially in the summer months and on weekends. Besides swimming, the waters also provide anglers with ample opportunity for fishing. Waterfront property owners have purposely left long stretches of the shore free for a path, so visitors can take leisurely strolls around

Above: Sorb women in the Spreewald still weave flax in traditional manner.

the lake. Only the odd tree or uncooperative owner obstructs the view or the path.

Theodor Fontane, who hiked over all the trails in the March of Brandenburg, walked around this lake in the spring of 1870: "It was a wonderful path; the blue skies arched over the blue water, and the sparse reeds lining the shore were hung with equally sparse shreds of foam which constantly swayed back and forth in the sharp east wind," he later remembered. Nowadays sailboaters, windsurfers and other aficionados of aquatic activities come and enjoy the lake.

Bad Saarow has been an exclusive health spa ever since 1910, when healing mud and the **Solequelle** (brine) spring were discovered. In past years, the military, particularly the upper echelons of the former GDR National People's Army, used it as a spa and sanatorium; the political bigwigs of the time also held the lake in high esteem – the SED Central Committee had a little community of bungalows built and maintained here for their own private use.

But Bad Saarow has its best years behind it: in the 1920s many celebrities of Berlin society spent time here relaxing from their busy lives, among them boxer Max Schmeling, actress Käthe Dorsch, and Harry Liedtke, whose request to be buried in Bad Saarow was finally fulfilled. And in 1922-23 the Russian writer Maxim Gorky came here to take the waters. A little museum has been set up recalling his visit. Since reunification, however, Bad Saarow has been crawling its way back to the top of the social heap, see, for example, the five-star Kempinski Hotel Sporting Club Berlin, with a sailing school, golf and tennis courts.

In the summer, if you look out from the deck of the passenger steamer cruising from Wendisch-Rietz to Bad Saarow, you will see enchanting water lilies peeking through the reeds.

The **Rauen Mountains** rise in the north. Miners dug lignite here from the 1840s till about 1905. One of the few remaining witnesses to this mining history, the **Steigerhaus**, stands under monument protection at Chausseestr. 35 in the small community of **Rauen**. A massive 13th-century fortified church built of fieldstone dominates the village green.

Rauen first became known for its **giant boulders** brought down from Sweden by ice age glaciers. Architect Schinkel commissioned the sculpting of the larger of the two stones into a huge **granite bowl** nearly 100-feet (30 meters) in circumference. In 1834 it was exhibited in front of the old museum in the Berlin *Lustgarten*. The smaller stone and what remains of the larger one still attract admirers to the Rauen Mountains.

In the fall, when the summer guests gradually depart, mushroom pickers take over the huge forest area between Königs Wusterhausen and **Halbe**. Armed with pocketknives and baskets, they roam the woods hunting for edible mushrooms, sometimes selling their harvest on Sundays at highway rest stops.

To the Spreewald

The marshy Spree river region, which in parts almost resembles a dense jungle, attains a width of up to seven miles (eleven km) in the **Spreewald** – the Spree Woods. Several hundred canals, arms of the Spree and many smaller streams intertwine to form the extensive network of waterways for the local inhabitants, the *Spreewäldler*. As in Venice, most local traffic and transportation is carried out on the water and every house has its own little dock. The "capital" of the Spreewald, **Lübbenau**, where the majority of boats dock, boasts the largest harbor.

The *Spreewäldler* have lived from fishing and vegetable cultivation for ages, and they now supply Berlin households with horseradish, cucumbers and onions. Since 1908 tourism between May and October has also been a fairly important source of income.

The enchanting **open-air museum** in **Lehde** provides a information on the history of the Spreewald region. The other villages and towns in the Spreewald area are also prepared for visiting crowds. One of the obligatory activities when coming here is being punted through the labyrinth of canals by a Spreewald lady dressed in traditional garb.

The ancient, over three-foot-thick (one meter) oaks and the dark **log cabins** with their garlands of onions create a veritably timeless atmosphere. But inevitably the inhabitants of the Spreewald will soon have to readjust to new economic times brought about by the great political and social revolution of the early 1990s. Much of the agriculture in this region is no longer competitive. The government of the state of Brandenburg will be hard pressed to effectively protect this unique culture. Whether the *Spreewäldler* manage to maintain the balance between their traditional way of life and tourism – combined with the effects of German reunification – remains to be seen.

POTSDAM
The area code for Potsdam is 0331.

Transportation
By **car**, Potsdam is accessible from one of the exits of the Berlin Stadtring peripheral road, over the Glienicker Bridge or via the AVUS (A115) and the exits **Kreuz Zehlendorf** and **Potsdam-Babelsberg**. A **train** to Potsdam goes from the S-Bahn station Wannsee, and a **bus** also leaves from there (No. 199) arriving at Bassinplatz. The **ships** of the **Weisse Flotte** are also a great deal of fun in summer. The pier is at the S-Bahn station Wannsee. The ships sail hourly.

Tourist Information
Potsdam Information, Touristenzentrale am Alten Markt, Fr.-Ebert-Str. 5, 14467 Potsdam, tel. 27 55 80. Apr-Oct: Mon-Fri 9 a.m.-8 p.m., Sat 10 a.m.-6 p.m., Sun and holidays 10 a.m.-4 p.m., Nov-March: Mon-Fri 10 a.m.-6 p.m., Sat, Sun 10 a.m.-2 p.m. The **Tourist Service** offers city tours, castle tours, group programs, tickets for court concerts in the castle theater, as well as a **direct booking service** for private quarters, hotels and vacation apartments.

Accommodation
Arcona Hotel Voltaire, Friedrich-Ebert-Str. 88, tel. 231 70. **art'otel Potsdam**, Zeppelinstr. 136, tel. 9815-0. **Dorint Hotel Sanssouci & Congresszentrum**, Jägerallee 20, tel. 27 40. **Hotel Mercure Berlin-Potsdam**, Lange Brücke, tel. 27 22. **Schlosshotel Cecilienhof**, in the Neuer Garten, tel. 370 50.

Post, Important Phone Numbers
Car Rentals: Europcar, Lange Brücke (in the Hotel Mercure), tel. 29 82 40.
Lost and Found: Friedrich-Ebert-Str. 79, tel. 289 15 87.
Taxi: tel. 29 22 31/-32/-33, 81 04 04.
Breakdowns: tel. 01850-10 11 12.
Main Post Office: Platz der Einheit, tel. 270 70 89.

Museums, Parks, Sights
Dampfmaschinenhaus (Steam Engine House), Breite Strasse, tel. 969 42 48, Sat, Sun and holidays 10 a.m.-noon, 1-5 p.m. Uhr.
Einstein Tower, Telegrafenberg, tel. 29 17 41.
Film Museum Potsdam, Marstall, Breite Strasse/Schlossstr. 1, tel. 27 18 10, Tue-Fri 10 a.m.-5 p.m., Sat, Sun and holidays 10 a.m.-6 p.m.
Film Park Babelsberg, August-Bebel-Str. 26-53, entrance Grossbeerenstrasse, tel. 721 27 50, daily 10 a.m.-6 p.m. Winter break from Nov 1, 1998 till March 6, 1999.

Friedenskirche, Marylgarten, Am Grünen Gitter 3, tel. 97 40 09.
Heilandskirche Sacrow stands about nine miles (14 km) north of Potsdam in Sacrow, near Fährstrasse, and is accessible by car on the road to Falkensee; Tue-Sun and holidays 11 a.m.-6:45 p.m., call in advance for tours, tel. 50 38 27.
Kirche St. Peter und Paul, Bassinplatz, tel. 2 80 49 42, call in advance for tours.
Kulturhaus Altes Rathaus Potsdam, (Old Town Hall) Am Alten Markt 9, tel. 29 31 75, Tue-Sun 10 a.m.-6 p.m.
Potsdam Museum, Breite Str. 13, tel. 289 66 00, indefinitely closed for renovations.
St.-Nikolai-Kirche, Alten Markt, tel. 270 31 68.
Südwest Friedhof (Southwest Cemetery) **Stahnsdorf**, Bahnhofsstr., tel. 03329/623 15, daily 7 a.m.-8 p.m. Unpolished piece of land with the tombs of, amongst others, Heinrich Zille and Walter Gropius, and the mausoleums of many Berlin industrialists of the 19th century.

Potsdam's Castle
Visitors' Center and **Information**: at the *Historische Mühle* (Historic Mill), located in Sanssouci Park, tel. 969 42 02, Apr-Oct, daily 8:30 a.m.-5 p.m.; Nov-March, daily 9 a.m.-4 p.m.
Schloss Cecilienhof, Memorial to the Potsdam Treaty, Neuer Garten, tel. 969 42 44, Apr 1-Oct 31, 9 a.m.-5 p.m., Nov-Mar, 9 a.m.-4 p.m.
Schloss Sanssouci is open daily except Monday: Apr-Oct 9 a.m.-5 p.m., Feb, Mar 9 a.m.-4 p.m., Nov-Jan 9 a.m.-3 p.m., noon break 12:30-1 p.m.
Marmorpalais (Marble Palace) in the Neuer Garten near Cecilienhof, Apr-Oct, Tue-Sun 10 a.m.-5 p.m., Nov-Mar only weekends 10 a.m.-3 p.m.
Schloss und Park Babelsberg, tel. 969 42 50, Apr-Oct, Tue-Sun 10 a.m.-5 p.m.; Nov-Mar weekends only, 10 a.m.-4 p.m.

Restaurants, Cafés and Bars
Villa Kellermann, Mangerstr. 34-36, tel. 29 15 72, Tue-Sun noon to midnight (fine Italian cuisine in a villa on the Heiliger See). **Juliette**, Jägerstr. 39, tel. 270 17 91, daily 12:30-11:30 p.m., (French of a better class). **Hofgarten Restaurant in the Hotel Voltaire**, Friedrich-Ebert-Str. 88, tel. 231 70 (fine cuisine on the edge of the Dutch Quarter). **La Madeleine**, Lindenstr. 9, tel. 270 54 00, daily noon-11 p.m. (crêperie of a special kind). **Waage**, Am Neuen Markt 12, tel. 270 96 75, Tue-Sat from 6 p.m., Sun from noon, earlier in summer (restaurant in historic setting). **Fritz-Kneipe** (Waldschloss), Stahnsdorfer Str. 100, tel. 71 91 40, daily 6-11 p.m. (*Kneipe* belonging to the Fritz radio station in the Lindenpark, where events are held).

Culture and Entertainment

The immediate proximity of Berlin doesn't make it easy on the cultural movers and shakers of Potsdam. Worth a visit, however, is the **Hans Otto Theater**, with its stages **Theaterhaus Am Alten Markt**, **Bühne Zimmerstrasse** (Zimmerstr. 10), **Studiobühne** (Heinrich-Mann-Allee 103) and, from Oct '98, the **Reithalle A** on Schiffbauergasse. In addition, the Theater plays in the *Säulenhof* of the Orangery in the park of Sanssouci (open-air, Sundays in July and August). Tickets for all venues are available in the Theaterhaus Am Alten Markt, tel. 27 57 10 (Mon-Thu 10 a.m.-6 p.m., Fri, Sat 10 a.m.-1 p.m.).

Kabarett Am Obelisk, Charlottenstr. 31 (tel. 29 10 69).

Schlosstheater im Neuen Palais (in Sanssouci Park), tel. 280 0693.

Rock and Pop Concerts: **Lindenpark**, Stahnsdorfer Str. 76, tel. 747 97 48; **Kunstfabrik**, Hermann-Elflein-Str.10, tel. 280 04 89, Wed-Fri 10 a.m.-4 p.m., Sat, Sun 2-7 p.m.; **Waschhaus**, Schiffbauergasse 1, tel. 271 56 26, Wed-Sun 4-8 p.m.

Around Potsdam

Weisse Flotte Potsdam, Lange Brücke, tel. 275 92 10. The ships dock for various excursions and for trips to Berlin, Caputh, Werder, Phöben and into the Havelland.

Haveldampfschiffahrt Potsdam, Heinrich-Mann-Allee, tel. 270 62 29, 544 61 40. Castle tours in a historic Havel steamship (weekends only).

Werder: information at the Rat der Stadt (City Council), Eisenbahnstr. 13/14, tel. 03327/2331.

Fruit Cultivation Museum of Werder, Karl-Marx-Platz 2, tel. 03327/2331 (appointment only).

MARCH LANDSCAPES

Oranienburg: **Fremdenverkehrsverein Oranienburg e.V.** (tourist information, Lehnitzstr. 21c, 16515 Oranienburg, tel. 03301/70 48 33). In Oranienburg do not miss the **memorial** and **museum** of **Sachsenhausen**; the exhibition on the concentration camp has the following hours: Tue-Sun 8:30 a.m. till 18 p.m., from Oct-Mar only till 16:30 p.m. (Strasse der Nationen 22, tel. 03301/80 37 18.

Bernau: **Tourist Office**, Marktplatz 2, 16321 Bernau, tel. 03338/36 53 88, for accommodation, sights and city tours; **Steintor Museum** (Berliner Strasse, tel. 03338/29 24; open May-Oct: Tue-Fri 9 a.m.-noon and 2-5 p.m., Sat, Sun 10 a.m.-1 p.m., 2 p.m.-5 p.m.); and the **Executioner's House Museum** (Am Henkerhaus), tel. 03338/22 45; same opening times, but open all year.

Eberswalde: **Tourist Information** is located in the Museum of the Adler Apotheke (Steinstr. 3, 16225 Eberswalde, tel. 03334/64520). Worth seeing: **Eberswalde Zoo**, **Niederfinow ship elevator**, **Chorin Monastery**.

Strausberg: **Tourist Information** also for accomodation (August-Bebel-Str. 1, tel. 03341/ 31 10 66, 15344 Strausberg). **Buckow**: **Brecht-Weigel-Haus** Bertolt-Brecht-Str. 29. **The Environment and Tourist Office Märkische Schweiz** gives information on the **Naturpark Märkische Schweiz** (Wriezener Str. 1a, 15377 Buckow, tel. 033433/575 00).

Königs Wusterhausen and Spreewald

The **Fremdenverkehrsverband Dahmeland e.V.** (Am Nottekanal, 15711 **Königs Wusterhausen**, tel. 03375/29 12 69, 29 48 74) has information on hotels and sights in the **Dahmeland** region. A good network of buses and trains connects KW with the area, as well as with the Spreewald, Potsdam and Berlin.

In **Bad Saarow** you can find further information at the **Kur- and Fremdenverkehrs GmbH** (Lindenstr. 5, 15526 Bad Saarow-Pieskow, tel. 033631/86 80) and the **Tourist Bureau** (Seestr. 36, tel. 033631/ 21 42).

A pier of the **Scharmützelsee Schiffahrtsgesellschaft** is on the Schwanenwiese (ticket sales, too, tel. 2419).

Spreewald (about 60 miles/100 km southeast of Berlin). Besides the German population, you will also find the Slav **Sorbs** here, with their own language and customs still intact today. The Spreewald has been under UNESCO protection as a biosphere reservation since 1991.

Lübbenau is the largest town and the best-known "Gateway to the Spreewald." Worth seeing in *Lubnjow* (Lübbenau in Sorbian) is the historic center of the **Old Town**, the Baroque **Nikolaikirche**, the **Postal Column of 1740**, the **Gatehouse of 1784** and the **Spreewald Museum** in the former court chambers of the castle complex.

The Lübbenau precinct of **Lehde** is a typical Spreewald village with thatched wooden houses, recommended is the **open-air museum** on an island.

Paddle boats are for rent from April to October from various businesses in Lübbenau. **Spreewald canoe rides**: Frank's Kahnfahrten (Dammstrasse, tel. 03542/36 73), the Kahnfährhafen Dammstrasse (tel. 035 42/22 25) and at the small harbor of the Spreeschlösschen (Spreestrasse, tel. 03542/27 10).

Further Information: **Spreewald-Fremdenverkehrsverein Lübbenau und Umgebung e.V.**, Ehm-Welk-Str. 15, 03222 Lübbenau, tel. 03542/36 68.

SHOPPING IN BERLIN

Berlin is an excellent place to indulge in shopping: consumers in this city have a choice between expensive boutiques and freaky bargain basements, between huge department stores and wild, trendy shops. In fact, all of Berlin appears to be one big and scrambled market where any and every consumer wish can be filled.

The Kurfürstendamm and its Side Streets

The Kurfürstendamm is still a great shopping boulevard, not only for tourists but also for many Berliners – even if they don't always want to admit it. The side streets have changed a lot in recent years, they've grown somewhat more chic and are usually more attractive than the Ku'-damm itself.

Preceding page: The Pergamon Altar. Left: Way-out articles are to be had at Schrill's department store.

The most elegant side street is **Fa-sanenstrasse**, particularly the section between the Ku'damm and Lietzenburger Strasse. Everything with name and rank in the fashion world has established itself here: Cartier, Chanel, Louis Vuitton and Rena Lange. Other international fashion designers have set up shop right on the Ku'damm, specifically between Olivaer Platz and Schlüterstrasse: Jil Sander, Yves Saint Laurent, Valentino, Gianni Versace (near Kramberg) and René Lezard. On Fasanenstrasse, too, besides all the high-class fashion shops, the arts have representatives: the London-based auction house **Christie's**, **Galerie Pels-Leusden** in Villa Grisebach and the **Käthe Kollwitz Museum**.

Make a point of going window-shopping on **Bleibtreustrasse**, especially near Lietzenburger Strasse. On the corner of the Ku'damm are two first-class men's stores, **SOR** and **Selbach**, and the jeweler **Axel Sedlatzek**. Nearby, the small, exquisite lingerie store **Nouvelle** beckons seductively. Crazy threads, accessories, fashion jewelry and unusual neckties are sold at **Kaufhaus Schrill**. At Bleibtreustrasse, the S-Bahn arcades begin at the S-Bahn bridge, where shops, cafés and restaurants have gone into business. Here you are close to the shops on Savignyplatz and its side streets.

Consumer Boulevard Tauentzien and KaDeWe

Tauentzienstrasse, which runs between Breitscheidplatz and Wittenbergplatz, is a veritable shopping strip with numerous, though hardly original, shops. On rainy days the place to go is the **Europa Center**, a mall with over 100 shops.

Berlin's most famous temple of consumerism is the **KaDeWe** (*Kaufhaus des Westens*) on Wittenbergplatz. Opened in 1907, the store now has almost 200,000 square feet (24,000 sq meters) of floor space and over 380,000 articles, making it the largest department store on the continent. Its **gourmet floor**, opened in 1956, has once and for all proven its exclusiveness, attracting primarily members of the "upper ten thousand." With its 22,500 square feet (7000 sq meters) and 33,000 different items, including 400 kinds of bread and 1300 kinds of cheese, this department of KaDeWe is Europe's largest gourmet paradise.

Friedrichstrasse

Friedrichstrasse, once a famous promenade, is scheduled to be polished up again. Construction work is still in progress on many parts of the two-mile (three km) street. A lot, however, has already been completed. Along the section extending from the U-Bahn stations Französische Strasse and Stadtmitte, businesses are looking for high-end consumerism. The new **Friedrichstadtpassagen** (an arcade between Französischestrasse and Mohrenstrasse) embodies sheer luxury, with its quarters Nos. 205,

206 and 207: fully glazed, furnished with Italian marble, and boasting an 830-foot (260-meter) underground shopping street. The French department store **Galeries Lafayette** (with its impressive cone of light), Jean-Paul Gaultier, Gucci, and Donna Karan have already moved in. There is still a lot of commercial space available in this beautiful arcade.

Not far away from Friedrichstrasse, on Potsdamer Platz in Berlin's new center, **Postdamer Platz Arcade**, an American-style shopping mall, opened in the fall of 1998.

The Hackesche Höfe

The combination residential and commercial complex **Hackesche Höfe**, built in 1905 on the Hackesche Markt in Mitte, was elaborately renovated during the early and mid-1990s. A host of shops have settled in the yards of the complex and in the surrounding streets (Rosenthalerstrasse, Oranienburgerstrasse and Auguststrasse). Emphasis is on young Berlin fashion makers, unconventional designers, and wild second-hand shops. Since this area is one of the "in" places to go in the city, daytime shoppers can easily move into the night scene. For true made-in-Berlin items, drop into Respectman (men's wear), the Kostümhaus (women's designer wear), Trippen (unusual wooden shoes) or NIX (Berlin designer).

Antiques and Art

Treasures from all periods are massed in Berlin's antique shops, illustrating the city's changing history. High-quality antiques are concentrated on **Keithstrasse**, just behind Wittenbergplatz. Here, and also on **Eisenacherstrasse**, **Motzstrasse**, and **Goltzstrasse**, the stores are lined up one after the other, as they are on **Suarezstrasse** in Charlottenburg. The area around **Ludwigkirchplatz** in Wilmersdorf, and along the S-Bahn arcades on

Georgenstrasse and **Friedrichstrasse** in Mitte are also good places to browse for the odd treasue. Those who are keener on antique art can pick up that bust of Nefertiti for their living room from the *Gipsformerei* **Plaster Casting Works of the Foundation of Prussian Cultural Heritage**. And if you want to dine like the Hohenzollern princes in your own livingroom, a shop on Unter den Linden sells **Meissen Porcelain**.

Second-Hand, Junk Stores and Markets

On **Winterfeldtplatz**, where one of Berlin's most attractive open-air markets takes place, vendors offer a wide spectrum of wares twice a week, from vegetables to ceramics. This is undoubtedly Berlin's most beautiful market, together with the **Türkenmarkt** on the Maybach-

Above: The flea market on the Strasse des 17. Juni, one of many places in Berlin where one might find a genuine treasure.

ufer in Neukölln. Another very popular market is the **Trödel- und Kunstmarkt** (Flea and Art Market) on Strasse des 17. Juni, S-Bahn station Tiergarten.

The **Berliner Kunst- und Nostalgiemarkt** (Art and Nostalgia Market) on the Museum Island, at the Zeughaus (arsenal) and Kupfergraben is an upscale flea market held against a historic backdrop. Exciting, too, is the flea market held in the yard of the **Kulturbrauerei**, an events venue for the scene. Every weekend, the **Grosse Marktfreiheit 17** (Great Market Freedom 17) is proclaimed in this former brewery in Prenzlauer Berg. The cheapest threads, however, are definitely found at Tati. This French annex to Woolworth recently opened a branch at the Kottbusser Brücke right near the Türkenmarkt mentioned above. In Kreuzberg, at **Mauerspechts Staatsauflösung** (in the House at Checkpoint Charlie), you can find authentic stuff from the days of the GDR under the heading "palpable history," that is, if that really *is* an authentic piece of the Wall.

SHOPPING

Besides the **Ku'damm** and **Friedrichstrasse**, every district has its larger or smaller shopping centers. Shopping centers "out in the sticks" can be found at the city limits. The best-known shopping mall in the city opened its doors to the public in autumn 1998: **Potsdamer Platz Arcade**, located on the famous square. More malls are being planned or have opened recently. **Well-known shopping streets**: **Wilmersdorfer Strasse** (pedestrian zone) in Charlottenburg, **Schlossstrasse** in Steglitz, and **Karl-Marx-Strasse** in Neukölln. Berlin's largest consumer shrine: **KaDeWe** (Schöneberg, Tauentzienstrasse 21, tel. 212 10), **Galeries Lafayette** (Friedrichstrasse/Französische Strasse, Mitte, tel. 20 94 80). "trendy shopping": **Hackesche Höfe** (Mitte, Rosenthaler Strasse 40/41), and **Bergmannstrasse** in Kreuzberg.

International Designer Boutiques and Fashion Houses

Chanel, Fasanenstr. 30, tel. 885 14 24; **Donna Karan**, Friedrichstadtpassagen, Quartier 206, tel. 20 94 60 10; **Gucci**, Friedrichstadtpassagen, Quartier 206, tel. 201 70 20; **Jean Paul Gaultier**, Friedrichstadtpassagen, Quartier 206, Friedrichstrasse, tel. 20 94 79 38; **Jil Sander**, Kurfürstendamm 185, tel. 886 70 20; **Joop! Store**, Steglitz, Schlossstr. 27, tel. 791 12 57; **Kramberg**, Kurfürstendamm 185, tel. 885 74 60; **Louis Vuitton**, Fasanenstr. 27, tel. 882 52 72; **Rena Lange**, Fasanenstr. 29, tel. 882 62 08; **René Lezard**, Kurfürstendamm 48/49, tel. 885 46 01; **Valentino**, Kurfürstendamm 27, tel. 882 76 77; **Yves Saint Laurent**, Kurfürstendamm 52, tel. 883 39 18.

Fashion "Made in Berlin"

Evelin Brandt, Charlottenburg, Savignyplatz 6, tel. 313 80 80, classical fashion; **Durchbruch**, Charlottenburg, Schlüterstr. 54, tel. 881 55 68; **Fiebelkorn/Chapeaux**, Charlottenburg, Bleibtreustr. 4, tel. 312 33 73; **Kostümhaus**, Mitte, Rosenthaler Str. 40/41, tel. 282 70 18; **Molotow**, Kreuzberg, Gneisenaustr. 112, tel. 693 08 18, Berlin designer; **Monella**, Charlottenburg, Ludwigkirchstr. 4, tel. 883 18 45; **NIX**, Mitte, Auguststr. 86, tel. 281 80 44; **Respectman**, Mitte, Neue Schönhauser Strasse 14, tel. 283 50 10; **Trippen**, Mitte, Rosenthaler Strasse 40/41.

Accessories, Gifts, Shoes, Jewelry, Art

Ararat, Charlottenburg, Schlüterstr. 22, tel. 312 44 45. **Budapester Schuhe** (shoes), Charlottenburg, Kurfürstendamm 199, tel. 881 17 07 (men's classic wear) and Bleibtreustr. 24, tel. 881 70 01 (exclusive and unusual women's shoes); **Cartier Berlin**, Charlottenburg, Fasanenstr. 28, tel. 882 16 00; **dadriade**, Mitte, Rosenthaler Str. 40/41, tel. 28 52 87 20, (contemporary designer items); **Da Vinci**, Kurfürstendamm 216, tel. 88125 47 (beautiful Italian shoe salon); **Günther Lambert**, Charlottenburg, Uhlandstr. 181, tel. 881 30 36, accessories, furniture; **Juwelier Axel Sedlatzek**, Kurfürstendamm 45, tel. 881 16 27; **Kaufhaus Schrill**, Charlottenburg, Bleibtreustr. 46, tel. 882 40 48; **Lila**, Bleibtreustr. 47; **Mauerspecht Staatsauflösung**, Kreuzberg, Friedrichstr. 44, tel. 253 72 50, everything from GDR days; **Ricardo Cartilione**, Charlottenburg, Savignyplatz 5, tel. 312 97 01, Italian shoe design; **Rio**, Charlottenburg, Bleibtreustr. 52, tel. 313 31 52, amusing fashion jewelry; **Roeckel-Handschuhe** (gloves), Charlottenburg, Kurfürstendamm 216, tel. 881 53 79; **Schuhtick**, Schöneberg, Tauentzienstr. 5, tel. 211 79 69 (unusual shoes; numerous branches); **Warner Bros. Studio Store**, Charlottenburg, Tauentzienstr. 9, tel. 25454-104.

Antiques, Books, Records

Berliner Universitätsbuchhandlung am Alex (University Bookshop), Mitte, Spandauer Str. 2, tel. 240 94 31; **books in Berlin**, Charlottenburg, Goethestr. 69, tel. 313 12 33, also English-language; **British Bookshop**, Mitte, Mauerstr. 83/84, tel. 238 46 80, English Books and media; **Bücherbogen am Savignyplatz**, Charlottenburg, Stadtbogen 593, tel. 312 19 32; **Düwal**, Charlottenburg, Schlüterstr. 17, tel. 313 30 30; **Gipsformerei der SMPK** (plaster molding), Charlottenburg, Sophie-Charlotten-Str. 17/18, tel. 321 70 11; **Dussmann**, Mitte, Friedrichstr. 91, tel. 2025-0, open until 10 pm; **Hugendubel**, book store, Tauentzien/corner of Rankestrasse; **Kiepert**, Charlottenburg, Hardenbergstr. 4/5, tel. 311 00 90; **Kiepert** (in the center) Friedrichstr. 63, tel. 208 25 11; **Meissen Porcelain**, Mitte, Unter den Linden 39b, tel. 204 35 81; **WOM**, World of Music, Charlottenburg, Augsburger Str. 36, tel. 885 72 40

Markets

Berliner Kunst- und Nostalgiemarkt (Art and Nostalgia Market), Mitte, on the Museumsinsel (Sat, Sun 11 a.m.-5 p.m.); **Grosse Marktfreiheit 17**, in the yard of the Kulturbrauerei, Prenzlauer Berg, Knaackstr. 97 (Sat, Sun 10 a.m. to 6 p.m.); **Trödel- und Kunstmarkt** (Flea and Art Market) Strasse des 17. Juni, Tiergarten (Sat, Sun 10 a.m.-5 p.m.); **Winterfeldtplatz Market** Schöneberg, Wed, Sat 8 a.m.-2 p.m.; **Türkenmarkt**, Neukölln, Maybachufer, Tue, Fri noon-6:30 p.m.

BERLIN'S MUSEUMS
The World in a Room

The first "long night of the museums" was held in August 1996, when about two dozen Berlin museums stayed open till after midnight. Strolling about under a star-lit sky on the historic **Museumsinsel** (Museum Island) – which, together with the **Kulturforum** in the Tiergarten and the museums in Dahlem constitute the most important sites in Berlin's museum landscape – was a very special thrill. Trudging over to the **Hamburger Bahnhof** to see the blue and green lighting artwork of its façade after sunset was well worth the effort. The **Museum der Gegenwart** (Museum of the Present) lodged here boasts the Marx collection, presenting works of Beuys, Rauschenberg, Twombly and Warhol, as well as works from the National Gallery.

Since the fall of the infamous Wall, the process of bringing together collections that were divided for decades and reorganizing them has been in high gear. The three museum centers in Berlin will have various tasks in the future.

Those wishing to take in Berlin's rich museum life are going to have to accept temporary closures and substitute exhibition space during moving procedure, which may well take years. One example of this art-on-the-move is the following: the part of the **antiquities collection** exhibited in Charlottenburg until 1996 have been placed together with items from the **Pergamon Museum** in the **Altes Museum** since May 1998. The famous Pergamon Altar and a few other pieces will stay in the Pergamon Museum, however. The **Museum für Spätantike und Byzantinische Kunst** (Museum for Late Antiquity and Byzantine Art) will relinquish its current space in Dahlem and

Left: The Pergamon Museum boasts numerous treasures from antiquity.

join the other part of the collection in the Bode Museum, which will be closed from 1999 till mid-2004. Only partial reopening is scheduled for 1999. The **Gemäldegalerie** (Picture Gallery) moved out of both Dahlem and the Bode Museum in June 1998. Its works are now being exhibited in the new picture gallery in the Kulturforum (Mattäikirchplatz). As for the **Berlinische Galerie**, it was forced to finally vacate the **Martin Gropius Building** at the beginning of 1998.

Many of the museums and collections have been gathered in foundations. The *Staatliche Museen zu Berlin, Preussischer Kulturbesitz* (State Museums of Berlin), or SMPK for short, founded in 1957, administers the museums on the Museumsinsel in Mitte, the Hamburger Bahnhof in Tiergarten, the museums and other establishments in the Kulturforum, the museums in Dahlem, the **Kunstgewerbe Museum** (Arts and Crafts Museum) in Schloss Köpenick (closed from 1998 to 2002), the **Ägyptisches Museum** (Egyptian Museum) in Charlottenburg, the **Galerie der Romantik** in Charlottenburg Castle, and the **Berggruen Collection**. The latter, one of the finest collections of classical modern works, is now displayed in the Stüler Wing opposite Charlottenburg Castle. Until 2006 the exhibition will focus on "Picasso and His Times" – over 100 works (paintings, sculptures and works on paper) by seven artists in classical modern style, as well as some works of tribal African art.

Over a dozen museums have gathered under the aegis of the **Stiftung Stadtmuseum** (City Museum Foundation, short for *Stiftung Stadtmuseum Berlin – Landesmuseum für Kultur und Geschichte Berlin*), which was founded in 1995 and, in spite of its long and erudite name, is once again the focus of critical debate. It administers the **Märkisches Museum** (Museum of the March), the **Berlin Museum**, closed until 1999 for renovations, the **Jüdisches** (Jewish) **Museum** (cur-

rently awaiting completion of its future domicile, the Libeskind Building beside the Berlin Museum), the **Ephraim Palais**, the **Düppel Village Museum**, the **Domäne Dahlem**, and the **Industrial Design Collection** in the **Kulturbrauerei**, an exciting venue for events in Prenzlauer Berg.

Treasures of the World on One Island

The Museum Island is partly in desolate shape, as renovation costs for the buildings are astronomical. But Museum Island's attractiveness remains unaffected by the general dilapidation, thanks primarily to the world-famous **Pergamon Museum**, which took its name from the "Altar of Pergamon," erected as a victory monument sometime between 180 and 159 B. C. in the ancient eponymous city in Asia Minor.

Above: Museum Island, obligatory for visitors to Berlin and school classes. Right: The Porcellain Room in Charlottenburg Palace.

Between 1878 and 1886, on a commission from the former Royal Prussian Museums, archeologists excavated the entire temple complex and brought it to Berlin. Shortly before the turn of the century a museum had been built on the island between the Spree and the Kupfergraben, but it was too small for the altar, so the present Pergamon Museum was constructed between 1912 and 1930.

After the monumental altar, the true crown of the collection from classical antiquity, the most popular attraction is the **Market Gate of Milet** in the hall of Roman architecture. The gate was built during the reign of Emperor Hadrian as the entrance to the city of Milet's southern market. In the well-lit and beautifully arranged museum hall, all the hustle and bustle of this ancient city in Asia Minor seems to echo in your ears. The Pergamon also houses the **Museum of Islamic Art** and of the **Museum of Asia Minor**.

The **Altes Museum** (Old Museum) was opened as Berlin's first museum in 1830 opposite the City Castle. The **Neues**

Museum (New Museum) is attached, surviving as a complementary building as a cost-intensive ruin from the days of reconstruction. The **Bode Museum** will be shut down from January 1999 to mid-2004. And the **Alte Nationalgalerie** (Old National Gallery), which closed in February 1998, placed a selection of its works in the Altes Museum; from 2001 it will exhibit 19th-century art. When the Bode Museum reopens, it will house the collection of sculptures, the coin collection, the children's gallery and, as already mentioned, the museum for late antiquity and Byzantine art. In addition, until the Neues Museum is renovated, the Bode Museum will also carry the Ägyptisches (Egyptian) Museum and the collection of papyri.

The Kulturforum and the Dahlem Museums

The **Kulturforum** has inherited the **Neue Nationalgalerie** (on Potsdamer Strasse), the **Kunstgewerbe Museum** (Museum of Arts and Crafts), the **Kupferstichkabinett** (Copperplate Engraving Cabinet), the **Kunstbibliothek** (Art Library), the **Neue Gemäldegalerie** (New Picture Gallery), and the **Musikinstrumenten Museum** (Musical Instrument Museum) next to the Philharmonic.

The New National Gallery, with its 1960's architecture by Mies van der Rohe and now regarded as a classic, presents changing exhibitions of modern art and painting and has a permanent collection of art from the 19th and 20th centuries. It is the only building Mies van der Rohe designed in Germany after emigrating to the US in 1937.

In the utilitarian Museum of Arts and Crafts (*Kunstgewerbe Museum*) built in 1985, four floors hold exhibits from all areas of European arts and crafts, from the Middle Ages to the present day. A part of the exhibition is displayed in the **Kunstgewerbe Museum** on the **Schlossinsel** (Palace Island) **Köpenick**. Until 1944 the works were in the Berlin City Castle, which was destroyed at that time.

The **Staatsbibliothek zu Berlin – Preussischer Kulturbesitz** (State Library) is in two buildings. Haus 1 in Mitte and Haus 2 in an edifice by Hans Scharoun, in fact one of the largest library buildings in Europe, standing to the southeast of the Kulturforum.

Berlin's museum system has a third base in **Dahlem** where, at the beginning of the 20th century, the State Museums of Berlin built an external branch of the Asian Museum. After World War Two and the construction of the Wall, Dahlem was systematically expanded to become West Berlin's museum center. Building after building was erected, ultimately giving rise to Berlin's largest Berlin complex. Until recently it included the **Museum of Islamic Art** (in the Pergamon Museum since May 1998) and the museums of **Indian Art** and **Far Eastern Art** (closed from May 1998 to April 2000), collections that reveal Dahlem's wide spectrum of fascinating exhibitions. New acquisitions are no exception: in 1989 the Museum of Islamic Art purchased a "Relief Tile with Inscription in Quadratic Kufi" from West Turkestan (Samarkand) dated A. D. 1386. The Museum of Indian Art is proud of a miniature from the heroic epic *Shahnama of Firdausi*, painted in the art school of a North Indian sultanate around A.D. 1450, while the Museum of Far Asian Art boasts exhibits covering such topics as "Divine Providence and Earthly Happiness: Chinese New Years' Pictures from the Wallenstein Collection."

But the real must is a visit to the **Museum für Völkerkunde** (Museum of Anthropology), whose collections from pre-Columbian America, South and East Asia, Africa and the South Sea islands have impressed generations of visitors. Its approximately 350,000 objects make it the world's largest museum of its kind.

Right: The bust of Nefertiti attracts crowds to the Egyptian Museum.

Most of the exhibits are presented in skillfully arranged rooms. Cones of light bring many a long-forgotten godhead back to life in almost frightening fashion.

Schloss Charlottenburg, with its small and large orangeries, has become the temporary abode of the famous **Galerie der Romantik** (Gallery of the Romantic Era) and the **Museum für Ur- und Frühgeschichte** (Museum for Prehistory and Early History; in the Langhans building). Since early 1997 the chambers of King Friedrich Wilhelm IV have also been on display here. Located opposite is the **Ägyptisches** (Egyptian) **Museum** (the two collections have not yet been joined on Museum Island). The bust of Nefertiti is what attracts the public in droves and sells hundreds of thousands of postcards, but it's by no means the greatest treasure in the collection.

Modern Art and Architecture, Archives and Allies

The **Bauhaus Archives**, which doesn't seem like a museum at all, fascinates even those not particularly enthusiastic about architecture. The exhibits demonstrate the complexity of the training at the Bauhaus School, and what theater, film, design and such a practical piece of furniture as a rocking chair actually have in common. The institution also possesses an outstanding archive on the Bauhaus School and its masters.

Then there is the wealth of material in the **Martin Gropius Building**, home until recently of the **Berlinische Galerie**, the **Jüdische Museum** and the **Werkbund-Archiv**. The *Werkbund-Archiv* provides unusual insight into everyday life in the 20th century. And the Jüdische (Jewish) Museum does not restrict itself to the period of German history infamous for the genocide committed against the Jewish people but, beyond that, also recalls the loss of Jewish culture, once so alive in Berlin.

The Martin Gropius Building closed in January 1998 for renovations, but should reopen in mid-1999 as the site of a permanent exhibition on the history of the Federal Republic of Germany. The Jewish Museum will move into the Libeskind Building in late 1999. The Berlinische Galerie and the Werkbund Archiv are slated to move onto the grounds of the Schultheis brewery in Kreuzberg.

The **Brücke Museum** specializes in Expressionist art. It was named for the artists' group founded in Dresden in 1905. Another museum, the **Verborgenes Museum** (Hidden Museum), has also specialized in a very special branch of art that has all too rarely met the eye of the public: art produced by women; art that has been forgotten, suppressed, underestimated, and has by and large gone unrecognized.

The **Georg Kolbe Museum**, in the late sculptor's studio (plus annex), is not exclusively dedicated to the works of this artist, but does include them. Kolbe, who lived from 1877 to 1947, was particularly

influenced by the French sculptor Auguste Rodin. Georg Kolbe's sculptures are considered by art historians among the most important in the first half of the 20th century, and not solely because of his idealistic philosophy.

The **Bröhan Museum**, by contrast, is in no danger of being forgotten. This museum's paintings and sculptures, as well as its glass and ceramic objects and even furniture, which are all fashioned in Art-Nouveau, Art-Deco and functionalist style, have kept it popular over the years.

With the title "More than a Suitcase Remains," the **Alliierten Museum** (Allied Forces Museum) on Clayallee traces the relationship of Berliners to the Allies over the years (see also page 231).

Nature and Technology

Several other museums display fascinating exhibits of quite another character. Unconcerned with the artistic aspects of culture, they depict the world in which we live. Topping the list is the **Museum**

für Naturkunde (Natural History Museum), which has displayed its collections, which now number 60 million objects, for 250 years. Its largest specimen is also the largest of its kind in the world: the 38-foot (12-meter) tall, 74-foot (23-meter) long skeleton of a *Brachiosaurus brancai*. The museum also owns the actual fragment of pitchblende in which the mineralogist Martin Heinrich Klapproth discovered uranium in 1789. A whole department is dedicated to meteorites.

The **Botanisches Museum** (in the Botanical Gardens), which reopened in spring 1991, confronts its visitors with those things that nature has made small, like petals, root hairs and leaf stems. They are shown here in magnification – sometimes thousandfold.

The Post and Communications Museum is closed until 1999. The exhibits, however, are on view in Schöneberg.

Above: A Brachiosaurus skeleton in the Museum of Natural Science.

The Wall: History and Myth

The **Forschungs- und Gedänkstatte Normannenstrasse** (Research and Memorial Rooms), located in the former Stasi headquarters, not only shows the work room of boss Erich Mielke, but also provides insight into the workings of the snooping procedures of the "listen and snatch people's corporation," as it was known familiarly.

The **Berlin Wall** has, of course, achieved museum status by now. Leftovers of the former city divider still stand on Schlesische Strasse in Kreuzberg, where the **Museum der Verbotenen Kunst** (Museum of Forbidden Art) has exhibitions in the last remaining watch tower.

The **East Side Gallery** in Friedrichshain is not really a museum, but is rather more of an open-air gallery. Graffiti-sprayed bits of the Wall have also been set up in the Mauerpark in Prenzlauer Berg, not far from the new Max Schmeling sports hall.

The **Haus am Checkpoint Charlie** also shows related items in its regular exhibition "The Wall from August 13, 1961, till Today." And right nearby, on Niederkirchnerstrasse, you can still see a few meters of the Wall, which was, after all, 96 miles long (155 km) in all.

The **Deutsches Historisches Museum** (German History Museum) is headquartered in the Baroque *Zeughaus* on Unter den Linden. It fulfills it's assigned task of "educating and understanding our common history," with changing exhibitions on German and European history.

Recently, two legacies of famous silver screen stars arrived in Berlin, one from Marlene Dietrich and the other from comedian Heinz Rühmann. The **Marlene Dietrich Collection**, with clothes, jewelry, letters and other momentos, is planned to be housed in the new Film Museum on Potsdamer Platz once it opens in the year 2000.

BERLIN STATE MUSEUMS OF PRUSSIAN CULTURAL HERITAGE

Tel. 20 90 55 55, Tue-Fri 10 a.m.-6 p.m., Sat-Sun 11 a.m.-6 p.m. Museums on Museum Island and Picture Gallery Tue-Sun 10 a.m.-6 p.m.

Ägyptisches Museum (Egyptian) and **Papyrussammlung**, Charlottenburg, Schloss Str. 70 and in Mitte, Thu until 8 p.m.; **Bode Museum**, on Museum Island, entrance Monbijou Bridge; **Altes Museum**, Mitte, Bodestr. 1-3 Museum Island; **Alte Nationalgalerie**, Museum Island, Bodestr.1-3; **Antikensammlung** (antiquities), Altes Museum, Museum Island; **Bode Museum**, Museum Island, entrance Monbijou Bridge; **Galerie der Romantik**, Charlottenburg, Schloss Charlottenburg, in the Knobelsdorff wing; **Gemäldegalerie** (Picture Gallery), in the Kulturforum, Tiergarten, Matthaikirchplatz 8; **Hamburger Bahnhof – Museum für Gegenwart** (Museum of the Present), Tiergarten, Invalidenstr. 50-51; **Kunstgewerbe Museum** (Arts and Crafts) in Köpenick Castle (closed until 2002) and in the Kulturforum, Matthäikirchplatz; **Kupferstichkabinett** (Copperplate Engraving Cabinet), Tiergarten, Matthäikirchplatz; **Münzkabinett** (Coin Collection), Mitte, in the Bode Museum, Museum Island; **Museum für Indische Kunst** (Indian Art), Zehlendorf (Dahlem), Lansstr. 8 (closed until year 2000); **Museum für Islamische Kunst** (Islamic Art), Mitte, Pergamon Museum, Museum Island and Zehlendorf (Dahlem), Lansstr. 8; **Museum für Ostasiatische Kunst** (Far Eastern Art), Zehlendorf (Dahlem), Lansstr. 8; **Museum für Stätantike und Byzantinische Kunst** (late antiquity/Byzantine art), Mitte, Bode Museum, Museum Island; **Museum für Völkerkunde** (anthropology), Zehlendorf (Dahlem), Lansstr. 8; **Musikinstrumenten Museum** (musical instruments), Tiergarten, Tiergartenstr. 1; **Neue Nationalgalerie**, Tiergarten, Potsdamer Str. 50; **Pergamon Museum**, Museum Island, entrance Kupfergraben (Thu until 8 p.m.); **Berggruen Collection**, "Picasso and His Times," Stüler Wing, opposite Charlottenburg Castle, Charlottenburg, Schloss Str. 1; **Skulpturensammlung**, Mitte, Bode Museum, Museum Island; **Vorderasiatisches Museum** (Asia Minor), Mitte, Pergamon Museum, Museum Island.

BERLIN CIY MUSEUMS

Berlin Museum, Kreuzberg, Lindenstr. 14 (closed till 1999); **Domäne Dahlem**, Zehlendorf, Königin-Luise-Str. 49, tel. 832 50 00, Wed-Mon 10 a.m.-6 p.m.; **Ephraim-Palais**, Mitte, Poststr. 16, tel. 240 02-0, Tue-Sun 10 a.m.- 6 p.m.; **Jüdisches** (Jewish) **Museum** (opens 1999 in the Libeskind Building), Kreuzberg, Stresemannstr. 110, tel. 25 48 65 16,

Tue-Sun 10 a.m.-8 p.m.; **Märkisches Museum**, Am Köllnischen Park 5, tel. 308 66-0, Tue-Sun 10 a.m.- 6 p.m.; **Düppel Village Museum**, Zehlendorf, Clauertstr. 11, tel. 802 66 71, Apr-Oct: Thu 3-7 p.m., Sun and holidays 10 a.m.-5 p.m.

FOUNDATION FOR PRUSSIAN PALACES AND GARDENS, BERLIN-BRANDENBURG

Schloss Charlottenburg, Schloss Str., tel. 32 09 11, Tue-Fri 9 a.m.-5 p.m., Sat, Sun 10 a.m.-5 p.m.; **Belvedere** (Berlin Porcellain), Tue-Sun 10 a.m.-5 p.m. (May-Oct), Tue-Fri 11 a.m.-3 p.m., Sat, Sun 10 a.m.-3 p.m. (Oct-May); **Schinkel-Pavillon**, Tue-Sun 10 a.m.-5 p.m. (May-Oct), Tue-Fri 11 a.m.-3 p.m., Sat, Sun 10 a.m.-3 p.m. (Oct-May).

OTHER MUSEUMS AND EXHIBITIONS

Alliierten Museum (Allied Forces), Clayallee 123, Dahlem, tel. 818 19 90, daily 10 a.m. to 6 p.m.
Bauhaus-Archiv, Tiergarten, Klingelhöferstr. 14, tel. 254 00 20, Wed-Mon 10 a.m.-5 p.m.
Berlinische Galerie (formerly in the Martin Gropius Building in Kreuzberg; new location to see the Schultheis brewery in Kreuzberg).
Botanisches Museum, Steglitz, Königin-Luise-Str. 6-8, tel. 83 00 61 27, Tue-Sun 10 a.m.-5 p.m.
Bröhan Museum, Charlottenburg, Schloss Str. 1a, tel. 321 40 29, Tue-Sun 10 a.m.-6 p.m., Thu till 8.
Brücke Museum, Zehlendorf, Bussardsteig 9, tel. 831 20 29, Wed-Mon 11 a.m.-5 p.m.
Haus am Checkpoint Charlie, Kreuzberg, Friedrichstr. 43-44, tel. 25 37 25-0, daily 9 a.m.-10 p.m.
Das Verborgene Museum (Hidden Museum), Charlottenburg, Schlüterstr. 70, tel. 313 36 56, Tue-Fri 1-7 p.m., Sat, Sun noon-4 p.m.
Deutsches Historisches Museum, Mitte, Unter den Linden 2, tel. 215 020 (closed until 2002).
Deutsche Guggenheim, Mitte, Unter den Linden 13-15, tel. 20 20 93-0, daily 11 a.m.-8 p.m.
Forschungs- und Gedenkstätte Normannenstrasse, Lichtenberg, Ruschestrasse 103 (Haus 1), tel. 553 68 54. Tue-Fri 11 a.m.-6 p.m., Sat, Sun 2-6 p.m. Exhibition in the former Stasi headquarters.
Gedenkstätte Haus der Wannsee-Konferenz, Zehlendorf, Am Grossen Wannsee 56-58, tel. 805 00 10, Mon-Fri 10 a.m.-6 p.m., Sat-Sun 2-6 p.m.
Georg Kolbe Museum, Charlottenburg, Sensburger Allee 25, tel. 304 21 44, Tue-Sun 10 a.m.-5 p.m.
Museum der Verbotenen Kunst (Forbidden Art), Treptow, Puschkinallee/Schlesiche Str., tel. 204 20 49, Wed-Sun and holidays noon-6 p.m.
Museum für Naturkunde, Mitte, Invalidenstr. 43, tel. 20 93 85 91, Tue-Sun 9:30 a.m.-5 p.m.
Deutsches Technik Museum Berlin, Kreuzberg, Trebbiner Str. 9, tel. 25 48 40, Tue-Fri 9 a.m.-5:30 p.m., Sat, Sun 10 a.m.-6 p.m.

OASES OF NATURE

First-time visitors to Berlin generally explore the part of the city between the Ku'damm and the Reichstag and between Unter den Linden and Alexanderplatz. In the middle of the city, Berlin seems grey. But this first impression is deceptive, for the city has quite a number of green areas. Unbeknownst to most, a quarter of Berlin's urban surface consists of woods and lakes, rivers, parks and other green areas. It's highest elevations are the Müggelberge (368 feet/115 meters) and the Teufelsberg, the largest lake is the Grosse Müggelsee, the longest river is the Spree (28 miles/45 km), and the longest canal the Teltowkanal (18 miles/29 km). Not included in this list are the many trees that line the streets of the city, especially when compared to other cities. Berlin had over 397,000 trees at last count, which,

Left: The Greenwich Promenade on Tegel Lake. Right: One of many establishments that offer the wanderer refreshments.

needless to say, is great news for the male contingent of Berlin's 87,000 dogs!

East or west, the Berliners' love of nature is legendary. A genuine Berliner is someone who enjoys a "drive into the greenery" on the weekend, or who withdraws into the petit bourgeois idyll of his *Laubenpieper* – the slang name for Berlin's typical small garden plots layed out in suburban colonies.

Palaces, Parks and Zoos

Berlin's first official parks were those created by the Hohenzollern princes as enchanting areas of greenery behind their palace walls. Berlin holds the claim to having Germany's first Baroque garden, which is behind **Schloss Charlottenburg**. In 1695 Friedrich I, Prussia's first king, gave his wife Sophie-Charlotte a little palace as her summer residence. Later, this basic construction was repeatedly expanded on the model of Versailles. The park was redesigned as an English garden in the 19th century.

Aerial bombing in World War Two severely damaged the buildings and park facilities, so that it now gives only a faint idea of its original appearance. But a stroll through the park is still a delight. The path around the **Carp Pond**, past the **Mausoleum** and to the **Belvedere**, or a walk along the Spree shore can be quite charming. Many excursion ships cruising on Berlin's waterways dock at the palace bridge.

In the 1920s the city had several parks laid out, among them the **Volkspark Jungfernheide**, located north of the palace below Tegel Airport. One bank of the park's lake is an open-air swimming area, the other boasts a small artificial sand beach. In contrast to the Jungfernheide, the tranquility of the **Plötzensee** in the **Volkspark Rehberge** is never disturbed by planes landing at Tegel.

Berlin's most famous park is, of course, the **Tiergarten**, which was designed by one of Europe's greatest landscape architects, Peter Joseph Lenné. At the western tip of the Tiergarten is the

Zoological Garden, Germany's oldest zoo. Today it has over 1700 species, making it the world's most varied zoo. The adjacent **Aquarium** is a good tip, with its crocodile hall and insectarium.

The Lichtenberg district also has a zoo, the **Tierpark Berlin-Friedrichsfelde**, located in the park bearing the same name, which was also designed by Lenné. The Tierpark's long-time director, Prof. H. Dathe, cleverly adopted Lenné's design idea, providing a harmonious home for about 8500 animals.

The **Botanical Garden** in the south of Berlin is a green idyll of a completely different sort. For over three centuries now, species of plants from all over the world have been displayed and researched here. The botanical garden was originally over on Potsdamer Strasse, where **Kleistpark** is now located. Its ancestor was the City Castle's park, laid out in 1646. Shortly before the end of the 19th century work began on the new garden in Dahlem. This botanical garden is one of the most important in the world, featuring about

20,000 species, many of which grow in their natural surroundings, sometimes arranged in huge glass arboretums. Anyone who can cope with the heavy moist air of the tropics should take a stroll through the Victoria House to see the royal water-lily from the Amazon basin, or inspect the new medicinal garden and learn about the healing powers of plants.

The Southeast: Köpenick and the Müggelsee

Köpenick's fame in Germany rests squarely on the "Captain of Köpenick," Carl Zuckermayer's wild literary character who has featured in many a film and play. The traveler to this, Berlin's largest district, will be pleased by the almost village-like atmosphere of the area around the **Rathaus** (City Hall), which stands in the middle of the old town on an island in the Spree. The steamers pick up pas-

Above: Wintry landscape where the Spree ships berth on the Wannsee.

sengers for their tours here. South of the old town is a peninsula, the **Schlossinsel**, where **Schloss Köpenick** stands. Part of the collection of Berlin's Museum of Arts and Crafts is on display here.

Köpenick's precinct of Friedrichshagen lies directly on a lake, the **Grosser Müggelsee**. This body of water is simply called "the big bathtub" by Berliners and, indeed, it is Berlin's largest lake at 1892 acres (766 ha). A *Kleiner* (Small) *Müggelsee* exists as well.

The water really draws crowds in summer: thousands come to the **Freibad Müggelsee** beach to swim, steamers sail by on their tours, and ferries shuttle from one side of the lake to the other. On the southern shore of the Müggelsee are some restaurants popular with daytrippers, the **Rübezahl** and the **Müggelseeperle**.

One important event in Köpenick is the rowing regatta held in the **Grünau** precinct on the course used for the rowing competition during the 1936 Olympic Games. Grünau's **Freibad** (public beach)

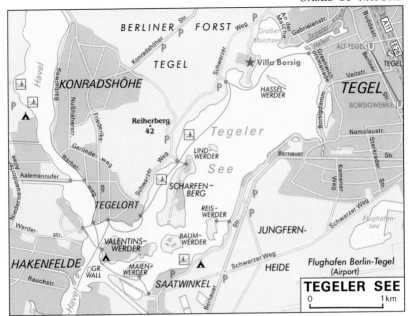

TEGELER SEE
0   1 km

is nearby, and on the northern shore you'll find another beach, the **Freibad Wendeschloss**.

In the middle of Köpenick's lake district lies the nature preserve **Müggelberge**. The 100-foot (30-meter) **Müggelturm** perched atop the "mountain" offers a wonderful view of the entire region of up to 31 miles (50 km) on clear days.

The **Dahme** is the river flowing through Köpenick. To the southwest of the Köpenick forest it is called the **Langer See** (Long Lake), and even has an (uninhabited) island in it called *Kleiner Rohrwall*.

Pure Nature in Berlin's North

Pristine nature as it existed in Berlin's environs a hundred years ago is rare today: but if it can be found anywhere, then it is in the northern outskirts of the city, in **Tegel**, where the metropolis gradually fades into the March of Brandenburg. One of the most beautiful hiking routes leads around **Tegeler See** (Lake

Tegel). An approximately three-hour hike along its shores is best begun at the **U-Bahn station Tegel** (line 6). From there, the route passes through the old village of Tegel, whose form still recalls the old village green, to **Greenwich Promenade**, which leads north along **Tegel Harbor**. After passing the little cove called **Grosse Malche**, the journey continues on the opposite shore on the **Schwarzer Weg**, an asphalt path. From here, trees block the view of the lake, so turn left onto the little shore path leading to a small peninsula. **Villa Borsig** hides there among shadowy trees behind a park wall. It was built in 1905 for the family of a captain of industry. Nowadays it is used by a research institute and, unfortunately, is closed to the public.

The trail along the shore continues south, past the public swimming area – the **Freibad Tegeler See** – and the dock of the car ferry to **Scharfenberg**, the largest island in the lake. Scharfenberg is reserved for the pupils of the boarding school located there.

171

The Schwarzer Weg continues to **Tegel Ort** (Tegel Village), where every hour a ferry takes strollers across to the villages of **Valentinswerder**, **Maienwerder** and **Saatwinkel** on the other shore. Arriving in Saatwinkel, take a break in one of the restaurants or follow the shoreside trail to **Reiswerder**. This route leads past a swimming area in idyllic surroundings. The trip back to Tegel can be done on foot or with the 113 bus on **Bernauer Strasse**.

The U-Bahn station Tegel is also the starting point for a hike through the **Tegeler Fliess** conservation area, which extends to the northeast of Berlin. This little river rises near Bernau and empties into the Tegeler See. It winds from Tegel to **Lübars** over a distance of nearly six miles (ten km), and a three-hour hike along its shores, through meadows and small patches of forest, is among the most beautiful ways to experience the nature Berlin has to offer. In some places, particularly on the other side of **Kienwerder**, the landscape is so spellbinding that you can easily forget you are hiking on the northern edge of a major city.

The Green South: Grunewald and Wannsee

In contrast to the landscape in Tegel, which is still relatively untouched and free of masses of scurrying tourists, **Grunewald** and the shores of the **Wannsee** are so well known that you can never enjoy nature alone.

Given snow in the cold season, crowds press onto the **Teufelsberg** (Devil's Mountain) for sleigh rides. Paragliding is another sport popular to the area. Berlin's airspace will also be watched from the top of this 368-foot (115-meter) "mountain."

Nonetheless, the Grunewald forest has its subtle charms; its stock of game animals is nearly as large as it was 400 years ago when Elector Joachim II first rode

out to hunt in the *Grüner Wald* (Green Woods). Every year boars emerge from the depths of the forest, only to show up in Zehlendorf's gardens, where they tear up the flower beds – always a big event for the local press in the "silly season." It is even said that, in their search for food, boars have torn plastic bags from the hands of strollers. But these are isolated and heresay events; normally the only boars you will encounter are those kept in large enclosures. They prefer to laze about in the mud.

Another popular destination in Grunewald is Joachim II's **Jagdschloss Grunewald** (Grunewald Hunting Lodge) on Lake Grunewald; it houses a museum with a collection of paintings.

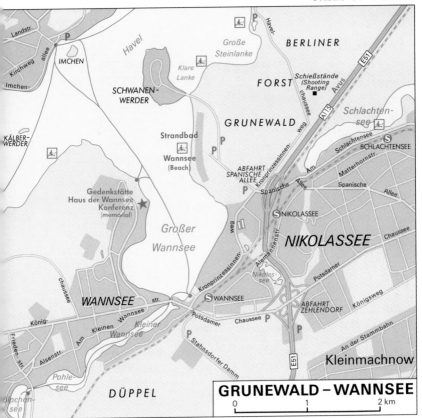

GRUNEWALD – WANNSEE

0   1   2 km

To experience Grunewald by car, start from the **Havelchaussee**, which follows the shore of the Havel. This street was the site of one of Berlin's most amusing political farces. The Social-Democratic and Green Party coalition with the Senate majority banned all car traffic from the Chaussee, but the district office in Zehlendorf refused to put up the appropriate traffic signs. Finally the Senate Department of Construction – now with a conservative Christian Democratic majority – carried out the task in spite of the protests of the Zehlendorfers. In March, 1991, the new Senate had the signs removed again in a great hurry: this time the Senate was afraid of new protests from the opposite side.

The Havelchaussee leads past the **Grunewaldturm** (tower), whose viewing platform offers a panorama of Berlin. Continuing south on the Chaussee, you'll arrive at **Lieper Bucht**, whose lovely sandy beach is great for swimming. The Havelchaussee then meets up with **Kronprinzessinweg**, which quickly takes you to the **Strandbad Wannsee** (Wannsee Beach), Europe's largest inland swimming area. Up to 40,000 Berliners crowd together here on weekends. The nearby **Schlachtensee** and **Krumme Lanke** offer a real alternative to the masses on the Wannsee's artificial sand beach. Both lakes can be comfortably circled on foot; and while the best-known meadows are filled with sunbathers on warm summer

173

weekends, there are also innumerable hidden swimming spots.

The road leaves the southern cove of the Wannsee behind and goes past the excursion boat docking facilities and through Wannsee village. A bus shuttles along the **Pfaueninsel-Chaussee** to the ferry to **Pfaueninsel** (Peacock Island). In 1794 Friedrich Wilhelm II once again gave irrefutable evidence of the Hohenzollern dynasty's passion for palaces amid greenery, ordering the construction of a little palace in the form of an artificial ruin on the diminutive island. Two decades later, Peter Jospeh Lenné gave the island its finishing touches by creating a fashionable English garden. With its proud peacocks, the island is considered one of the most beautiful spots in all of Berlin.

The **Volkspark Glienicke**, accessible via **Nikolskoer Weg**, sprawls south of the Pfaueninsel. Its real value has

Above: The panda bear is still one of the zoo's most beloved dwellers.

emerged with the fall of the Wall. The park was originally part of the Sanssouci Palace grounds! It is hardly any wonder that the **Glienicke Palace** is reminiscent of the atmosphere in Sanssouci.

Nature in the City's Parks

Many of Berlin's districts have municipal parks. Small but attractive is Neukölln's **Körnerpark**, which was once a quarry. To access its charms, you will have to go down wide stairs, as the park lies up to 22 feet (seven meters) below the level of the surrounding houses. The **Orangery**, which is used as an exhibition room, is a special gem. **Britzer Garten** is also located in Neukölln. The Federal Garden Exhibition was held there in 1985, a great honor in Germany. The grounds were thereafter turned into a recreational park.

The **Bürgerpark** in **Pankow** was laid out in 1854 as a private park. Broad meadows with picturesque clumps of trees straddle the shores of the **Panke river**, which gave the district its name. At one edge of the park is the "Park Library," Berlin's smallest.

Marzahn has its own **Erholungspark** for strollers and joggers, and **Weissensee** its green surface. In the late 19th century, Berliners used to come to wander about this pleasure garden, which included a music pavilion and a caroussel situated near the almost perfectly round **Weisser See** (White Lake).

In the middle of **Friedrichshain**, between the Friedensstrasse and Am Friedrichshain, is the district's eponymous **Volkspark**. Once again it was Lenné who drew up the plans and, in August, 1848, it was opened to the Berliners, but not before the casualties of the Revolution of March 1848 found their final resting place in the **Friedhof der Märzgefallenen**. Gustav Meyer, Berlin's first director of garden construction, had the park expanded between 1874 and 1875.

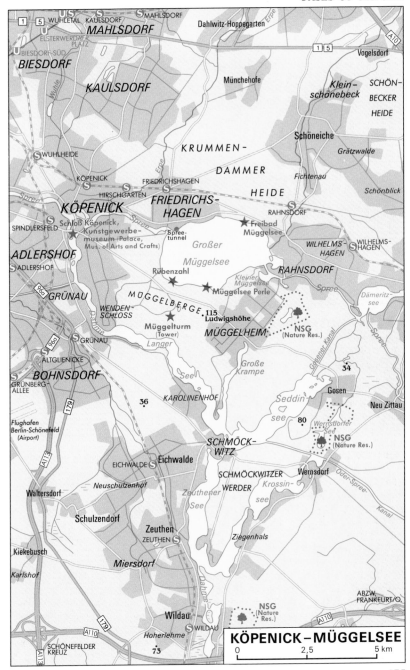

KÖPENICK–MÜGGELSEE

0   2,5   5 km

Later the **Märchenbrunnen** (Fairy Tale Fountain) provided it with a new entrance. The fountain, designed in neo-Baroque style, sports sandstone figures from the fairy tales collected by the Brothers Grimm.

After 1945 a million cubic meters of rubble from the city's ruins were piled up on the demolished Wehrmacht flak bunkers, thus producing two sizable hills. Maps designate them as **Grosser** and **Kleiner Bunkerberg** (Large and Small Bunker Mountain), but the Berliners nicknamed them **Mont Klamott**. A long sledding path winds its way down from the 153-foot (48-meter) plateau of the smaller mountain.

Treptow, bordered on the northeast by the Spree river, has three large parks: the **Köllnische Heide**, near the S-Bahn station Oberspree; the **Königsheide**, in the Johannistal quarter – both are natural forest areas with good hiking trails – and

Above: Cooling off on a summer boat ride across one of Berlin's many lakes.

Treptower Park. In 1896 Gustav Meyer began work on the Treptower Park beside the Spree. The Berlin Trade Fair was held here in the same year; its only remain being the giant telescope in the **Archenhold-Sternwarte**. The *Neues Gartenhaus an der Spree*, built in 1821-22 across from the observatory, is now called *Haus Zenner* after its celebrated manager.

Near the abbey bridge, rowboats or paddleboats are for rent for a row around the **Insel der Jugend** (Island of Youth). The **Soviet Memorial** to the 5000 Soviet soldiers who died in the battle for the city is also in the park.

The passenger ships of the **Weisse Flotte** (White Fleet) cruise from Treptow Harbor out onto the Spree and Havel rivers, and into the countryside to **Köpenick**, one of Berlin's "green lungs," as it were. The **Langer See, Seddinsee, Dämmeritzsee** and, finally, **Kleiner** and **Grosser Müggelsee** are stops on its big lake journey. Of course you can do the same route in your own boat.

PALACES, PARKS AND LAKES

Palaces, Parks, Zoos and other Sights

Botanical Garden, Steglitz, entrances: Königin-Luise-Platz and Unter den Eichen, tel. 83 00 60, Nov-Jan daily 9 a.m.-4 p.m., Feb till 5 p.m., March-Oct till 6 p.m., Apr, Aug, Sept till 8 p.m., May-July till 9 p.m., although the greenhouses close an hour earlier.

Britzer Garten, Neukölln, tel. 700 90 60; entrances: Buckower Damm, Mohriner Allee, Tauernallee, Sangerhauser Weg, Nov-Feb 9 a.m.-4 p.m., March till 5:30 p.m., Apr, Sept to 7 p.m., May-Aug till 8 p.m., Oct till 5 p.m..

Grunewaldturm (Tower), **Wilmersdorf**, Havelchaussee 61, on Karlsberg, daily 10 a.m. till sunset, height: 172 feet (55 meters), 204 steps lead up to a lookout platform.

Jagdschloss Grunewald (hunting lodge), Zehlendorf, on Lake Grunewald, tel. 813 35 97, mid-May to mid-Oct Tue-Sun 10 a.m.-5 p.m., mid-Oct to mid-May Sat, Sun 10 a.m.-4 p.m. (museum, hunting weapons exhibition).

Müggelturm (tower), Köpenick, in the Müggelberge, near Müggelheimer Damm, daily 9 a.m.-5 p.m., lookout platform at 100 feet (30 meters), 126 steps, tel. 651 65 12.

Charlottenburg Palace, Luisenpl., tel. 32 09 11 **Museums in the Palace**: the palace grounds are open Tue-Fri 9 a.m.-5 p.m., and Sat, Sun 10 a.m.- 5 p.m.

Friedrichsfelde Palace, Lichtenberg, Am Tierpark 125 (on the grounds of the Tierpark), tel. 513 81 42, Museum (17th- and 18th-century art), Tue-Sun 10 a.m.-18 p.m., Sat, Sun 1 p.m.-4 p.m. Concerts, too (see p. 209).

Glienicke Palace and Park, Zehlendorf, Königstr. 36, tel. 805 30 41; Palace Museum Sat, Sun 10 a.m.-5 p.m., Park, daily 7 a.m. till sunset.

Köpenick Castle, Schlossinsel (Castle Island), tel. 657 26 51, Museum of Arts and Crafts, Wed-Sun 10 a.m.-18 p.m.

Pfaueninsel Palace, Zehlendorf, Pfaueninselchaussee tel. 805 30 42, Palace: tours every half-hour: Tue-Sun 10 a.m.-1 p.m. and 1:30-5 p.m.

Spreepark Berlin, Treptow, Kiehnwerderallee, entrance: Neue Krugallee, tel. 53 33 50, Spring/Summer daily 9 a.m.-7 p.m. A new recreational park suited for families.

Tierpark (zoo) **Berlin-Friedrichsfelde**, Lichtenberg, Am Tierpark 125, tel. 51 53 10, entrance at the U-Bahn station Tierpark and at Friedrichsfelde Palace, daily 9 a.m. till sunset.

Zoological Garden, Tiergarten, entrances: Hardenbergplatz 8 (Lion Gate) opposite Zoo Station and on Budapester Str. 34 (Elephant Gate), tel. 25 40 10, Nov-Feb daily 9 a.m.-5 p.m., March till 5:30 p.m., Apr-Sept till 6:30 p.m., Oct till 6 p.m.

Treptower Park, Puschkinallee, S-Bahn: Treptow Park; sights: Soviet memorial and Archenhold Sternwarte (Wed-Sun 2-4:30 p.m.).

Aquarium, Tiergarten, Budapester Str. 32 (at the Elephant Gate), tel. 25 40 10, open daily from 9 a.m.-6 p.m.

Outing Destinations, Restaurants, Cafés

Alter Dorfkrug Lübars, Reinickendorf, Alt-Lübars 8, tel. 402 71 74, Wed-Fri noon-10 p.m., Sat, Sun from 11:30 a.m., in summer till 11 p.m. Nice, cozy restaurant with country-village atmosphere.

Forsthaus Paulsborn, Zehlendorf, at Grunewald hunting manor, tel. 818 19 10, Tue-Sun 11 a.m.-11 p.m., Sun from 9 a.m.

Eierschale Zenner, Treptow, Alt-Treptow 14-17., tel. 533 73 70, Sun-Thu 9-2 a.m., Fri, Sat till 4 a.m.

Loretta am Wannsee, Zehlendorf, Kronprinzessinnenweg 260, tel. 803 51 56, daily 9 a.m.-midnight.

Rübezahl/Müggelseeperle, Köpenick, on the Grosser Müggelsee (lake), tel. 65 88 22 00, daily 6:30 a.m.-11 p.m., gigantic terrace in summer, with a view of the lake.

Wirtshaus Schildhorn, Zehlendorf, Havelchaussee/Strasse am Schildhorn 4a, tel. 305 31 11, daily from 11 a.m. Good establishment with a beer garden on the Wannsee.

Schleusenkrug, Tiergarten, Müller-Breslau-Strasse, tel. 313 99 09, from 11 a.m. Popular beer garden in the Tiergarten.

Wirtshaus zur Pfaueninsel, Zehlendorf, Pfaueninselchaussee 100, tel. 805 22 25, in summer daily 9 a.m.-11 p.m., in winter Wed-Mon 10 a.m.-8 p.m.

Brauhaus Joh. Albrecht (brewery), Reinickendorf, Karolinenstr. 12, tel. 433 50 10, and in Neukölln, Glasower Str. 27, nice beer garden, tel. 626 88 80, daily from 10 a.m.

Ships

Spreefahrt Horst Duggen, tel. 394 49 54. Excursions on the Spree and in the canals beginning at the Congressional Hall.

Reederei Bruno Winkler, Tiergarten. Levetzowstr. 12a, tel. 391 70 70, at the Schlossbrücke, Charlottenburger Ufer.

Reederei Riedel, Kreuzberg, Planufer 78, tel. 691 37 82, at the Hansabrücke, Märkisches Ufer. City tours through historical Berlin, at Wannsee tour of the seven lakes.

Stern- und Kreis-Schiffahrt, Treptow, Puschkinallee 16/17, tel. 536 36 00, from Tegel, Wannsee, Treptow.

SPORTS IN BERLIN: TRADITION AND RECORDS

Berlin's oldest sports club is what is refered to as a "shooting club," the Spandau Shooting Guild, which was founded in 1334. It was a good beginning, perhaps, but a somewhat more active world of sports came to life only centuries later, and the place was once again Berlin. The world owes its first public gymnasium to Friedrich Ludwig Jahn, a sports teacher and "Father of Gymnastics," as he has since been known in Germany. It was dedicated in the spring of 1811 in the **Hasenheide**, a recreational park in Neukölln.

New Athletic Venues

Is Berlin also a center of sports besides being a world-class metropolis? Indeed, no city seems to offer as much to the ac-

Above: The annual Berlin Marathon passes through the Brandenburg Gate, of course!

tive or passive sportsperson as Berlin, be that high-performance sports or the more recreational type. In spite of having failed to become an Olympic city again, it does boast two new first-class venues: the **Max Schmeling Halle** was erected in the **Friedrich Jahn Sportpark**; and the **Velodrome** (cycling stadium) was built on the grounds of the former Werner Seelenbinder Hall on Landsberger Allee. The great tradition of Berlin's **Six-Day Bicycle Races** was revived here in January 1997. The European premiere of the Six-Day Races took place in the stadium at the Zoo on March 15th, 1909. After 86 starts, the races were temporarily stopped in 1990.

The basketball players of *Alba Berlin* regularly play their games in the Max Schmeling Halle before 9000 spectators and avid fans. They were the first German team to win a European cup. In addition, in 1997 they became German champions and national cup winners. They're also Berlin's most popular team at the moment.

Soccer Rising

For years Berlin was the only European capital without a top league soccer team. Traditional associations, such as Hertha BSC, Tennis Borussia and FC Union Berlin were better known for their scandals than their athletic achievements, and hovered about in the second or even third leagues. A ray of hope has appeared, however, that Berlin might climb the ladder of German soccer. Hertha BSC actually made it into the federal league with the help of their sponsor Ufa and an improved environment. The fans honored this by capacity appearance at the Olympic stadium on the first day of play. The Berliners have already started dreaming of *Juventus Torino* and *AC Milano*, and of the construction of a brand new stadium.

Ultimate Performances and VIPs

Don't cry for Berliners. Great soccer is in fact an annual event, viz the German Soccer League (DFB) Cup Final, which is held in the oval of the Olympic stadium, when a crowd of 76,000 shows up and turns the place into a veritable sea of colors. The place has well earned the nickname "the Wembley of Germany," recalling the London stadium where the British Cup Final is held. The city can offer its visitors a first-league smorgasbord of 20 types of sports with numerous German champions. Berlin regularly sends an impressive contingent of athletes to the Olympic summer and winter games. In Atlanta, every fifth German competitor was a Berliner. The city's most famous and popular sports stars are the swimmer Franziska von Almsick, the former world champion boxer Graciano Rocchigiani and the gymnast Andreas Wecker.

Even the teams of the city offer top performances and have strings of successes to show: ice hockey is represented at federal level by eastern and western teams, the *Eisbären Berlin* and *Berlin Capitals* respectively. The *Capitals* use the skating rink in Jafféstrasse, the *Eisbären* are stationed at the Sportforum Berlin in Hohenschönhausen. The *Eisbären* succeeded in showing the *Capitals* which way the wind blows in 1997 for the first time during the play-offs. Ice racing competitions are also held regularly in the Sportforum.

Berlin women's and men's teams are also well represented when it comes to volley ball, water polo and hockey. The Berliner cannot complain of a dearth of major sporting events either.

The **Berlin City Marathon** reached its peak in 1990: over 27,000 people wanted to run the course, which, for the first time, led through the Brandenburg Gate; only 25,000 were allowed for reasons of space. This huge number of participants makes the Berlin marathon the third-largest in the world. Incidentally, the second marathon race ever to be staged in Germany was scheduled to take place in Berlin in 1904. It had to be called off, however, because only seven runners registered. Berlin, of course, boasts myriad other events as well: in August, the city hosts the Republic's most important track-and-field competition (**ISTAF**), which has been held since 1937 and attracts up to 50,000 spectators. Recommendable as well is the **German Harness-Racing Derby** (first weekend in August) and the international **German Tennis Championship for Women**, which is traditionally held at Whitsun in Grunewald.

On the other hand, the **Hoppegarten** will come to life again. This galloping track from the days of the Kaiser is once again justifying its reputation as the most beautiful riding facility east of Paris. The first German Derby ever was held here in 1895. In addition, there are also the **Mariendorf Harness-Racing Track** and the **Karlshorst Harness-Racing Track**.

Because of the great space needed, golf could only get a toehold in Berlin after unification. The world elite of golf now meet once a year in Motzen (near Berlin) for the **German Masters** tournament.

Berlin's Nautical Pleasures

Early on, the Markish water courses caught the attention of Elector Friedrich III, who later became King Friedrich I, and lured him into buying so-called "pleasure yachts." Nowadays these vessels look very different. Most are registered in the 122 sailing clubs that have come into existence throughout Berlin. 20,000 sports boats (masted boats, sailboats, rowboats and windsurfing boards) ply the waves of the innumerable lakes in and around Berlin. And that does not include the sailing buffs not registered in clubs! Other water sports fans are also well-off. At the beginning of the 19th

Above: Model-airplane enthusiasts test their planes on the Teufelsberg.

century Berliners who wanted to swim had to jump into the Spree or the Schafgraben (Sheep Ditch), known since as the Landwehrkanal. Today, in the western part of Berlin alone, over 30 so-called *Freibäder* (in natural waters) and **open-air swimming pools** offer Berliners a place in the sun. In winter they can choose from 35 public indoor swimming pools throughout Berlin. In addition, there are numerous official and officious swimming holes on the many lakes and rivers around the city.

Berlin's most famous beach is **Strandbad Wannsee**, the largest inland pool in Europe with a beautiful sand beach and even wicker beach chairs.

The **Sport and Recreation Center** (SEZ), is an early showcase project that was commissioned by the SED "for the good of the people" in 1980. Besides swimming in the huge pool, the SEZ also offers courses in dancing for senior citizens, aerobics for beginners, martial arts, body-building and ice skating in the building's own "polarium."

SPORTS

Gyms, Stadiums, Skating Rinks

Eisstadion Jafféstrasse (ice skating), Charlottenburg, tel. 30 69 69 69 (ticket service).

Eisstadion Wilmersdorf (ice skating), Wilmersdorf, Fritz-Wildung-Str. 9, tel. 824 10 12.

Erika-Hess-Eisstadion (ice skating), Wedding, Müllerstr. 185, tel. 45 75-55 55.

Horst-Korber-Zentrum, Charlottenburg, Glockenturmstr. 3-5, tel. 30 00 60.

Max-Schmeling-Halle (gym), Prenzlauer Berg, Am Falkplatz, service tel. 44 30 44 30, basketball, boxing.

Olympic Stadium, with swimming, riding and hockey stadiums, clock tower and stage in the woods, Charlottenburg, Olympischer Platz, tel. 304 74 72, tours: daily 8 a.m. until sunset, ISTAF track-and-field venue.

Sportforum Berlin, Hohenschönhausen, Weissenseer Weg 51-55, information, tel. 97 17-0. Most sports events in eastern Berlin take place here. The *Eisbären Berlin* play hockey here.

Velodrom (cycling track), **Prenzlauer Berg**, Ernst-Riedel-Str. 53, tel. 44 30 44 30. 6-Day Races.

Recreational Centers, Golf, Minigolf

Public Golf Center, Berlin-Mitte, Chausseestr. 94, Mitte, tel. 285 70 01. Golf for Everyman.

Freizeitforum Marzahn (recreational center), Marzahn, Marzahner Promenade 55, tel. 54 70 41 70. Bowling, gym, swimming pool, sauna.

Freizeit – und Erholungszentrum Wuhlheide (recreational center), Köpenick, Eichgestell, tel. 63 88 72 97. Skating rink, swimming lake and lawn; many cultural events.

Golfpark Schloss Wilkendorf, Wilkendorfer Str. 19A, Wilkendorf, 0 33 41/33 09 30. Largest golf center in the proximity of Berlin.

Sport- und Erholungszentrum (recreational center), Friedrichshain, Landsberger Allee 77, tel. 42 28 33 20/21 (info telephone). Berlin's largest recreational center: seven pools, sauna, solarium, fitness center, bowling alley, billiards, ice-skating rink, rollerblade and skateboard rink, restaurants.

Tennis-Squash-City, Wilmersdorf, Brandenburgische Str. 53, tel. 873 90 97. Tennis, badminton and squash courts.

Indoor and Outdoor Pools, Saunas

blub Badeparadies, Neukölln, Buschkrugallee 64, tel. 609 06-0, Mon-Thu 10 a.m.-11 p.m., Fri 10 a.m.-midnight, Sun 9 a.m.-midnight

Freibad Halensee (outdoor swimming area) Wilmersdorf, Koenigsallee 5a, tel. 891 17 03.

Freibad Oberhavel (outdoor swimming area), Spandau, Havelschanze 29, tel. 335 26 20.

Freibad Tegeler See (outdoor swimming area), Reinickendorf, Schwarzer Weg, tel. 434 10 78.

Haus Paulsborn, Wilmersdorf, Eisenzahnstr. 14, tel. 892 70 20, regular saunas, "bio-sauna" (not so hot) and a women-only sauna.

Stadtbad Charlottenburg, Charlottenburg, Alte Halle, Krumme Str. 10, tel. 34 30 32 14. These municipal baths were built in 1899 and thanks to expensive renovations, are among the most beautiful in Berlin. The walls are decorated with luscious Art-Nouveau couples that gaze down at the swimmers.

Hallenbad am Spreewaldplatz (indoor pool), Kreuzberg, Wiener Str. 59H, tel. 25 88-58 15.

Stadtbad Neukölln (municipal baths), Ganghoferstr. 5, tel. 68 09 26 53, Berlin's first municipal baths with separate pools for men and women.

Stadtbad Tiergarten (municipal baths), Tiergarten, Seydlitzstr. 7, tel. 39 05 40 18.

Strandbad Wannsee (lakeside beach and marked-off swimming area) Zehlendorf, Wannseebadweg 25, tel. 803 56 12. Has a very long and beautiful beach, beach chairs, restaurants, etc.

Thermen am Europa-Center (spa), Schöneberg, in the Europa-Center, tel. 261 60 31, Berlin's largest sauna.

Equestrian Sports

Hoppegarten, Dahlwitz-Hoppegarten, Goetheallee 1, tel. 0 33 42-3 89 30 (S-Bahn No.3 Hoppegarten).

Trabrennbahn Karlshorst (harness-racing), Lichtenberg, Treskowallee 129, tel. 509 92 92/5 00, Tue 6 p.m., Sat 2 p.m.

Trabrennbahn Mariendorf (harness-racing), Tempelhof, Mariendorfer Damm 222, tel. 740 11, Wed 6 p.m., Sun 1:30 p.m., German Trotters' Derby.

Sports Information Ticket Sales

Messe Berlin GmbH, Charlottenburg, Messedamm 22, tel. 30 38 44 44; tickets for major events such as the ISTAF.

Berlin Marathon, registration: SCC Berlin, Charlottenburg, Waldschulallee 34, tel. 302 53 70.

Landessportbund Berlin, Charlottenburg, Jesse-Owens-Allee 1-2, tel. 300 02. The LBS publishes a sports calendar twice a year.

Sportservice Berlin, Hohenschönhausen, Konrad-Wolf-Str. 45, tel. 97 17-20 00, Mon, Wed 8 a.m.-5 p.m., Tue, Thu 8 a.m.-3 p.m. and Fri 8 a.m.-2 p.m. Otherwise refer to the usual sales offices.

CULINARY DISCOVERIES

Berlin's much-maligned culinary landscape is gradually reaching a level that might be expected of a place purporting to be a world-class metropolis. Even the fare peddled by snack bars is more varied than elsewhere. However, the entrenched *Currywurst* (sausage with curried ketchup), a postwar creation, has sounded the retreat. In its low-brow place are multicultural tidbits such as sushi, tapas and other savory exotica.

This hardly means that there are no longer any establishments where one can find down-to-earth Berlin-style fare set in the appropriate ambiance. Generally, however, they are only visited by travel groups. Basic Berlin cuisine (with standard-issue grumpy waitresses) can best be enjoyed at **Hardtke**, on Meinekestrasse. It opened during the 1950s – as can be

Preceding pages: Classical music in the "Waldbühne." Above: Street-side café scene on a summer day in Berlin.

seen if you take a closer look at the somewhat worn decor – with its own butcher's shop that still offers good meat and sausages à la Berlin.

The majestic menu at the **Spree Athen** is further enhanced by a program of entertainment including typical Berlin street songs, ballads and chansons. Another old-fashioned place, as far as decor and food go, is **Radkes Gasthaus Alt-Berlin**. Other restaurants with hearty Berlin dishes are gathered around the Gedächtniskirche and in the pretty Nikolaiviertel in former East Berlin.

Berlin's Gourmet Shrines

Since reunification, however, the number of haute cuisine shrines that have popped up in the capital and where the connoisseur with a distinguishing palate can be sure to find quality dishes has increased considerably.

Whether Siegfried Rockendorf and his restaurant **Rockendorf** in Waidmannslust to the north of the city still occupies the number one slot is a matter of debate. It only boasts a single Michelin star now, but the average patron will be hard pressed to notice a drop in the quality. The wine list is superb and well worth the somewhat long drive there.

The eternal number two of Berlin's gastronomic hierarchy is still thought to be **Frühsammer's Gasthaus** in Nikolassee. Its new-style German cuisine will also amply reward the drive down to the south of Berlin.

Fighting its way up the gourmet ladder is the **Bamberger Reiter** in Schöneberg. Besides the restaurant, it also has an adjacent bistro with cheaper but no less tasty fare.

The top places are increasingly being taken over by some of the restaurants located in Berlin's finest hotels, such as the **Vivaldi** in the Schlosshotel Vier Jahreszeiten or the **Quadriga** in the Brandenburger Hof.

In any event, since the mid-1980s extravagant nouvelle cuisine mixed with a soupçon of Italian and French cuisine has established itself in the city in spite of the conservative Berliners. Typical for Berlin these days is the pairing up of relatively good food with high prices in pubs, bars and trendy meeting places. The light restaurants with bare walls around the Ku'damm and Savignyplatz by and large belong in this category, as do an increasing number of restaurants in Mitte. The **Paris-Bar**, a traditional meeting place for intellectuals and jet-setting stars, serves up basic French dishes and a proper selection of wines. The waiters even speak French!

Nationality is not an issue at **Bovril**, on the other hand, where the kitchen has a definite international hue. The Bovril has been the revolving door for journalists and artists for years now, or simply for people who are proud to make the place their headquarters. Anyone in Berlin with a palate for southern German cuisine heads to the **Florian**. Strangely enough,

this seems to be the circle of filmmakers and their entourages. *Riesling* (a dry white wine) is served until the wee hours of the morning there.

There are two excellent Italian restaurants downtown, **Tucci** and the new **XII Apostoli**, in both of which the waiters' attitude tends to be either fawningly friendly or very much *noblesse oblige*. Tucci's has been successful with the same rustic menu for years; as for the Apostoli, which stays open 24 hours a day, it really does serve twelve different kinds of pizza, each named after one of the twelve disciples.

The **Borchardt** on Gendarmenmarkt in Mitte has a wonderful atmosphere and genuine cosmopolitan flair. Food is without equal. Also on gendarmenmarkt is the **Vau**, which even has a Michelin star now.

The **Modellhut** near the Hackesche Höfe is more *en vogue*; it's one of those new, upwardly mobile restaurants in Mitte which seduce with their unusual interior design and good cooking. The slightly Mediterranean **Mare Bê** is in the same category. New restaurants seem to be opening on a weekly basis in this trendy area anyway.

Culture, many Berliners think, can also be ingested via the esophagus, hence they are increasingly gravitating toward more exotic cuisine. A surefire bet is the little **Foyer**, which produces Turkish specialties in its outdoor setting.

Fofi's Estiatorio has a long tradition in the city. It has moved to Mitte now, but the world still meets there for Greek wine and food. Cooler heads in town sample the imaginative menus in the Spanish **Carpe Diem**, or at least go for a portion of tapas with a cocktail at the bar.

The growth of Berlin's international community is spawning a hunger for more high-brow American cooking and for Tex-Mex food, which has been gaining popularity throughout Europe. At any rate, quite a few restaurants are trying to

fill the vacuum in the market sector lying beyond hamburgers and apple pie. The **Nola**, situated in Moabit a district hardly known for its gastronomic fireworks, is worth a try. The classy southwestern cooking easily justifies the upper-level prices. The fashionable Mexican of the moment is the **Tres Kilos** on Marheineckeplatz in Kreuzberg. Forget eating there without a reservation!

California freestyle is served in the **Frisco** in sleepy little Schmargendorf, where dishes with Asian and Mexican influences are served in a fantasy Wild-West ambiance. By the way, Australia is represented in Berlin, too, so reservations are indeed advised if you want to try the **Woolloomooloo**. In good home style, the menu includes all sorts of dishes from down under: kangaroo steaks, ostrich meat, a selection of Australian beers and wines, all accompanied by the deep piping sound of the digeridoo.

Above: The Altes Zollhaus cooks up affordable German and French dishes for its patrons.

Neighborhood Haute Cuisine

Over the past few years many of Kreuzberg's finest restaurants have either gone out of business or changed locations: the **Maxwell** has moved to Mitte; the Exil, the Hasenburg and the Vineria Franzotti have closed down. Nevertheless, there are still quite a number of good places that have stayed in their old spots or survived. The **Altes Zollhaus** and the **Abricot** have above-average German and French dishes at affordable prices. Also very good are the Italian **Chamisso** and the trendy **Osteria No. 1**, which overcame its crisis and can once again be patronized.

Another Italian place, and a popular one at that, is the **Trattoria Lappeggi** on Kollwitzplatz in Prenzlauer Berg. Just a few steps away is the **Pasternak**, which has a contrasting menu of Russian specialties in a pub-like atmosphere.

In Schöneberg, the **Storch** offers tasty Alsatian food, and the mood is very relaxed.

RESTAURANTS

Gourmet Restaurants with International Cuisine

Reservations may be necessary at these restaurants:

Alt-Luxemburg, Charlottenburg, Windscheidstr. 31, tel. 323 87 30, Mon-Sat 7 p.m.-1 a.m.

Bamberger Reiter, Schöneberg, Regensburger Str. 7, tel. 218 42 82, Tue-Sat 6 p.m.-1 a.m.

Bovril, Charlottenburg, Kurfürstendamm 184, tel. 881 84 61, Mon-Sat 11-1 a.m.

Frühsammer's Gasthaus, Zehlendorf, Matterhornstr. 101, tel. 803 27 20, daily 7-9:30 p.m.

Quadriga, in Hotel Brandenburger Hof, Wilmersdorf, Eislebener Str. 14, tel. 21 40 50.

Rockendorf's Restaurant, Reinickendorf, Düsterhauptstr. 1, tel. 402 30 99, Tue-Sat from noon on, meals noon-2 p.m. and 7-21:30 p.m.

Vau, Mitte, Jägerstr. 54/55, tel. 20 29 73-0, Mon-Sat noon for lunch, from 7 p.m. for dinner.

Vivaldi, in Hotel Vier Jahreszeiten, Wilmersdorf, Brahmsstr. 10, tel. 89 58 45 20/21, Wed-Sun 6 p.m.-midnight; meals till 10:30.

German and Nouvelle Cuisine

Abricot, Kreuzberg, Hasenheide 48, tel. 693 11 50, daily 11-1 a.m.

Altes Zollhaus, Kreuzberg, Carl-Herz-Ufer 30, tel. 692 33 00, Tue-Sat from 6 p.m.

Borchardt, Mitte, Französische Str. 47, tel. 20 39 71 17, daily 11:30-2 a.m., food served till midnight.

Florian, Charlottenburg, Grolmanstr. 52, tel. 313 91 84, daily 6 p.m.-4 a.m. (food till 1 a.m.).

Hardtke, Charlottenburg, Meinekestr. 27, tel. 881 98 27, daily 10-12:30 a.m.

Maxwell, Mitte, Bergstr. 22, tel. 280 71 21, daily noon-1 a.m.

Meineke, Meinekestr. 10, tel. 882 31 58.

Modellhut, Mitte, Alte Schönhauser Str. 28, tel. 283 55 11, daily from 6 p.m.

Offenbach-Stuben, Prenzlauer Berg, Stubbenkammerstr. 8, tel. 445 85 02, daily 6 p.m.-2 a.m.

Radkes Gasthaus Alt-Berlin, Charlottenburg, Marburger Str. 16, tel. 213 46 52, daily 11-2 a.m.

Reinhard's, Mitte, (in the Nikolaiviertel), Poststr. 28, tel. 242 52 95, daily 9-1 a.m.

Spree-Athen, Charlottenburg, Leibnizstr. 60, tel. 324 17 33, Mon-Sat from 6 p.m.

American and Australian Cuisine

Frisco, Wilmersdorf, Warnemünder Str. 8, tel. 823 47 62, daily 7-2 a.m.

Jimmy's Diner, Wilmersdorf, Pariser Str. 41, tel. 882 31 41, daily 4 p.m.-3 a.m. (Fri, Sat until 5 a.m.). American diner atmosphere.

Nola, Tiergarten, Dortmunder Str. 9, tel. 399 69 69, daily 5 p.m.-1:30 a.m., service from 6 to 11:30 p.m.

Woolloomooloo, Charlottenburg, Röntgenstr. 7, tel. 34 70 27 77, daily 5 p.m.-1 a.m.

French Cuisine

Cour Carré, Charlottenburg, Savignyplatz 5, tel. 312 52 38, daily noon-2 a.m.

Paris-Bar, Charlottenburg, Kantstr. 152, tel. 313 80 52, daily from noon on.

Rosenbaum, Prenzlauer Berg, Oderberger Str. 61, tel. 448 46 10, daily from 6 p.m.

Storch, Schöneberg, Wartburgstr. 54, tel. 784 20 59, daily 6-11:30 p.m.

Alt Luxemburg, Windscheidstr. 31, tel. 323 87 30.

Greek Cuisine

Fofis Estiatorio, Mitte, Rathausstr. 25, tel. 242 34 35, daily 11:30-1 a.m.

Ypsilon, Schöneberg, Hauptstr. 163, tel. 782 45 39, daily from noon on. Big terrace open in summer.

Italian Cuisine

Chamisso, Kreuzberg, Willibald-Alexis-Str. 25, tel. 691 56 42, daily 6 p.m.-1 a.m.

Hosteria del Monte Croce, Kreuzberg, Mittenwalder Str. 6, tel. 694 39 68, Mon-Sat from 7:30 p.m.

Osteria No. 1, Kreuzberg, Kreuzbergstr. 71, tel. 786 91 62, daily noon-2 a.m.

Trattoria Lappeggi, Prenzlauer Berg, Kollwitzstr. 56, tel. 442 63 47, daily from noon on.

Tucci, Charlottenburg, Grolmanstr. 52, tel. 313 93 35, daily 11-1 a.m.

XII Apostoli, Charlottennburg, Bleibtreustr. 49, tel. 312 14 33, open 24 hours a day.

Ponte Vecchio, Spielhagenstr. 3, tel. 342 19 99.

Spanish and Mexican Cuisine

Carpe Diem, Charlottenburg, Savingypassage, Arch No. 576, tel. 313 27 28, Tue-Sat noon-1 a.m.

Los Tres Kilos, Kreuzberg, Marheinekeplatz 3, tel. 693 60 44, daily 6 p.m.-2 a.m.

Mare Bê, Mitte, Rosenthaler Str. 46, tel. 283 65 45.

Turkish and Russian Cuisine

Foyer, Charlottenburg, Uhlandstr. 28, tel. 881 42 68, daily 5 p.m.-12:30 a.m.

Pasternak, Knaackstr. 24, tel. 441 33 99, daily noon-2 a.m.

BARS: WILD HANGOUTS AND WORKINGMEN'S PUBS

The place where the two halves of Berlin knitted back together fastest seems to be the *Kneipen*; the bars and pubs. For many Berliners, both from the east and from the west, the local *Kneipe* is simply an extension of their own living room. And if the beer is good, the pot roast is well-done and the *Schnapps* is cheap, they'll even walk a couple blocks further. Old-fashioned Berlin *Gemütlichkeit* can be found even today in any bar on any corner. In all Berlin that includes the 5200 bars, pubs, cafés and trendy meeting-places.

The Charlottenburg Scene: Too Cool

The hub of Berlin's nightlife is around Savignyplatz, in the heart of West Berlin's downtown. At least, that is what those people think who like to frequent the bars and restaurants that exude an icy kind of elegance. One place the visitor will never find the Charlottenburg crowd is on the Ku'damm. The boulevard may be an inviting place for a stroll in the evening, but it's little more than a bar strip for charter tours.

Charlottenburgers like to meet around Savignyplatz, which is also called the "Savigny Triangle," for three streets (Grolmannstrasse, Knesebeckstrasse and Carmerstrasse) meet here, and every kind of pub can be found in this area.

Right next to Savignyplatz, where Grolmanstrasse starts, there is the **Zwiebelfisch**, which still attracts veterans of the events of 1968 and other thirsty barflies. Most of the local places are restaurants, but some of them, like **Tucci**, are also good as bars.

Right next door is the diminutive **Le Bar**, which used to be an insider's tip when its owner, Pascale Jean-Louis, still tended the bar. These days, on weekends,

Above: Berlin still has a number of typical, old-fashioned corner "Kneipen."

it is usually frequented by a noisy *nouveau riche* clientele – but on weekdays it is an alternative to the large, cold bars in the Tiergarten district.

Café Savigny, a few steps further on, is a good place to go in order to get a nice *café au lait*. The locale is spartanly furnished, but they do have a wide selection of newspapers.

Dralle's is on the corner of Pestalozzi and Schlüterstrasse, and is frequented by full-time bar-flies. Night for night, you will see the same people, mostly from the media, yuppies and their classy girl friends. The leather benches are red, as are the walls, from which giant posters of American jazz legends stare down at the crowd while their music booms from loudspeakers. The waitresses are pretty, too, and unpredictable.

On Knesebeckstrasse you will find one of the city's finest bars, **CUT**. This small place, very much in the style of an American cocktail bar, has a panoply of 300 exquisite cocktails on offer. It is quite popular with the VIP crowd. Its furnishings consist of mirrors, black marble and granite.

At the end of the street, right on Savignyplatz, the **Gainsbourg** competes with the CUT for the rank of best cocktail. The atmosphere here is good as well. In addition, in summer, the little garden in the front is open from 6 p.m. onward.

If you're still up for it, check out the **Filmbühne** on Steinplatz, mostly frequented by students engaged in animated and intelligent conversation before taking in the latest arty movie at the adjacent cinema.

Don't miss the **Diener** either, towards Ku'damm at the beginning of Grolmanstrasse: since the postwar years, Berlin's theater celebrities have been meeting here to be harassed by moody waiters. But they are accustomed to the treatment, and the wine is good.

Zillemarkt, on Bleibtreustrasse, has a different kind of ambience, a little more touristy in fact. It used to be a stopping place for coaches. All that has survived from that era is the cobblestone floor – so watch out if you are wearing high-heeled shoes! Then there's **Ali Baba's Minipizza**, where, until the wee hours of the morning and in an easygoing atmosphere, you will be served the best minipizza in the city.

Before leaving Savignyplatz, don't miss at least one of the bars under the S-Bahn arches between Bleibtreustrasse and Knesebeckstrasse. The **Bogen** is particularly pleasant, with excellent wines at good prices and live piano music. The architectural crowd meets right next door at **Café Aedes**.

Schöneberg:
A Somewhat Different Scene

Schönebergers tend to turn up their noses at Charlottenburg. They think that the elegant Westerners are much too snobby to know how to enjoy a real Berlin *Kneipe*. And thus the Schöneberger scene is less elegant than elsewhere in Berlin West, but not quite as eccentric as in Kreuzberg.

The focal point of Schöneberg's nightlife is around Winterfeldplatz and Nollendorfplatz. **Café Swing** is where rock musicians, students and married men from Schöneberg out on their own rub shoulders. Then there's **Café M** on Goltzstrasse, the entertainment street of the neighborhood, favored particularly by the young and the unconventional. Café M tends to be crowded, and during the summer customers simply move outside.

Café Sidney, a spacious establishment on Winterfeldtplatz, also moves its steel tables out into the street during the summer. Diagonally across the square is the traditional **Slumberland**, which once housed the *Dschungel*. The crowd starts to gather here on market Saturday as early as mid-afternoon in an attempt to forget the cold: you cross over to the bar on genuine white sand.

The **Rössli-Bar** is situated a little out of the way, yet is ideal for skiing fanatics: one of the walls is covered by a panorama of the Alps made of papier-mâché. The **Pinguin-Club** is where a lot of Berlin's top music crowd meet up for drinks and chatter. The place has a reputation for friendly service and a relaxed atmosphere.

Kreuzberg Traditions

According to one popular old ditty, which has been sung to death, "Kreuzberg nights are long." There is no doubt that Kreuzbergers are perhaps a little more inclined to celebrating than other Berliners. What is even more true is that there is a number of traditions that coexist alongside one another in Kreuzberg: there are the old, stuffy corner *Kneipen*, which the "in" crowd avoids like the plague; there are the pretentious bars for the district's social climbers; and then there are the bars for the punks and university students.

Leydicke is a Kreuzberg institution, even though it is actually located in Schöneberg. This hundred-year-old drinking establishment is still a popular meeting-place for Berliners, and for curious tourists and school classes. It is less noisy on weekdays, and also more authentic. The strawberry and rasperry wines are home-made productions served in simple glasses, which make them taste even better.

Bar Centrale and **Café Wirtschaftswunder** are for the more established Kreuzberg residents. Bar Centrale has adopted a somewhat clean, streamlined Italian look, while the Wirtschaftswunder (Economic Miracle) is, logically, in 1950s garb.

Right: Trendy places notwithstanding, the traditional pub is still the old favorite.

If you want to experience pure, unadulterated Kreuzberg at its best, drop in at the **Bierhimmel**, located on Oranienstrasse and Heinrichplatz. It is the alternative crowd's most popular meeting place. Just what is heavenly here, as the name "Himmel" would seem to suggest, no one actually knows, especially as the candles on the walls are more reminiscent of a funeral.

For harder music, try out the **Wild at Heart**, a wittily-furnished bar on Wienerstrasse. And for interesting, cultivated drinks, you have the **Morena** diagonally opposite.

The remnants of the 1968 generation gathers piously at the **Rote Harfe** on Heinrichplatz, an institution that has since been rejuvenated in some ways.

The Oranienburgers

Very soon after the fall of the Wall, the once deserted Oranienburger Strasse turned into one of the most fast-paced – as well as one of the most exciting – night spots in Berlin. Curious nighthawks and the counter-culture crowd from West Berlin, who were beginning to tire of Kreuzberg, as well as artists and prostitutes, started discovering the area. Since the days of the East's new beginning, much has changed in the area: the streetwalkers have disappeared, and bus loads of tourists are shepherded along the Oranienburger.

Yet this spot at the heart of Spandau (sometimes also referred to as the *Scheunenviertel*, or "Barn District") remains exciting. Much will probably change in the future, too, as it has one of the best locations in downtown Berlin. The **Silberstein** is still a place where GDR intellectuals and artists meet. Further on are the **Café Orange** and the **Café Oren**, where you can get kosher food until the wee hours. In summer the café is virtually hidden by the crowd out on the street, but this crowd happens to

be trying to get into the **Obst und Gemüse**, a bar-cum-*Kneipe*. Why hundreds of pleasure-seekers are standing around in the hope of getting in, no one really knows. Maybe it is due to the beautiful young east Berlin women drinking cheap white wine or GDR beer here.

Right across the street is the **Tacheles**, an arts and events center founded by a group of squatters in the ruins of an old department store, with a café, bar and discotheque.

On the side streets, especially Auguststrasse and Tucholskystrasse, there are other bars, including the **Verkehrsberuhigte Ostzone**, the "Reduced-traffic Eastern Zone." Its decor includes an amusing collection of old bus seats. Then there's **Hackbarth's**, frequented by Humboldt University students. Not far from here you will find numerous discotheques.

Clärchens Ballhaus, a real Berlin institution, is a little way up Auguststrasse: this place has been around since the 1930s. Elderly gentlemen still slide their ladies with fancy hairdos over the polished dance floor. Petit bourgeois happiness in the midst of chaos.

Prenzlauer Berg: Trendy for Trendy's Sake

So far, Prenzlauer Berg has pretty much been spared by tourism and curious Berliners from the west side of town. The crowd here seems to rotate around its own axis anyway. The nightlife is increasingly concentrated in the streets around **Kollwitzplatz**. In summer, the crowd here wandering from bar to bar along the sidewalk is reminiscent of those on the Ramblas in Barcelona – much to the dismay of the local residents.

In **Café Kyril** on Lychener Strasse you can get an idea of what life was like before the fall of the Wall. A great number of bookish types meet here to reminisce about the good old days of resistance in the underground GDR movement. Frequently there are readings on weekends, which are quite bearable if you take them

with a glass of beer. On the other hand, the guests at **Café Anita Wronski** and **Kommandantur**, both on Knaack-strasse, are more relaxed and quite free of ideology. Even though the names of these cafés are political, the guests are young and apolitical – despite one or two preferring to wear a flat cap and red star. The scene that goes along with that particular crowd already has to be searched for here.

The well-mixed crowd that frequents the **Krähe**, a watering hole from way back, tends to be somewhat on the colorful side.

Just about every imaginable type of trendy bar can be found around Helmholtzplatz. The **Torpedokäfer** is a rather chic place, with a stainless steel bar and some solid wooden furniture. The Cuban-influenced bar **La Bodeguita del Medio** has borrowed a fair amount from Hemingway. Walls covered in graffiti

and drawings, as well as the good cocktails that are served up here, make for some fine entertainment. Another nice trendy bar, this one with good food to boot, is the **Oderquelle**.

In the **Schlot**, on Kastanienallee, the jazz fans of the area come together. A very diverse program, from weird to conventionally good, is offered on a factory level in the second rear courtyard. The **Prater**, just a few steps further, was recently revived, a pleasure parlor with a long tradition, a big beer garden, a dance club, theatrical performances and teas with dancing.

If you think the crowd is too noisy here or elsewhere in Prenzlauer Berg, you may want to walk over to Husemann-strasse: there you will find the **Restauration 1900**. Even when it's crammed full, it's guaranteed to stay quiet and decorous. Faces from the old GDR days pop in, visitors from the west side of town lean against the bar, and slowly the two sides come closer as the night grows long and the beer flows.

Above: The "1900," where the "in" crowd meets in Art-Nouveau decor.

CAFÉS, BARS AND PUBS

Ali Baba, Charlottenburg, Bleibtreustr. 45, tel. 881 13 50, daily 11:30-3 a.m.

Bar Centrale, Kreuzberg, Yorckstr. 82, tel. 786 29 89, Mon-Sat from noon on.

Bierhimmel, Kreuzberg, Oranienstr. 181, tel. 615 31 22, daily 3 p.m.- 3 a.m., bar Wed-Sun from 2 p.m.

Bogen, Charlottenburg, Savignypassage, Arch No. 597, tel. 313 77 04, Tue-Sun 15-3 a.m.

Café Aedes, Charlottenburg, S-Bahnbogen 599, tel. 312 55 04, daily 10 a.m.-midnight.

Café Anita Wronski, Prenzlauer Berg, Knaackstr. 26-28, tel. 442 84 83, daily 10-3 a.m.

Cafe Kyril, Prenzlauer Berg, Lychener Str. 73, tel. 444 16 57, daily 11-3 a.m.

Café M, Schöneberg, Goltzstr. 33, tel. 216 70 92, daily from 8 a.m.

Café Orange, Mitte, Oranienburger str. 32, tel. 282 00 28, daily from 9 a.m.

Café Savigny, Charlottenburg, Grolmanstr. 53, tel. 312 81 95, daily 10-2 a.m.

Café Sidney, Schöneberg, Winterfeldtstr. 40, tel. 216 52 53, Sun-Thu 9-2 a.m., Fri/Sat 9-3 a.m.

Café Swing, Schöneberg, Nollendorfplatz 3-4, tel. 216 61 37, daily from 11 a.m.

Clärchens Ballhaus, Prenzlauer Berg, Auguststr. 24/25, tel. 282 92 95, Tue-Sat from 7:30 p.m.

CUT, Charlottenburg, Knesebeckstr. 16, tel. 313 35 11, daily 10 p.m.-6 a.m.

Deichgraf, Wedding, Nordufer 10, tel. 453 76 13, daily 9-4 a.m. Somewhat remote student place.

Diener, Charlottenburg, Grolmanstr. 47, tel. 881 53 29, daily from 6 p.m..

Dralle's, Charlottenburg, Schlüterstr. 69, tel. 313 50 38, daily 1 p.m.-2 a.m., Fri, Sat 1 p.m.-4 a.m.

Filmbühne am Steinplatz, Charlottenburg, Hardenbergstr. 12, tel. 312 90 17, daily 10-4 a.m.

Gainsbourg, Charlottenburg, Savignyplatz 5, tel. 313 74 64, daily from 6 p.m.

Geierwally's Stieftochter im Ausland, Weissensee, Prenzlauer Promenade 3, tel. 471 30 17, daily 5 p.m.-3 a.m.

Grossbeerenkeller, Kreuzberg, Grossbeerenstr. 90, tel. 251 30 64, Mon-Fri 4 p.m.-1 a.m., Sat 6 p.m.-1 a.m. Original Kreuzberg with local politicians.

Hackbarth's, Mitte, Auguststr. 49a, tel. 282 77 06, daily 9-3 a.m.

Kastanie, Charlottenburg, Schloss Str. 22, tel. 321 50 34, daily noon-2 a.m. Near the palace.

Kilkenny Irish Pub, Mitte, Hackescher Markt (S-Bahn arches), tel. 282 20 84. Thu-Mon 11-2 a.m.

Kommandantur, Prenzlauer Berg, Knaackstr. 20, tel. 442 77 25, daily from 6 p.m.

Krähe, Prenzlauer Berg, Kollwitzstr. 84, tel. 442 82 91, Mon-Fri 5:30 p.m.-1 a.m., Sat/Sun from 10 a.m.

La Bodeguita del Medio, Prenzlauer Berg, Lychener Str. 6, tel. 441 74 12, open daily from 6 p.m.

Le Bar, Charlottenburg, Grolmanstr. 52, tel. 312 87 02, daily from 7 p.m.

Lentz, Charlottenburg, Stuttgarter Platz 20, tel. 324 16 19, daily 9-2 a.m. Relaxed family place.

Leydicke, Schöneberg, Mansteinstr. 4, tel. 216 29 73, daily from 5 p.m., Sat from noon on.

Monrena, Kreuzberg, Wiener Str. 60, tel. 611 47 16, daily 9-4 a.m.

Obst und Gemüse, Mitte, Oranienburger Str. 48/49, tel. 282 96 47, daily from 11:30 a.m.

Oderquelle, Prenzlauer Berg, Oderberger Str. 27, tel. 448 25 96, daily 2 p.m.-3 a.m.

Oren, Mitte, Oranienburger Str. 28, tel. 282 82 28, Sun-Fri 10-1 a.m., Sat 10-2 a.m.

Pinguin-Club, Schöneberg, Wartburgstr. 54, tel. 781 30 05, daily 9 p.m.-4 a.m.

Prater, Prenzlauer Berg, Kastanienallee 7-9, tel. 448 56 88, Mon-Fri 6 p.m.-1 a.m., Sat/Sun noon-1 a.m.

Restauration 1900, Prenzlauer Berg, Husemannstr. 1, tel. 449 40 52, open Mon-Sat 4 p.m.-midnight.

Rössli-Bar, Schöneberg, Eisenacher Str. 80, tel. 784 63 45, daily from 6 p.m.

Rost, Charlottenburg, Knesebeckstr. 29, tel. 881 95 01, daily 9-2 a.m. Classy bar for actors.

Rote Harfe, Kreuzberg, Oranienstr. 13, tel. 618 44 46, daily 10-3 a.m.

Schlot, Prenzlauer Berg, Kastanienallee 29, 2. Hinterhof, tel. 448 21 60, daily from 8 p.m.

Silberstein, Mitte, Oranienburger Str. 27, tel. 281 20 95, daily from 4 p.m.

Slumberland, Schöneberg, Goltzstr. 24, tel. 216 53 49, Sun-Fri from 9:30 p.m., Sat from 11 a.m.

Tacheles, Mitte, Oranienburger Str. 53-56, tel. 282 61 85.

Torpedokäfer, Prenzlauer Berg, Dunckerstr. 69, tel. 444 57 63, daily from 11 a.m.

Tucci, Charlottenburg, Grolmannstr. 52, tel. 313 93 35, daily noon-1 a.m.

Van Loon, Kreuzberg, Urbanhafen/Carl-Herz-Ufer, tel. 692 62 93, daily 10-1 a.m. Restaurant-ship docked on the Landwehrkanal.

Verkehrsberuhigte Ostzone, Mitte, Auguststr. 93, no telephone, daily 24 hours.

Wild at Heart, Kreuzberg, Wiener Str. 20, tel. 611 70 10, daily from 4 p.m.

Wirtschaftswunder, Kreuzberg, Yorckstr. 81, tel. 786 99 99, daily 3 p.m.-5 a.m.

Zillemarkt, Charlottenburg, Bleibtreustr. 48a, tel. 881 70 40, daily 9-1 a.m.

Zwiebelfisch, Charlottenburg, Savignyplatz 7-8, tel. 313 73 63, daily noon-6 a.m.

MAKING THE SCENE –
DAY OR NIGHT

Berlin's nightlife is just as fast-paced as it ever was. Night clubs change their names, move or adopt a new style at a dizzying rate. They also trade places at the top of the "in" scale at a high rate. This might be typical of the 1990s, it might also be a sign of the birth of a new city. Berlin's younger crowd is currently at its most capricious, constantly on the search for wild parties and the newest club.

When national and international television cameras broadcast Berlin's Love Parade, it dawned on the world at large that Berlin is not only the city with the largest annual dance event in Europe, but also the German capital of nighthawks, ravers, dance fanatics and pleasure-seekers. Hundreds of thousands of mainly young people come to this annual summer street party, the **Love Parade**, from Germany and other (mostly European) countries, to dance on the Strasse des 17. Juni. Young girls in shorts and bikini tops and gays in leather garb let their half-naked bodies swirl to techno music – and this in broad daylight! The highlights to this massive event are the huge parties that take place in the evening. You can't say you've "made the scene" until you've hit all the right Love Parade mega-parties!

Christopher Street Day, which takes place simultaneously in Berlin and Cologne on the last weekend of June, is a gay and lesbian celebration featuring wittily-provocative parades, street dances and parties.

The multinational **Carnival of Cultures**, which was brought to life by groups of immigrants and foreigners' associations, has been gaining in popularity in Berlin. The Carnival of Culture takes place at the end of May.

Above: Hair style fit for the Love Parade.
Right: The city's best cocktails are served at Harry's New York Bar.

Another annual event is called **Clubs United**. With a single ticket, the participant can extensively navigate Berlin's musical scene by shuttle bus to over 20 clubs and no less than 80 events (in late summer; for specific dates, consult tourist information).

If you new to Berlin, or are a tourist, you'll have a difficult time discovering the depths of Berlin's party-volcano without the assistance of a Berlin nightowl. Taking a look at the city magazines *Tip*, *Zitty* or *Prinz* that are available at newsstands can also help, or picking up the two free events and "scene" magazines *030* and *Weekly*, or the fliers that can be found in cinemas, bars and clubs.

Berlin Bars – Cool and Wild

Berlin has no official closing time. Of its 10,000 gastronomic operations a number of bars and discotheques have developed that are nearly always worth a visit. Modern cocktail aficionados begin their evening at the **Bar am Lützowplatz**

at about 10 p.m. Many a guest has the first-class cocktails to thank for ending his evening here again but juiced. A bar like this was long overdue in Berlin, as the architecture, drinks list and staff are mixed into a classic fun cocktail themselves in this long bar. Behind the 50-foot (16-meter) bar the bartenders work their shakers. In front of the bar the chic clientele relaxes on bar stools of dazzling chrome. The preferred topic of conversation: the difference between Jim Beam and a 12-year old whiskey from the Scottish highlands, or which aluminum rims go best with the new convertibles.

If you are not in the right age or income bracket for its atmosphere, just stroll over to Hotel Esplanade, which is right around the corner. There you will find the Berlin branch of the legendary **Harry's New York Bar**. The bartenders, male and female, wear white uniforms, and the walls are adorned with pictures of all 42 American presidents. And every night of the week, in real Dixie style, American jazz pianists or tubby soul

singers sit down at the piano and entertain the over-40s.

A nice establishment in Prenzlauer Bergn is the **Akba Lounge**. On weekends it turns into a dance club with alternating DJs. Another bar that begins filling up around 10 p.m. is the little **Zoulou Bar**. It has the feel of Hemingways African expeditions. One of the finest places for cocktails, however, and an absolute must for nightowls, is the **Green Door** on Winterfeldtplatz. Happy hour for the usually carefree, stylish crowd that gathers here starts at 6 p.m.

The **Fischlabor** (Fish Laboratory) is also located in Schöneberg. Its decor – if that is how one can refer to it – is in grey. Grey furry rugs hang from the walls, and the curtains are in grey, too. The fridge is well stocked with "Space" beer.

Even before midnight Schöneberg's **Kumpelnest 3000** is a lively place, a bar decked out in bordello colors and materials. Things get really steamy at about 4 a.m., when the bartender plays wild 1970s music on his cassette deck and guests start to dance spontaneously at the bar while holding on to their glass of Beck's beer. Finally, for a bit of something chic, try the **ZeoBar** under the protective eaves of the Hackesche Höfe.

Small Cabarets and Hot Shows

There are plenty of cabarets, such as **Chez Nous** and **La Vie En Rose**, where you can simply lean back comfortably and let yourself be entertained in style. When the "Ladies" at Chez Nous aren't on tour in the western German provinces, they like to joke around with the audience and tell all kinds of anecdotes from the transvestite daily grind. La Vie En Rose offers performances several times a night – a mixture of travesty and magic show, dancing and tasteful striptease. Under the bright red lights you'll see lots of naked skin, bare breasts and gyrating derrières only fleetingly covered by feather boas.

Above and right: Show girls and boys, and a good transvestite show at La Vie en Rose.

Discotheques in the West

Nights spent on Berlin's dance floors are even more strenuous, especially since the scene in the eastern districts has blossomed and become a paradise for DJs and owners of new clubs. Since then, thousands of dance fanatics from all over the city set out every weekend on their pilgrimage to the "Wild East."

But ever since some of the better-known clubs, such as the Bunker or the E-Werk, closed there, the western districts have once again recouped some of their former popularity. One of the most recent clubs to try to attract the E-Werk's party crowd is the **Hangar II**. This locale, with over 42,000 square feet (4000 sq meters) spread out over two futuristically designed levels in the Tempelhof airport, attracts some of the world's most famous DJs, such as Westbam.

The old and venerable dance and concert shrine **Metropol** underwent a kind of rebirth. Legendary concerts were held here, and until reunification, the Metropol was West Berlin's top mega-disco. Things then quieted down. It was renovated, and now shines like a newly-polished gem. In addition to its new Egyptian image, the establishment added 650,000 watts of lighting and over 40,000 watts of music power.

Beginning at 11 p.m. and lasting until dawn are the giant parties held every Friday and Saturday at the **BKA tents**. Techno adepts have the most fun here, though the crowd and the music is quite mixed. Special events such as "Fish Seeks Bicycle" parties are held here as well. For salsa and merengue grooves, the place to go is the basement club **El Barrio**. It's one of the few dance clubs open six nights a week (closed Mondays), and is a place where people older than 30 will feel comfortable.

For years now the best place to dance in the western section of the city has been the little **Blue Note**. Prices here are reasonable, entrance is even free, and the flirt factor is quite high. Music tends to be anything that can be danced to.

Even though the controversial Indian guru Bhagwan Shree Rajneesh died some time ago, the disco **Far Out** on Lehniner Platz is indestructible, and is still operated by his Berlin disciples. It looks bright and airy like all the other Bhagwan discos: from Thursdays to Saturdays believers and non-believers alike put down their glasses and take to the dance floor, which vibrates to hundreds of dancing feet as the DJ starts playing the hits of yesterday's and today's charts.

Kreuzberg Discotheques

During the summer months Far Out regulars prefer Kreuzberg's **Golgatha**, a mixture of beer garden, discotheque and daytrip pub. It's right on Kreuzberg's "slope" and is definitely worth seeing, if only because it is so close.

Above: The 90°, where the trendy crowd meets in club ambience. Right: Facial artwork at a gay party in Kreuzberg.

If you continue on to Kreuzberg's downtown area, you will hit come across a rather unusual place: the **MS Sanssouci**, a ship docked along the Gröbenufer in Kreuzberg near the Oberbaumbrücke. The ship is a combination bar, café and restaurant. It has everything from Sunday brunches to jazz concerts on tap, or even house parties and gay tea dances.

The DJ at the **Schnabelbar** on Oranienstrasse has total control of the tiny dance floor of his hot spot. Drum 'n' Bass and music by black artists is what keeps the dancers moving here.

The **Sage Club**, situated on the "border" between Kreuzberg and Mitte, is regarded as perhaps the best of the capital city's clubs. The beautiful people of the late night scene can amuse themselves here on two dancefloors; and after working up a sweat they can cool down with cocktails at one of club's three bars. This rather high-class and impressively-designed nightclub exudes a truly metropolitan atmosphere.

Downtown Berlin:
Techno Beat and House

On weekends, house music and techno fans tend to go to one of their techno temples such as the **Tresor**. The Tresor was number one among Berlin's techno dance floors for a couple of years. Top international DJs worked here, and more often than not one would hear the British accent of young house fans; the American rap icon, Guru, from the band Gang Starr, even dropped in on occasion, grabbed the microphone and launched into a rap about social problems in distant American cities that still haven't reached Berlin.

Then came the **E-Werk**, and along with it a genuinely metropolitan night club. Now that the young ravers have gotten used to paying ten to 15 marks to get in, the doormen ask for 20. The E-Werk has gone out of business in the meantime. A special staging of Don Giovanni was recently put on here, trying to bridge the yawning canyon between techno and classical opera. Still, there is no lack of unusual places for sweaty dance activity in nocturnal Berlin. Good house and techno parties with high voltage and wattage are regularly held in the **Matrix**, for example, in *Gewölbe* (vault) No. 3, right under the U-Bahn station Warschauer Strasse. The uninitiated might have a hard time finding their way to the entrance around construction fences. A good party address and a guarantee for unusual events is the **Kalkscheune**. Everything worth dancing to is represented here, from house and techno to tango fever and drag queen shows.

Friendly Clubs for People
who Like to Talk

As a consequence of this party inflation, many night clubbers who are older than 20 long for a fair amount of intimacy and a chat at the bar. They don't want to

just dance their feet hot, they want to move their tongues, too. Berlin's party volcano immediately spat out the right kinds of clubs for those wanting communication together with their beer at the bar, and gave these clubs a new label: Creative Clubbing.

Bob Young's **90°** is one of them. He turned an old garage and its mechanic's atmosphere and uneven cement floor into an insider's place with a parquet dance floor. On weekends people who have a membership card have a better chance of getting past the doorman than those who don't. The DJ plays soul and house, and at the crowded bar regular guests discuss the interior decoration of the bar, which has changed yet again.

The **Hafenbar** in Mitte has been in business for 30 years now, and has served as a disco since 1993. The atmosphere is by and large relaxed here, soft lighting instead of flashing, blinding bulbs all over the place. On Fridays the DJ pulls out standards from the 1980s or hit songs. Prices are civil, the party mood is A-1.

199

It was the **Delicious Doughnuts Research** dance club on Rosenthaler Strasse that actually coined the phrase "creative clubbing." After a thorough renovation, this club, which was there at the start, is as much in demand as ever, and, moreover, it's one of the few places open seven days a week. On weekdays, Doughnuts sometimes stages "Jazz Poetry Performances" for insiders and enthusiasts. These can turn out to be very interesting cultural events in an intimate atmosphere.

You had better get there before midnight on weekends, otherwise you won't have a chance to make it past the inevitable long line in front, as this place is now one of the most popular spots to dance and talk. The later the hour, too, the more difficult it is to actually get a drink at the bar. The musical selections are on the soft side, generally, and are

good for dancing. A good tip for the evening hours is the bar in the front section of the club.

Shortly after opening in the summer of 1997, the **Oxymoron** hit the top of the club charts. Located in the restored Hackesche Höfe, in the midst of an "in"part of town, the establishment serves as a restaurant, then as a bar in the evening, and after 11 p.m. it becomes a club. Parties are held here on weekends. A special event is the "Pasta Opera" every Thursday, with pasta served up to classical opera arias.

At the end of their tour of Berlin's party scene, dance tourists will have an additional 30 miles (about 50 km) on their car odometers and at least twice that amount of marks less in their wallets. You may also have a crashing headache, and if you don't have at least two club stamps on the back of each hand, you will probably have missed the hottest party in town. But as the sun rises every morning, it sets every evening – and that's when things really get going in Berlin.

Above: Sweating it out in east Berlin – on the tiny Sophienclub dance floor.

LATE NIGHT BARS

Bar am Lützowplatz, Tiergarten, Lützowplatz 7, tel. 262 68 07, daily 5 p.m.-4 a.m.

Berlin Bar, Wilmersdorf, Uhlandstr. 145, tel. 883 79 36, daily 10 p.m.-7 a.m.

Caracas, Schöneberg, Kurfrstenstr.9, tel. 261 56 18, daily from 10 p.m.

Clärchens Ballhaus, Mitte, Auguststr. 24, tel. 282 92 95. This is more of a traditional dancing establishment.

Fischlabor, Schöneberg, Frankenstr. 13, tel. 216 26 35, daily 9 p.m.-5 a.m.

Green Door, Schöneberg, Winterfeldtstr. 50, tel. 215 25 15, daily 6 p.m. - 3 a.m.

Harry's New York Bar in the Grand Hotel Esplanade, Tiergarten, Lützowufer 15, tel. 26 10 11, opens daily at noon

Kumpelnest 3000, Tiergarten, Lützowstr. 23, tel. 261 69 18, daily 5 p.m.-5 a.m.

Morena, Kreuzberg, Wiener Str. 60, tel. 611 47 16, daily at 9 a.m.-4 a.m. Mexican bar.

Niagara, Kreuzberg, Gneisenaustr. 58, tel. 692 61 72, opens daily at 8 p.m.

Schnabelbar, Kreuzberg, Oranienstr. 31, tel. 614 53 56, opens daily at 9 p.m.

Tom's Bar, Schöneberg, Motzstrasse 20, tel. 213 45 70.

ZeoBar, Mitte, Rosenthaler Str. 38/39, tel. 283 46 81, opens daily at 6 p.m.

Zoulou Bar, Schöneberg, Hauptstr. 1, tel. 784 68 94, daily 10 p.m.-6 a.m.

MUSICAL VARIETY THEATERS

La Vie En Rose in Tempelhof Airport, Tempelhof, Platz der Luftbrücke, tel. 69 51 30 00. Show times Tue-Sun 9 p.m.

Cabaret Chez Nous, Charlottenburg, Marburger Str. 14, tel. 213 18 10, Shows daily around 8:30 and 11 p.m.

Kleine Nachtrevue, Schöneberg, Kurfürstenstr. 114, tel. 218 89 50, shows daily except Sun at 10:30 p.m. and 12:30 a.m.

DISCOTHEQUES

Abraxas, Charlottenburg, Kantstr. 134, tel. 312 94 93, Tue-Sun 10 p.m.-5 a.m. Nice little disco for Latin and Afro fans.

Akba Lounge, Prenzlauer Berg, Sredzkistr. 64, tel. 441 14 63, opens daily at 7 p.m.

BKA-Zelt, Mitte, Schlossplatz.

Far Out, Wilmersdorf, Kurfürstendamm 156 (on Lehniner Platz), tel. 320 007 23, daily 10 p.m.- 3:30 a.m., Fri and Sat until 5:30 a.m.

Blue Note, Schöneberg, Courbièrestr. 13, tel. 214 12 37, Wed-Sat opens 10 p.m.

Delicious Doughnuts, Mitte, Rosenthaler Str. 9/ Ecke Auguststrasse, tel. 283 30 21, Tue-Sun 10 p.m.-5 a.m.

Golgatha, Kreuzberg, Dudenstrasse 48-64, (at the Kreuzberg), tel. 785 24 53, daily 10 p.m.-6 a.m.

Hafenbar, Mitte, Chausseestr. 20, tel. 282 85 93; Fri/Sat opens 9 p.m.

Hangar II in Tempelhof airport, Tempelhof, Columbiadamm 2-6. Watch for announcements.

Loft, in Columbia Fritz, Tempelhof, Columbiadamm 9-11, concert hall, live music.

Kalkscheune, Mitte, Johannisstr. 2, tel. 28 39 00 65, Fri/Sat opens at 10 p.m. Events are announced.

Knaack Club, Prenzlauer Berg, Greifswalder Str. 224, tel. 436 23 51, Fri-Mon, Wed 10 p.m.-6 a.m.

Lime Club, Mitte, Dircksenstr. 105, tel. 281 45 85, Fri/Sat opens 11 p.m. Small club nestled in the S-Bahn arches.

Lipstick, Charlottenburg, Richard-Wagner-Platz 5, tel. 342 81 26. Relaxed gay disco.

Matrix, Friedrichshain, Warschauer Platz 18 im Gewölbe 3. Watch for announcements.

Metropol, Schöneberg, Nollendorfplatz 5, tel. 216 27 87, opens Fri und Sat at 10 p.m.

MS Sanssouci, Kreuzberg, Gröbenufer/Schlesisches Tor auf dem Wasser, tel. 611 12 55, Fri opens at 10 p.m., opens Sat at 11 p.m., Sun at 8 p.m.

90°, Schöneberg, Dennewitzstr. 37, tel. 262 89 84, opens Wed-Sun at 11 p.m.

First, Charlottenburg, Joachimstaler Str. 26, tel. 882 26 86, daily, exc. Mon, 11 p.m.-6 a.m.

Orpheuo, Schöneberg, Marburger Str. 2, tel. 211 64 45, opens daily 11 p.m.

Oxymoron in the Hackesche Höfe, Mitte, Rosenthaler Str. 40-41. Club opens at 11 p.m.

Sage Club, Kreuzberg, Brühenstr./Köpenicker Str., Thu from 9 p.m., Fri-Sat from 11 p.m.

Schmaltzwald, in the Berlin Prater, Prenzlauer Berg, Kastanien Allee 7-9, tel. 448 56 88, opens Fri-Sun at 10 p.m. Weird club in 1970s style.

Sophienclub, Mitte, Sophienstr. 6, tel. 282 45 52, opens daily at 9 p.m.

Tränenpalast, Mitte, Reichstagsufer 17 (S-Bahn station Friedrichstrasse), tel. 321 10 22, parties are held irregularly in the former GDR border installations.

Tresor/Globus Bar, Mitte, Leipziger Str. 128a, no telephone, opens Fri-Mon at 11 p.m.

Note:
Most discotheques request DM 10 entrance fee, no drink included. The top bars and discos require proper attire, the others have no dress code. Most clubs are open to all age groups.

WORLD THEATER AND
THEATRICAL BERLIN

One thing that has made Berlin unique since reunification is the cohesion and conflict between two theater cultures which have undergone different development since 1945.

Compared with the theaters in the West, the stages in the East were more certain of the approval of their audiences. In a fairly subtle manner they functioned as forums for political information and frequently even as a substitute for newspapers. Now, since political theater lost its *raison d'être* by virtue of the change of systems, the stages in the city's eastern section are in search of a new identity. It may be that before long there won't be much to distinguish them from the stages in Berlin's western section.

As the capital city, East Berlin attracted the best directors of the former GDR, whereas West Berlin was just one theater city among many. The nearly 30 stages in unified Berlin *could* serve as the foundation for turning the city back into what it once was before the Nazis closed the theaters in 1944 – roughly half of which were destroyed during the war: Germany's theater capital (as it had been known since the turn of the century). In the 1920s it was even *the* European theater metropolis. Today the houses are struggling for cash, and some don't even know if they will survive the next season.

Still, the diversity of the theaters – about 30 stages and 100 independent groups – and of their concepts is staggering. Everything is represented from world-class theater to specialty stages to partly experimental, partly established fringe theater. Nonetheless, the city has not yet managed to step back into its former role as a true theater metropolis. This was especially apparent during the **Ber-**

Right: The Schauspielhaus served as a theater until 1944, then as a concert hall.

lin Theater Competition, which takes place annually in May. A jury selects what it deems to be the best German-language production. For the most part only the productions of the Schaubühne theater have made it through this competition, and since 1989 those of East German director Thomas Langhoff have always been at the top.

The Big Stages

The **Schaubühne** on Lehniner Platz is a private theater whose players hitherto enjoyed considerable input in the creative process. In 1997, however, the decision was made to dissolved the ensemble and hire the actors per play in the future. As a cultural showpiece, it is heavily subsidized and was for a long time thought of as one of the best theaters in the world. It was founded in 1962 as a left-leaning, socially-critical private theater, and was named simply after its location, *Schaubühne am Halleschen Tor*.

In 1970 a troup of actors and actresses centered around Peter Stein moved into the building. Their programming was generally in accord with the goals of the protest movements of 1968. The reputation of the Schaubühne is primarily based on the directing work of Peter Stein, who remained artistic director until 1985, and of Luc Bondy and Klaus Michael Grüber – as well as on the professionalism of the players themselves.

However, many critics believe that the Schaubühne broke with its political tradition and developed into a light entertainment theater when it moved from Kreuzberg to the Ku'damm.

Since the fall of the Wall, the **Deutsches Theater** in the former eastern section of the city has developed into the one of the top stages in Berlin. There is hardly another German-speaking theater which so enthuses critics and the public alike. This is due, not least of all, to a unique combination of sheer excellence in act-

ing, which can be admired in any of their porudctions. The name might bring to mind associations with a "national theater" but, since the merger with the former West Berlin state theaters, the Deutsches Theater has had to take over, albeit involuntarily, the role of Berlin State Theater. Although at its foundation in 1883 programming along these lines played a role, today, both classical and contemporary pieces from around the world are on the performance schedule. The theater has an unusually broad repertoire including some 30 lengthier productions.

When Max Reinhardt, the Deutsches Theater's owner, emigrated in 1933, he chose Heinz Hilpert to carry on with the good work. Hilpert was aware of the fact that the Nazis needed the Deutsches Theater and its accompanying Kammerspiele playhouse as a liberal "alibi," and lead both theaters with innocuous productions of classics through the war. Even so, occasionally Joseph Goebbels threatened: "Hilperts' stagings are concentration camps on vacation." However,

Hilpert would then counter: "Then you'll have to put Goethe in Oranienburg and Hebbel in a concentration camp." Soon after the war's end, the Deutsches Theater dared to leap into the political fray with contemporary dramas. The tradition of subtle political innuendo was continued by Thomas Langhoff, who in 1991 became general director.

Of course, just as they always have, star actors and actresses like to perform at the Deutsches Theater, but the spirit of the ensemble is also highly developed. A new generation is rising next to the venerable acting greats. The old separation between the Deutsches Theater and the Kammerspiele, which was almost exclusively used as an experimental stage, no longer exists. In both houses classics, contemporary drama and light entertainment pieces are performed today. The Baracke, the second rehearsal stage of the Deutsches Theater, has turned out to be one of the most experimental theaters in town. Besides Heiner Müller, who from time to time

203

produced his own work here, Alexander Lang was one of the most important directors ever, in the Deutsches Theater and in the former GDR.

The political world staged quite a scene about the theater in 1993. The Senate suddenly decided to close the **Berlin State Schauspielbühne** together with its flagship, the **Schiller Theater**, due to the city's grave financial situation. After weeks of protests and protracted legal proceeedings the Berlin House of Representatives confirmed the Senate's decision. Ironically, an audit one year later showed that this overhasty closure had in fact cost taxpayers ten million marks more than a gradual close-down would have. The Schiller Theater has meanwhile become a stage for musicals for a number of producers.

The **Maxim Gorki Theater**, though small, is also among the most successful stages, but it, too, is struggling for survi-

Above: Hamlet in the Deutsches Theater.
Right: The great Max Reinhardt.

204

val. The Gorki's namesake is also representative of the many other dramatists from Russia and other eastern European countries whose pieces are carefully produced in this theater. Alongside its meritorious director (and actor) Albert Hetterle, the current director Bernd Willms and Thomas Langhoff, who made theatrical history with George Tabori's political farce *Mein Kampf*, have shaped the house's style. In addition to political theater, good light entertainment pieces with excellent casts have become important in the repertoire, for example, the production of *Hauptmann von Köpenick* by Katharina Thalbach.

On the other hand, the **Berliner Ensemble** has been relying primarily on its past worldwide reputation since it drove away producer and director Ruth Berghaus in 1977. The Ensemble was founded by Bertolt Brecht in 1949, right after his return from exile. In 1954 the Ensemble received its own performance space, the **Theater am Schiffbauerdamm**, which Brecht developed into an avant-garde stage. After his death in 1956 the Berliner Ensemble remained specialized in Brecht dramas. It has also consistently tried out works written in his spirit by other dramatists. Despite the interesting concept and the dedicated work of its players, this stage – predestined for experimentation – has congealed into a kind of theater museum. The playwright Heiner Müller inspired the Berliner Ensemble until his death. Ever since, the Theater am Schiffbauerdamm has entertained the public best with headlines about its internal quarrels and its fights with Brecht's heirs. The attempt to place the house under the leadership of a five-man committee failed miserably. Artistic stagnation and chaotic leadership led to the departure of director Martin Wuttke (at the end of 1996), of chief dramatic advisor Carl Hegemann and of artistic directress Andrea Beth (1997). In spite of these storms, director Stephan Suschke planned a great 1998 for the public, the 100th anniversary of Brecht's birth. Everyone is also very curious whether Claus Peymann, the director of the Burg Theater in Vienna, will switch to the Berliner Ensemble for the 1999/2000 season.

"Art for the People" was the motto for the 1890 founding of the **Volksbühne** (People's Stage). Germany's first theatergoers' association erected its own building in 1914 on Bülowplatz – present-day Rosa-Luxemburg-Platz – from pennies donated by workers. Max Reinhardt was the first director; later Erwin Piscator became the theater's chief producer. After initial success the Volksbühne's pedagogical dramaturgy began wearing down the spirit and patience of its proletarian audience. At a time when Reinhardt was producing great art at the Deutsches Theater, essayist Hans Sahl mocked: "The workers went to Reinhardt to edify themselves with beauty after dull labor; the bourgeoisie went to Piscator to applaud the portrayal of their impending downfall."

PROFESSOR MAX REINHARDT.

Piscator's revolutionary impetus finally lead to a break with the Social-Democratic attitudes of the Volksbühne's directorate. He founded his own theater on Nollendorfplatz, where his *agitprop* (agitation/propaganda) productions of the time – toward the end of the Weimar Republic – made the theater hall into a battlefield. In 1954, after its reconstruction as the municipal theater – it had only the name in common with the older institution – the Volksbühne, under the direction of Brecht student Benno Besson, became the most innovative theater of the GDR during the 1970s. Director Frank Castorf, with his provocative productions, is now the artistic inspiration of the house. In addition, the Volksbühne has long been using more than one stage. More intimate plays and chanson recitals are held in the red and green salons. The ensemble also stages some remarkable works at the traditional old comedy institution Prater on Kastanienallee.

In 1953, when the Volksbühne was dissolved in the GDR because the Free

Above: Using the street as a stage – a guaranteed audience.

German Union Alliance took over the management of theater attendance, several of the former members in West Berlin founded their own peoples' stage association.

It managed to open its own theater by 1963: the **Freie** (Free) **Volksbühne**. Piscator worked here for a while after his return from exile, directing plays like *Der Stellvertreter* by Rolf Hochhuth, *In der Sache J. Robert Oppenheimer* by Heinar Kipphardt and *Die Ermittlung* by Peter Weiss, among others.

Ghetto, by Joshua Sobol, sparked a vehement discussion. Since 1986, however, the name Freie Volksbühne has been nothing more than a fake label. The old members of the audience association rejected the highly individualistic direction of Hans Neuenfels and ticket sales sank dramatically. Finally, the musicals producer Friedrich Kurz took over the Volksbühne and turned it into the **Musical Theater Berlin**. The production he imported from London, *Shakespeare and Rock 'n' Roll*, ultimately went bankrupt. In the autumn of 1997 the **Theater der Freien Volksbühne** ventured a new start. The good old house on Schaperstrasse has returned to the fold of Berlin cultural life with guest performances of musical shows, cabaret and plays.

The Theater am Halleschen Ufer has taken over the house of the **Theatermanufaktur**. It's a space for independent groups, its emphasis is on modern dance.

The cosy **Renaissance Theater**, built in 1926, is oriented toward the tastes of a broad public, serving up dramas by a wide variety of playwrights including Molière, Arthur Miller and Dürrenmatt in easily digestible form. Berlin's popular star Harald Juhnke has lent several of the productions a pinch of light entertainment theater. Occasionally on Sundays, celebrities from culture and politics deliver commentaries as part of the "Berliner Lectures" series. A workshop stage performs private theater as well; **das studio** presents contemporary drama.

The **Hebbel Theater** primarily hosts productions which stand slightly oblique of the commonplace, established theater. Here they find a distinctive, intellectual and mostly youthful audience, who – beyond the major guest productions – are interested in the latest influences from around the world, from plays to new opera productions to really off-the-wall performances. The Hebbel Theater has meanwhile made a name for itself with modern dance as well, and a renowned festival, the *Internationales Tanzfest Berlin – Tanz im August.*

Small Stages and Light Entertainment Theater

The **Hansa Theater**, the **Vaganten-Bühne** and the **Tribüne**, founded in 1919 as an attempt at a proletarian theater, favor more-or-less pretentious entertainment and popular pieces, but also harken gladly back to the tradition of the cellar theater of the 1950s, confronting their audiences with Samuel Beckett or Jean-Paul Sartre. The **kleines theater** is a self-proclaimed specialty stage. The unknown is rescued from oblivion there and is presented with a good helping of irony, some sarcasm and frequently music as well. They may even be setting a record, with over 1400 performances of the production of *Das Küssen macht so gut wie kein Geräusch* (Kissing Hardly Makes Any Noise At All).

Almost every theater in Berlin's eastern section includes intelligently produced light entertainment pieces in their repertoires. West Berlin, on the other hand, has two theaters which specialize in this sort of production, the **Theater am Kurfürstendamm** and the **Komödie**, which are part of the Wölffer entertainment dynasty. Neither, however, has managed to pull off a production which could persuade the genre's dyed-in-the-wool opponents that light entertainment theater isn't by definition stuffy. The audience backs up this impression: crowds of tourists are carted in on buses so that they can catch a few winks after a day filled with the stress of sightseeing. A more aggressive approach was tried out once with Alan Ayckbourn's *From Now On* directed by Peter Zadek in 1989, starring Otto Sander and Susanne Lothar.

Beyond the Big-Time: Fringe Theater

During the past two decades many independent groups have come into being and disappeared again, since only a few have managed to hold their ground and drum up a regular financial support. Among the more durable fringe stages are the **Theater zum Westlichen Stadthirschen**, **Transform Theater**, **Zan Pollo Theater** and **Freie Theateranstalt Berlin**. The latter is an exceptional phenomenon, having put on well over 1000 performances of *Ich bin's nicht, Adolf Hitler ist es gewesen* (It Wasn't Me, It Was Adolf Hitler). Many other independent groups have no performance space of their own, and only a few of them are up to the task of creating good, unconventional or even experimental theater.

Zinnober, an independent group, has moved to the **Theater o. N.**; the house's productions and guest performances are certainly worth a viewing. The same applies to the **Theater unterm Dach**, which stages modern dance and movement pieces. The unconventional productions of the small and self-deprecating **theater 89** not only keep the audience happy, but have also succeeded in earning the recognition of cultural journalists. The **Stükke** produces English- and German-language plays in the Höfe am Südstern (Kreuzberg). As far as English-language theater goes, it is the exclusive domain of the **Friends of Italian Opera**, whose works range from classic to experimental.

The **bat Studio Theater** in Prenzlauer Berg is, hardly a fringe theater, nonetheless it embodies all of the charming characteristics of the independent groups. The bat (*Berliner Arbeiter- und Studententheater* – workers' and students' theater) originated in 1961, when Wolf Biermann set up self-regulated "subotniks" – workers and students who wanted to do performances as an independent group. However, their very first première was forbidden, and the Communist regime expropriated the workers' theater.

The **Sophiensaele** started operating in the autumn of 1996 and attracts a regular audience thanks to its consistently exciting productions.

The **Grips** is an independent but regularly-supported group. Since the end of the 1960s it has been doing children's and youths' productions. Its musical *Linie 1* made it world famous. It is dedi-

Above: The musical "Linie 1" made the Grips a famous children's and young people's theater.

cated to political problems such as youth unemployment, alienation and estrangement in the big city, environmental protection and historic topics such as Germany's infamous Nazi past.

In addition to these two well-known theaters, there are a number of other independent troups for young Berliners who entertain and inform children and young-at-heart adults, such as **Klecks Theater** of Neukölln. The **carrousel – Theater an der Parkaue**, the former Theater der Freundschaft, also stages works for a younger crowd. Puppet theater is the name of the game at the **Schaubude** in Prenzlauer Berg. The unusual productions and guest appearances of other puppet and figure theaters are fare not only for the young.

Naturally the theaters are all competing for the public's favor. Competition enlivens not only business, but the arts as well. Accordingly, Berlin *is* on the right road to becoming the theater metropolis of Europe and a cultural turnstile between East and West.

THEATERS

The daily newspapers and magazines and the *Berlin-Programm* publish the schedules of the theaters. The current program is also announced on the phone, tel. 01156 .

Berliner Ensemble, Mitte, Bertolt-Brecht-Platz, tel. 282 31 60.

Deutsches Theater / Kammerspiele and **Baracke**, Mitte, Schumannstr. 13a, tel. 287 12, info: tel. 284 41-221/-222, box office: 282 84 65.

Freie Theateranstalten, Charlottenburg, Klausenerplatz 19, tel. 321 58 89.

Freie Volksbühne, Wilmersdorf, Schaperstr. 24, tel. 860 09 30.

Hansa Theater, Tiergarten, Alt-Moabit 48, tel. 391 44 60.

Hebbel Theater, Kreuzberg, Stresemannstr. 29, tel. 25 90 04-27.

Kleines Theater, Steglitz, Südwestkorso 64, tel. 821 30 30,

Komödie, Charlottenburg, Kurfürstendamm 206, tel. 47 02 10 10 or 883 10 03.

Maxim Gorki Theater/Gorki Studio, Mitte, Am Festungsgraben 2, tel. 20 22 11 15; entrance Gorki Studio: behind the Giesshaus.

Renaissance Theater, Charlottenburg, Hardenbergstr. 6, tel. 312 42 02.

Schaubühne am Lehniner Platz, Wilmersdorf, Kurfürstendamm 153, tel. 89 00 23.

Schiller Theater, Charlottenburg, Bismarckstr. 110, tel. 319 53 48.

Theater am Kurfürstendamm, Charlottenburg, Ku'damm 206-209, tel. 47 02 10 10 or 883 10 03.

Theater am Halleschen Ufer, Kreuzberg, Hallesches Ufer 32, tickets: tel. 251 09 41, info: tel. 251 06 55.

Theater der Freien Volksbühne, Wilmersdorf, Schaperstr. 24, Tel. 88 42 08 84.

Tribüne, Charlottenburg, Otto-Suhr-Allee 18-20, tel. 341 26 00.

Vagantenbühne, Charlottenburg, Kantstr. 12a, tel. 312 45 29.

Volksbühne am Rosa-Luxemburg-Platz, Mitte, Rosa-Luxemburg-Platz, tel. 247 67 72.

FRINGE THEATERS

carrousel – Theater an der Parkaue, Lichtenberg, Parkaue 29, tel. 55 77 52-52.

bat Studio Theater, Prenzlauer Berg, Belforter Str. 15, tel. 442 76 13.

Stükke, Kreuzberg, Höfe am Südstern, Hasenheide 54, tel. 69 40 98 69.

Friends of Italian Opera, Kreuzberg, Fidicinstr. 40, tel. 691 12 11.

Garn Theater, Kreuzberg, Katzbachstr. 19, tel. 786 43 46.

Grips Theater, Tiergarten, Altonaer Str. 22 (at the U-Bahn station Hansaplatz), tel. 391 40 04; they also perform at the Schiller Werkstatt (Charlottenburg, Bismarckstr. 110).

Klecks Kinder Theater, Neukölln, Schinkestr. 9, tel. 693 77 31.

Ratibor, Kreuzberg, Cuvrystrasse. 20, tel. 618 6199.

Schaubude, Prenzlauer Berg, Greifswalder Str. 81-84, tel. 423 43 14.

Sophiensaele, Mitte, Sophienstrasse 18, tel. 283 52 66.

Teatr Kreatur, Kreuzberg, Tempelhofer Ufer 10, tel. 251 31 16.

theater 89, Mitte, Torstr. 216, tel. 282 46 56.

theaterforum Kreuzberg, Kreuzberg, Eisenbahnstr. 21, tel. 618 28 05.

tik-Theater im Kino, Friedrichshain, Proskauer Str. 19, tel. 426 85 99.

Theater o. N., Prenzlauer Berg, Kollwitzstr. 53, tel. 440 92 14.

Theater im Schmalen Handtuch, Friedrichshain, Frankfurter Allee 91, tel. 558 46 59.

Theater unterm Dach, Prenzlauer Berg, Danziger Str. 101, at the House of Culture in Ernst Thälmann Park, tel. 42 40 10 80.

Theater Zerbrochene Fenster, Kreuzberg, Fidicinstr. 3, tel. 694 24 00.

Theater zum Westlichen Stadthirschen, Kreuzberg, Kreuzbergstr. 37, tel. 785 70 33.

Zan Pollo Theater, Steglitz, Rheinstr. 45, tel. 852 20 02.

Zaubertheater Igor Jedlin, Charlottenburg, Roscherstr. 7, tel. 323 37 77.

Theater Ticket Offices

Konzert und Theaterkasse im KaDeWe, Schöneberg, Tauentzienstr. 21, tel. 217 77 54.

Showtime Konzert und Theaterkasse bei Wertheim, Charlottenburg, Kurfürstendamm 231, tel. 882 25 00.

Centrum, Charlottenburg, Meinekestr. 25, tel. 882 76 11.

Berlin Ticket, Tiergarten, Potsdamer Str. 96, tel. 23 08 82 30.

Theater- und Konzertkasse City Center, Charlottenburg, Kurfürstendamm 16, tel. 882 65 63.

Theater- und Konzertkassen im Nikolaiviertel, Mitte, Am Spreeufer 6, tel. 241 46 35.

Hekticket, Mitte, Rathausstr. 1 (on Alexanderplatz) and in Zoo, Hardenbergstr. 29a, tel. 2431 2431, fax 2431 2430, E-Mail: ticket@snafu.de Half-price theater tickets.

Last Minute Theaterkasse, in the International Trade Center at the Friedrichstrasse train station, Mitte, Friedrichstr. 95, tel. 20 96 22 33. Up to 50 percent discount on tickets.

OPERAS AND ORCHESTRAS, VARIETY AND CABARET

Opera Houses

The **Deutsche Oper** may not be considered the most revolutionary of German opera stages, but no one would accuse it of being hackneyed. Director Götz Friedrich has, after all, always succeeded in getting young people interested in Wagner with his *Ring der Nibelungen.* The controversial stagings of Hans Neuenfels, John Dew and Günter Krämer seldom appear in the repertoire, however.

The **Staatsoper Unter den Linden** (State Opera) has the prettier house. It was designed in typical north German classicism by von Knobelsdorff in 1740. Daniel Barenboim conducts operas, ballets and concerts in the representative opera house these days. Besides the

Above: A performance at the German State Opera on Unter den Linden. Right: The Philharmonic in the Kulturforum.

standard works in the operatic repertoire, Unter den Linden has been emphasizing operas from the pre-Mozart era in period productions, music theater from the 1920s and contemporary works.

The **Komische Oper**, the Comic Opera (in whose productions only German is sung), is one of the most interesting in all of Germany. It celebrated its 50th anniversary in 1997. It was director Walter Felsenstein who made the opera house world famous. It owes its current standing to the innovative principal director Harry Kupfer.

The combined opera houses of Berlin offer the public about 60 ballet evenings in all per year. The Komische Oper is also involved in the annual "International Dance Festival – Dance in August," which is staged primarily in the **Hebbel Theater**. Another important dance stage in Berlin is the **Theater am Halleschen Ufer** (which hosts guest performances of varying quality). The **Tanzfabrik Berlin** has also long been a big name in the free dance scene.

Fringe Opera

The founding of the **Zeitgenössische Oper Berlin** (Contemporary Opera of Berlin) in 1997, conclusively proved how lively and up-to-date modern opera can be. That summer it produced Mozart's Don Giovanni under the direction of Katharina Thalbach in the legendary – though now closed down – "techno temple" E-Werk, offering serious music in harmony with pile-driving electronic beats.

New shores are also being ventured onto by several independent musical groups. The fringe scene is still small, but it includes the **Neuköllner Oper**, which puts on generally high-brow and worthwhile musical theater by its own ensemble and invites guest performances for chamber-size events, musicals, one-acters and musical cabaret, all in a former ballroom. Also active participants in musical theater life are the **Berliner Kammeroper** and the **Neue Opernbühne Berlin**.

The Philharmonic and Other Orchestras

The world-famous **Berlin Philharmonic Orchestra** has gathered quite a roster of superlatives. It was founded over a hundred years ago and is considered today one of the world's finest orchestras. It is housed in one of the most beautiful concert halls, the **Philharmonie**, built by Hans Scharoun and inaugurated in 1963. It is probably one of the century's most important constructions and has superb acoustics to boot. The tent-like building has been nicknamed the "Karajan Circus" after Herbert von Karajan, who acted as its musical director for decades and who shaped the orchestra's style. The musicians also seem to have inherited – by some kind of collective memory – the musical qualities of the ensemble's earlier conductors, Hans von Bülow, Arthur Nikisch and Wilhelm Furtwängler. Claudio Abbado, who took over after Karajan's death, places greater emphasis on contemporary works.

The **Berlin Symphony Orchestra** (BSO), whose musical expression was shaped by conductor Kurt Sanderling, is housed in the **Konzerthaus Berlin** (the Schauspielhaus on Gendarmenmarkt), which was designed by Schinkel. The Schauspielhaus is also used now and then by the **Staatskapelle Berlin**, which, after all, was once conducted by Furtwängler and von Karajan, and which performs in the Konzerthaus. In July the Gendarmenmarkt is the venue for the performances of the "Classic Open Air" festival.

Finally, there are two orchestras affiliated with Berlin radio stations that frequently travel abroad for guest performances: the **German Symphony Orchestra** under Vladimir Ashkenazy and the **Berlin Radio Symphony Orchestra**, from the eastern part of the city.

Music aficionados might even find more than they bargained for during **Berlin Festival** weeks. The event, which takes place in September, has been a part of the cultural scene for over 40 years now. The program usually devotes itself to a single theme, tending to a kind of earnest thoroughness. For example, works of Schönberg and Brahms might be played on a single program. For Berlin and its performing artists, the festival weeks serve as an important meeting point for eastern and western Europe.

The **Akademie der Künste** (Academy of Arts) and the **Künstlerhaus Bethanien** concentrate their efforts on contemporary music. The **Musik-Biennale** festival held in March plays its part as well.

The organizers of the **Berliner Kabarett-Anstalt** have come up with some intelligent compromises with regard to new music. Every Tuesday they put on a show called *Unerhörte Musik*, or "unprecedented music." The "fantastic" musical works are explained and discussed in a congenial atmosphere.

Right: Variety shows in the Friedrichstadtpalast are too tame for many.

Jazz and Rock Scene

Exactly the place you would expect to find a bit of room for some serious cultural border crossing seems to have fallen victim to the demands of the dreaded lowest common denominator. At the **JazzFest Berlin**, which is put on in November, the program is largely tailor-made for the stars who just happen to be on a European tour at the time. You rarely discover anything new there. **The Jazz Across the Border** festival is held in the House of the World's Cultures in Tiergarten in June and July. Another good tip for jazz sessions (outside the festival as well) is the **Quasimodo** jazz cellar, which often hosts VIPs of the international jazz scene.

Besides the mega-concerts held at the **Waldbühne** in the Olympic Stadium, rock and pop fans find all they need to hear at some of the smaller clubs, such as the **SO 36** or the **Knaack-Club**. Middle-range concerts are held at such places as the **Arena**, or at the **Tempodrom**, which will be moving from Tiergarten to Kreuzberg in 1999. The *Heimatklänge* (local sounds) at the Tempodrom are very popular.

Musicals, Variety Shows and Cabarets

The **Theater des Westens**, situated in a 19th-century palace, has developed into one of the best musical repertory stages in Europe through the efforts of director and choreographer Helmut Baumann. Also, musical revues and operettas have been made entertaining, even for those who otherwise would more likely turn up their noses at them. The performances range from *My Fair Lady* to *Dreamgirls* and *Gypsy*.

The **Metropol-Theater** on Friedrichstrasse tried to attract the public with a program devoted exclusively to operetta under the direction of René Kollo. In the

summer of 1997, however, it filed for bankruptcy. Its future was unknown at the time of printing.

Orgies of petty bourgeois conventionality are still being held on the stages of the **Friedrichstadtpalast**. The "greatest revue in Europe," as it promotes itself, has improved only marginally despite new directors and professional support from the US. For people who might enjoy seeing, say, *Strapse und Gänsehaut* (Garters and Goosepimples), the much more intimate **Nacht-Revue** (Night Revue) in the Friedrichstadtpalast offers an exciting variety show, including some thoroughly erotic numbers, around the witching hour.

In the 1920s Berlin was *the* European entertainment metropolis par excellence. There were over 150 variety theaters. Two very different establishments have resuscitated this tradition: the Wintergarten – Das Varieté and the Chamäleon Varieté. International artists under the direction of the great magician André Heller and Roncalli-founder Bernhard Paul present impressive performances in the **Wintergarten**: one of the program titles was *Donnerwetter, Tadellos!* (Faultless, by Jove!). The **Chamäleon** rejects the idea of arid reconstructions of the 1920s, offering instead a modern and witty variety, presented at the **Hackesche Höfe** with great elan and increasing professionalism by groups of young performers. A younger but very popular sister of these two is the **Bar jeder Vernunft** in the Spiegel tent on the parking deck of the former Freie Volksbühne. The Berlin cabaret artist Holger Klotzbach has turned this venue into a Berlin night scene contender with guest appearances by stars like Tim Fischer, Meret Becker, Georgette Dee, the Swiss Pfister siblings, Cora Frost and Max Raabe. After the show the tent is turned into a bar with live piano music, and on weekends young talents do their bit in the popular *Nacht-salon*.

The 40 amateur acrobats and clowns of the **ufaFabrik** have meanwhile achieved an admirable degree of professionalism.

In 1982 the alternative Ufa-Circus opened. According to their own advertising, their only predatory animal sits in the ticket booth.

In the 1920s Berlin was also a true metropolis of the political-literary cabaret as well. Among the most renowned of these was Max Reinhardt's *Schall und Rauch* (Sound and Smoke Fumes). In the cellar of the **Theater des Westens**, Trude Hesterberg's cabaret became famed as the "Wild Stage": Claire Waldoff and Ernst Busch sang Tucholsky chansons in the *Kabarett der Komiker* (Cabaret of the Comedian) – *Kadeko* for short. Nowadays the tone is set in Berlin's cabarets by glib regulars like Martin Buchholz who, as a master of the stale political joke, has become a Berlin institution. Like many other one-man acts he appears mostly at the **Wühlmäuse**.

The best cabaret, inasmuch as it's still truly satirical in the sense of Heinrich Heine ("Wit without seriousness is only a sneeze of the intellect"), is **Die Distel** (The Thistle) in the city's eastern section. And, though it has lost its favorite pincushion – the Communist regime – it certainly hasn't lost its spines. Die Distel is refreshingly biased, in stark contrast to the "balanced" cabaret of the **Stachelschweine** (Porcupines). An inside tip for people with a soft spot for crazy thinking is the **Berliner Kabarett-Anstalt** (**BKA**) in the BKA tents on Schlossplatz. Like the **Mehringhof Theater**, the **Podewil** is a venue for all kinds of productions. Here is the legendary place where rebellious artists from East and West appeared when the house was still under the thumb of the Communists. Entirely new in the city's eastern section is the café-restaurant **Kartoon**, in which semi-pro cabaret artists wait tables and then serve up nourishment for the intellect as dessert. Berlin today is far from having the diversity it once had, but it is a far cry from Balzac's laconic description of it in 1840 as the "capital of boredom."

Above: The highly recommendable Berlin cabaret Die Distel in the east of the city.

OPERAS AND ORCHESTRAS, VARIETY AND CABARET

Opera Houses and Musical Stages

Berliner Kammeroper, info: Kreuzberg, Kottbusser Damm 79, tel. 693 10 54.

Deutsche Oper Berlin, Charlottenburg, Bismarckstr. 35, tel. 341 02 49.

Friedrichstadtpalast, Mitte, Friedrichstr. 107, tel. 232 62-0.

Komische Oper, Mitte, Behrenstr. 55-57, box office: Unter den Linden 41, tel. 202 60-360, ticket service: tel. 47 02 10 00.

Neue Opernbühne Berlin, info: Schöneberg, Goltzstr. 13, tel. 215 35 89.

Neuköllner Oper, Neukölln, Karl-Marx-Str. 131-133, tel. 68 89 07 77.

Staatsoper Unter den Linden, Mitte, Unter den Linden 7, tickets: tel. 20 35 45 55, info: tel. 208 28 61.

Theater des Westens, Charlottenburg, Kantstr. 12, tel. 882 28 88.

Berlin Orchestras, Music Auditoriums

"Hanns Eisler" Music School, chamber music auditorium in Mitte, Charlottenstr. 55, tel. 203 09-20 03.

Hochschule der Künste, Charlottenburg, concert hall on Hardenbergstr. 33 and on Bundesallee 1-2, tel. 313 70 01.

Max-Beckmann-Saal, Wedding, Luxemburger Str. 20, tel. 03301/457 22 34.

Otto-Braun-Saal (in the State Library), Tiergarten, Potsdamer Str. 33, tel. 26 61.

Philharmonie und Kammermusiksaal (chamber music auditorium), Tiergarten, Kulturforum, Matthäikirchstr. 1, tel. 25 48 80.

RIAS Berlin, Schöneberg, Kufsteiner Str. 69, tel. 850 30.

Konzerthaus Berlin (Schauspielhaus am Gendarmenmarkt), Mitte, Gendarmenmarkt, tickets: tel. 203 09 21 01/-02.

Meistersaal, Kreuzberg, Köthener Str. 38, tel. 26 49 53 13. Chamber music.

Schloss Friedrichsfelde, Lichtenberg, Am Tierpark 125, tel. 513 81 42, ticket office at the palace entrance of the zoo.

SFB, large and small broadcasting halls, Charlottenburg, Haus des Rundfunks, Masurenallee 8-14, tel. 30 31-0.

Jazz and Rock, Modern Music

Akademie der Künste (Arts Academy), Tiergarten, Hanseatenweg 10, tel. 390 00 70.

Alabama, Wedding, Genter Str. 65, tel. 453 69 52. Blues, jazz, rock.

Arena, Treptow, Eichenstr. 4, tel. 533 73 33.

A-Trane, Charlottenburg, Bleibtreustr. 1, tel. 313 25 50.

Eierschale Dahlem, Zehlendorf, Podbielskiallee 50, tel. 832 70 97. Mixture of musical sounds, including jazz, dixieland and country.

Eierschale Zenner, Treptow, Alt-Treptow 14-17, tel. 533 73 70.

Flöz, Wilmersdorf, Nassauische Str. 37, tel. 861 10 00.

Knaack-Club, Prenzlauer Berg, Greifswalder Str. 224, tel. 442 70 60.

Künsterhaus Bethanien, Kreuzberg, Mariannenplatz 2, tel. 61 69 03-0.

Kulturbrauerei, Prenzlauer Berg, Knaackstr. 97, tel. 441 92 69.

Metropol, Schöneberg, Nollendorfplatz 5, tel. 21 73 680. Disco, concerts.

Tacheles, Mitte, Oranienburger Str. 54-56, tel. 281 61 19. Often unusual concerts.

SO 36, Kreuzberg, Oranienstr. 190, tel. 614 13 06.

Podewil, Mitte, Klosterstr. 68-70, tel. 24 74 97 77. Classical and jazz.

Quasimodo, Charlottenburg, Kantstr. 12a, tel. 312 80 86. Jazz sessions.

Variety, Dance and Cabaret

Bar jeder Vernunft, Wilmersdorf, Schaperstr. 24, tel. 883 15 82.

Berliner Kabarett-Anstalt (BKA), Kreuzberg, Mehringdamm 32-34, tel. 251 01 12.

BKA Tents, Mitte, Schlossplatz.

Chamäleon Varieté, Mitte, Rosenthaler Str. 40/41, tel. 282 71 18.

Distel, Mitte, Friedrichstr. 101, tel. 204 47 04.

Kartoon, Mitte, Französische Str. 24, tel. 204 47 56.

Mehringhof Theater, Kreuzberg, Gneisenaustr. 2a, tel. 691 50 99.

Scheinbar, Schöneberg, Monumentenstr. 9, tel. 784 55 39. Small stage and cabaret.

Die Stachelschweine, Charlottenburg, Europa-Center, tel. 261 47 95.

Tanzfabrik Berlin, Kreuzberg, Möckernstr. 68, tel. 786 58 61.

Tempodrom, Tiergarten, In den Zelten, tel. 394 40 45 (a move to the Anhalter Train Station in Kreuzberg is planned for 1999).

ufaFabrik, Tempelhof, Viktoriastr. 10-18, tel. 752 80 85.

Wintergarten – Das Varieté, Tiergarten, Potsdamer Str. 96, tickets can be purchased at Berlin Ticket: tel. 23 08 82 30.

Die Wühlmäuse, Wilmersdorf, Nürnbergerstr. 33, corner of Lietzenburger Str., tel. 213 70 47.

FILM CITY BERLIN

Once a year, in the midst of the murky Berlin February, black sunglasses suddenly start turning up on the street. They are the unmistakable sign of the international film jet-set who invade the city for ten days during the **International Film Festival**.

The couple of film stars and directors and a gigantic retinue of PR people arouse in the city the deceptive feeling that it is again a major film industry metropolis. Certainly the **Berlinale**, as the festival performance is casually referred to, has evolved into one of the major film festivals since its founding in 1951. However, as is true for the other major European festivals in Cannes and Venice, Berlin suffers from the general feebleness of German and European film. The **Forum des Jungen** (newer) **Films**, established in 1971, did not change the situ-

Above: Taking a break between shots during on-location filming in Berlin.

ation much: the works of unknown directors were well-meaningly accepted, but the broader public was more interested in productions from the dream factories in Hollywood. Nonetheless, the festival *is* an important event, especially since you are more likely to discover unusual and gripping small productions in Berlin than in Cannes, Venice or Hollywood.

The number of screens in Berlin was 182 in 1996, to which are added the open-air screens in summer (the largest being the Waldbühne at the Olympic Stadium). This makes Berlin the outright movie house capital of Germany. During the next few years mega-houses and multiplexes will provide another 5000 seats. Nonetheless, these figures appear rather modest in comparison with the those from the 1920s. In 1932 one could choose from among 358 cinemas. The major movie houses, in which – now as then – the premières are run (sometimes even with the director and actors present) are located on the Kurfürstendamm, where else?

Berlin: The City that Wrote Film History

There was a time when film history was made in Berlin's studios. The movies took their first tentative steps in Pankow when the brothers Emil and Max Skladanowsky began experimenting with the bioscope in 1892. In 1900 Berlin's first film producer, Oskar Messter, took Berlin's movie houses by storm with his silent films. Beginning in 1919 the German film industry developed a style of its own in Berlin based on Expressionism on the stage and in literature. Famous examples are Robert Wiene's *Das Cabinet des Dr. Caligari* and Fritz Murnau's equally bizarre *Nosferatu*. In the mid-1920s this style was extended to portray the extremity of a modern, technologized world, as in Fritz Lang's *Metropolis.*

The model for these and other films was partly Berlin's babylonian vivacity, as reflected in Walter Ruttmann's *Berlin, die Sinfonie einer Großstadt* (1927) or social criticism as in *Mutter Krausen's Fahrt ins Glück* (1929). At the beginning of the 1930s German film was a big export success; 52 percent of all foreign films in the US came from Germany – from Berlin at that! However, with the advent of the Nazi regime German film collapsed. The majority of directors had already emigrated to the United States by then. Films shot during the war were either harmless comedies, musicals or morale boosters. After the war a new German cinema only started up hesitantly. With *Die Mörder sind unter uns* or *Die Sünderin*, Wolfgang Staudte remained a maverick. And, after a brief renewal of the cinema in the 1960s, films like *Berlin Alexanderplatz* or *Der Himmel über Berlin* appeared to be blazing a new trail, though they turned out to be exceptions.

Today there are the **Deutsche Film- und Fernsehakademie** (German Academy of Film and Television) in Berlin and the **Hochschule für Film und Fernsehen** (College for Film and Television; moving to Filmstadt Babelsberg in 1999) in Potsdam, as well as the **Stiftung Deutsche Kinemathek** and the **Arsenal**, its affiliated cinema. All of these institutions offer the opportunity to get good training. However, the few German directors who have achieved international success tend to prefer working abroad. In addition, Berlin lacks proper film subsidy. The *Film- und Fernsehakademie* and *Deutsche Kinemathek* will probably move into the Sony Center on Potsdamer Platz soon. The **Berlinale** will also be centered on Potsdamer Platz in the future.

In the meantime, the studios are slowly decaying while living on the myths of their past. The acquisition of the **DEFA studios** in Potsdam-Babelsberg by a major French investor is helping to make Berlin's future as a film-making city somewhat rosier. Director Volker Schlöndorff is chairman of the supervisory board of the new Babelsberg studios, which are intended to tie into the good old days of the UFA studios. However, as an artist, he finds himself in the unwilling role of the broker who is forced to canvas door to door just to have films made in Babelsberg and thus bring in the big money. The once proud studios, which cover an area of 103 acres (43 ha) and include the largest inventory of props in the world (over 600,000 pieces), survive today from television and video productions, and from the daily cranking out of soap operas and talk shows for German TV. One major movie was made here recently: *The Neverending Story III.*

Filmpark Babelsberg (tel. 0331 / 721 2750) attracts half a million visitors a year to its theme park, which provides a behind-the-cameras look into the world of film production. Highlights include a stunt show, the virtual screen experience of *Show Scan Action* cinema, the *Cinefantastic* science fiction exhibition and a simulated film shoot.

ART AND LITERATURE

Berlin's gallery landscape, which has weathered a lot of changes through the storms of history, is noteworthy today primarily for its almost incomparable diversity. Its perpetual state of metamorphosis is its most impressive characteristic.

One thing is certain, however, the galleries of Berlin have something for every taste and pocketbook. Since the reunification of the two Germanys this has become even truer than ever.

While the heavyweight international art business is focused mainly in Charlottenburg, on and around the Kurfurstendamm, younger and more avant-garde galleries and artists have settled mainly in Mitte. Many of them used to be in Kreuzberg, but ever since reunification that district has lost its image as an innovative

center of the arts. Besides the approximately 250 galleries involved in vivacious artistic life of Germany's brand new old capital, a variety of sites are repeatedly used as part of the arts scene.

Exhibitions are held any place imaginable: in cafés and banks (whose generosity, by the way, leaves a lot to be desired), in churches, colleges and libraries, in the TV tower, or in train stations; for example, the **Dirty Windows Gallery** at the U-Bahn station Kurfürstendamm. A unique, open-air gallery for graffiti art, because it is perched on a piece of the Berlin Wall, is the **East Side Gallery** in Friedrichshain.

The art scene in Berlin has an exceptional liveliness due to the constant supply of new faces from the big academies and the exchange of artists. To find out how good they are, go to the changing exhibitions at the **daad-Galerie** (Tiergarten, Kurfürstenstrasse 58, tel. 261 36 40).

One information forum and a trading post for the international arts market is

Preceding pages: Summer lunch break.
Above: Berlin artist J. Grützke.

the **art forum berlin**. This arts trade fair, held in the fairgrounds near the Radio Tower, was opened in October 1996 and now draws the art world's attention to the city once every year.

Galleries around Oranienburgerstrasse

There are some forms of life existing in Mitte whose main means of expression is an unbroken will to fulfill their wishes. Since the fall of the Wall, unconventional gallery owners have settled here, mainly around Oranienburger Strasse. Galleries and museums in Mitte have started collaborating via the Internet (If you have Internet access, updated information can be clicked on at http://www.b.shuttle.de/art-bag/Berlin-Mitte/).

Matthias Arndt and Anna Lubinus, who established **Galerie Arndt & Partner** (Rosenthaler Str. 40/41, Hof III, tel. 280 81 23), found an unusual site for exhibiting their 1997 project "Storytellers." The gallery, which is located in the Hackesche Höfe (international contemporary art), chose the old transformer house of the building.

Also in Hof III (Third Courtyard), two women founded their own gallery, **Leo.Coppi** (tel. 283 53 31). They offer art (artists from the former GDR, figurative painting) at reasonable prices. **Architekturgalerie Aedes** (see "The Eccentric and the Bizarre" beginning on page 224) is also located in these venerable residential and commercial buildings.

Around the corner, at Sophienstrasse 21, you should drop into the artistically well-endowed **Sophien-Gips-Höfe**. Nicole Hackert and Bruno Brunnet run the **Contemporary Fine Arts** gallery (tel. 283 65 81), which presents young international and contemporary art in the shape of paintings, drawings, installations and sculptures. Right next door, in **Galerie Sophien Edition** (Sophienstr.

24, in the courtyard, tel. 282 82 33), you'll mainly find painters, sculptors and graphic artists being represented.

Galerie Johannes Zielke – the owner is one of the best-known Berlin gallerists (from the eastern side of town) – has moved from Prenzlauer Berg to Mitte. A terrific meetingplace for artists of all stripes is located at Gipstrasse 7 (tel. 282 98 02).

Strolling down Auguststrasse, passing by bars, wild and woolly fashion designers and galleries, you will run across **Galerie EIGEN + ART** (No. 26, tel. 280 66 05). This gallery was founded in Leipzig in 1983 and was one of the few private galleries in the former GDR. A project involving participation in temporary galleries in international art centers such as Tokyo, Paris, New York, London and Berlin resulted in a second office in Berlin-Mitte. The gallery displays the works of international and German artists. A special emphasis is placed on foreign artists living in Berlin who project their vision of the city in the future.

The basic work of **Galerie Wohnmaschine** (Tucholskystr. 35, tel. 30 87 20 15) consists of year-long projects between owner Friedrich Loock and young artists (many from Berlin). The name of the gallery means "Living Machine." In 1988 Loock was the first person ever to open a private gallery in his own living room (on Auguststrasse, a sidestreet off Tucholskystrasse).

In the neighboring district of Prenzlauer Berg there are two good sites for the connoiseur of art galleries. The **Kulturbrauerei** (Knaackstr. 97, corner of Danziger Strasse, tel. 441 92 69/70) is still a top address for exhibitions. And contemporary art has a forum all of its own in the **Galerie im Pferdestall** (literally, "in the horse stables") and the **Alte Schlosserei** gallery.

At Kollwitzstrasse 53 (right at the Jewish cemetery and opposite the *Kunstverein*, or art association, on Prenzlauer

Berg), art dealer Barbara Blickensdorff has been making a name for herself since October 1996 in her **Galerie Blickensdorff** (tel. 442 88 88). She exhibits some veritable classics, such as a selection of the works of British pop artist David Hockney, together with established Berlin artists (mainly constructivists) and young artists, some of whom actually live in "Prenzlberg."

For some, art should not be confined exclusively to the four (gallery) walls. At Blickendorff's most recent so-called city exhibition, the painter Magdalena Häfner took her colorful works and paraded them around the area to the tune of Scottish music. This artistic procession was appropriately entitled: "Art Gets Up and Takes a Walk – Led by a Bagpiper – Through the City Districts of Prenzlauer Berg and Mitte."

Above: Berlin artist Kurt Mühlenhaupt with one of his sculptures. Right: Renovation à la Kreuzberg, an artistic enterprise.

Incidentally, the space behind the façade of Kollwitzstrasse 53, which is under governmental preservation order, is also the home of the Theater o. N. (formerly the Zinnober theatrical group).

Galleries in Charlottenburg

Rudolph Springer (**Galerie Springer**, Charlottenburg, Fasanenstr. 13, tel. 312 70 63) is one of the few gallery owners in Berlin who has weathered all the changes on Fasanenstrasse during the past 50 years. Unimpressed by passing fashions, and strictly trusting only his own standards of quality, Springer still plugs away at his work in an old-fashioned but genial manner and mourns the passing of the days when things revolved more around art than money.

One of the most famous names in local art dealership is on the first floor of the old Berlin house at the corner of the Kurfurstendamm and Uhlandstrasse. In his **Galerie Brusberg**, gallery owner and art dealer Dieter Brusberg shows contemporary art and works from the classical modern period (Kurfurstendamm 213, tel. 882 76 82). Villa Grisebach on Fasanenstrasse 25 is home to the **Käthe-Kollwitz Museum** and **Galerie Pels-Leusden** (tel. 885 91 50), whose main thrust is on German Impressionism and Expressionism, as well as international contemporary art.

The end of the Wall spelled new blood for art in Berlin. Thomas Schulte from New York and Eric Franck from Geneva were two of the first artists spearheading an influx of international artists to Berlin at the beginning of the 1990s. Their work can be seen in **Galerie Franck + Schulte** (Mommsenstr. 56, tel. 324 00 44). The gallery, together with Galerie Volker Diehl around the corner (Niebuhrstr. 2, tel. 881 82 80), also belongs to the approximately 130 members of the *art forum Berlin*.

Wolf Vostell's son opened a gallery at Knesebeckstrasse 30: **Fine Art Rafael Vostell** (tel. 885 22 80) is focused on the *Fluxus* movement and shows the work of many young Berlin artists.

The range of Berlin galleries, with its diversity of international and experimental art, is also visible in other sections of Charlottenburg, in **Galerie Anselm Dreher**, for example (Pfalzburger Str. 80, tel. 883 52 49), **Galerie Georg Nothelfer** (Charlottenburg, Uhlandstr. 184, tel. 881 44 05) and **Galerie Nikolaus Sonne** (Charlottenburg, Kantstr. 138, tel. 312 23 55).

These are galleries which represent – with a certain commitment – artists who, on the one hand, are popular, like Andy Warhol at Sonne's, or thoroughly experimental, like Jochen Gerz at Dreher's. You will really be well taken care of at these places, and you can rely on their professional knowledge. These galleries are places that also cater to unconventional tastes.

Obviously this applies just as much to those galleries that sell paintings per-

fectly suited to exquisite furniture, among them the **Raab Galerie** (Schöneberg, Potsdamer Str. 58; tel. 261 92 17). They may have to be modern, but they can be exciting as well. The people there know what they have acquired and can display it without hesitation.

This list of galleries would be incomplete without mentioning **Eva Poll** (Tiergarten, Lützowplatz 7, tel. 261 70 91), who has remained loyal to realists like Ulrich Baehr and has represented Schang Hutter. She also looks after the daughter of Fred Thieler, H. C. Gabriel, just as she does several painters who already left the GDR well before the Wall actually fell. You will find Russians there who have had a broad public in Berlin for a long time.

And if you should want to purchase even more geographically defined art after surveying this vast selection, you will also find it if you ask for Latvian artists, for example, represented in the **InterArt** gallery (Schöneberg, Potsdamer Str. 93, tel. 262 88 10).

The Eccentric and the Bizarre

The **Aedes** architecture gallery (Charlottenburg, Savignyplatz, tel. 282 70 15) investigates the future of more than just Berlin architecturally. Models provide information on the ideas of both students and professors. It is possible to gain a real understanding from these models. Drawings illustrate their aesthetic concepts, and the adjacent café is by no means the worst place to mull over and discuss the possibilities of these interesting artistic designs.

The painter Dieter Fenz and the sculptor Michael Schuh have come up with a new and successful way of combining a café and a cultural experience. Their **Café Phillis** (Tiergarten, Pohlstr. 70, tel. 261 90 60, daily from 10-2 a.m.) attracts a variegated crowd of cocktail drinkers, art fans and coffee house intellectuals. It is a bunch that, according to Dieter Fenz,

Above: Berlin artists in their studio in Kreuzberg.

should be "lively, cosmopolitan and a little bit wicked." Fenz and his partner spent years working away at the dilapidated junk store ultimately turning it into a chic cultural meeting place with a bar and gallery. Once a week there is a special show; a jazz concert, a lecture, a performance or the opening of an exhibition.

If you prefer unusual combinations, you can also make your acquisition at **Gelbe Musik** (Charlottenburg, Schaperstr. 11, tel. 211 39 62) for a slightly higher price. Records and scores from visual artists are the unusual round-up of this gallery, which operates just as spectacularly as it does reclusively.

On the other hand, two other galleries are rather aggressive in their handling of the remains of a great past. The photography guild, which once had its home in Berlin, has to be satisfied with a single address at the moment. In the eastern section of the city, in Friedrichshain, the **Fotogalerie** at Helsingforser Platz 1 (tel. 296 16 84) still has its lens cap off, while in the western section of town only Ernst

Volland, with his **Galerie Voller Ernst** (Schöneberg, Innsbrucker Str. 37, tel. 782 68 03), provides the public with primarily humorous photographs.

In order to facilitate orientation through Berlin's art life, some operators have specialized in tours or special walks through the art and cultural landscape of the city. Rewarding and importantly up-to-date cultural walks through the gallery scene in Mitte are offered by **art:berlin** (Schöneberg, Kufsteiner Str. 7, tel. 85 72 81 82).

Berlin and Literature

In the 1920s there were almost 1000 publishing houses located in Berlin, and one quarter of all publications in German came from this city.

Today there are less than 200, and they are mostly small or alternative publishing houses. Not only publishing novels brings in big money these days; just as important are the large scientific and educational publishers, including Julius Springer, Walter deGruyter, Cornelsen, Langenscheidt, and Volk und Wissen, who together publish one fifth of all German-language scientific works.

Many of the traditional large publishing houses are returning now that the city is not only resuming its rightful place as the German capital, but also because of the new infrastructure going up. For example, after reunification Rowohlt opened up a branch publishing house in Berlin which specializes in eastern European culture and literature. And one of the riskiest new ventures, by Klaus Wagenbach, has turned into a publishing house of renown. In addition, there is the newly-founded Berlin-Verlag, which carries first-time Berlin authors as well as Nobel Prize winners in its catalogue, and has promoted new signs of life on Berlin's literary scene with this wild mixture.

At the same time, all large publishers from the former GDR, like Aufbau Ver-

lag, have not only succeeded in keeping their footing in the east of Germany after being privatized, but have also demonstrated an ability to break through to a certain extent in the very crowded market of western Germany.

Publishing in Berlin is a modest business and the great writers have stayed away, but there is no lack of opportunities for literary discussion.

There is, for example, the **Literaturhaus Berlin**, founded in 1986 in a private house from the founding years of the German Reich (Charlottenburg, Fasanenstr. 23, tel. 882 65 52), with its literary readings, moderated discussions and exhibitions.

Even the venerable **Literarische Colloquium Berlin** (Zehlendorf, Am Sandwerder 5, 816 99 60), which used to be the meeting place for *Gruppe 47*, is still a place where heated literary debates take place between authors – who sometimes live in this elegant villa at the Wannsee, too. Every year the city rents rooms to young writers on scholarships. Readings are part of the regular program. Berlin's art and literature panoply is further enhanced by the **Akademie der Künste** (Academy of Art) and the **Neue Gesellschaft für Literatur** (New Literary Society), with their Berlin authors' days, book shops and a variety of events.

The **Literaturforum im Brecht-Haus** (Mitte, Chausseestr. 125, tel. 282 20 03) is a very active participant in literary life. It offers readings, films and seminars. The house on Chausseestrasse also harbors a Brecht memorial; namely the rooms where he and Helene Weigl lived and worked. The Bertolt-Brecht-Archiv is also here, accessible to the public once again since November 1997.

At the Literaturforum and at the new **literaturWERKstatt berlin** (Majakowskiring 46/48, tel. 48 52 45-0), great talent still hopes to be discovered one evening – the one who will write the really great Berlin novel for the critics.

THE ALTERNATIVE SCENE

Almost everybody in Berlin complains about the counter-culture scene, but nobody, allegedly, is a part of it; it is always the *others*. Nevertheless, there is some concern making the rounds that it could dissolve into thin air, that the little niches in which it ekes out its subsidized existence might dry up, because the Senate is turning off the money-faucet. For all that, the counter-culture – which fills the normal citizens of Berlin with fear – has since become quite tame. In fact the counter-culture is dead. Berlin, stronghold of the counter-culture, rang in the era of the alternative conformist ten years ago already.

How it all Began

At the end of the 1960s, when the **Extra-Parliamentary Opposition** (APO)

Above: Student leader Rudi Dutschke in 1968. Right: Squatting old houses is passé.

was at its zenith, the alternative scene was going for the jugular of convention. They made a ruckus in an effort to banish the stench of the Adenauer era from peoples' living rooms. At the head of the pack was the **Socialist German Student League** (SDS), then headed by Rudi Dutschke. They took to the streets in a broad offensive against the *Notstandsgesetze* (national emergency laws), for democracy at the universities, the liberation of the so-called Third World, and against the Vietnam War. In Berlin the tension, which had already been long dammed-up, exploded during the 1968 International Vietnam Congress.

12,000 adherents of the SDS participated in its concluding demonstrations against the USA's war in Vietnam. The Springer Press mobilized against the protesters and proclaimed Rudi Dutschke an enemy of the people. On April 11, 1969, one Jürgen Bachmann fired shots at Dutschke – he died ten years later as a result of his injuries. There was a spontaneous reaction to the attempted assassi-

nation, committed by *Bild*-reader Bachmann. The same evening, thousands of students blocked deliveries of the tabloid *Bild* newspaper.

With this act they triggered a wave of violence that washed over other major cities. West Berlin became the driving force of the students' movement. However, the protest generation gradually moved from the universities into grassroots and trade union groups. Grandiose plans for a world revolution faded in favor of more modest changes in daily life. Self-administered day-care centers and youth centers were established in this way, as well as the – at that time exotic, but today entirely normal – *Wohngemeinschaft* (shared flat).

House-to-House Combat

In July 1971 the first successful squat began at Mariannenplatz in Kreuzberg, in the **Georg-von-Rauch-Haus**. The squatters wrote: "Hands off the Rauchhaus, otherwise City Hall will go up in smoke."

(*Rauch* = smoke). However, the real wave of squatting began eight years later, when the housing shortage became intolerable in West Berlin, while at the same time 20,000 apartments stood empty. The majority of these were the objects of speculation by owners who simply allowed the buildings to decay and were awaiting demolition permits so that they could erect new apartment buildings and then demand enormous rents. Within two years 170 buildings were occupied, and at the high point of the movement the number reached 281. The "maintainance occupiers," as they called themselves, waged a veritable war against the landlords. Since the beginning of the 1980s the street battles have had less and less to do with political protest. Every May 1 the "chaotics" celebrate for their own amusement a "street slaughter-festival," which alludes to the former battleground of Berlin's streets.

In 1981 Hans-Jochen Vogel, the governing Social-Democratic mayor at that time, drafted a set of rules which still apply today. According to these, the Senate makes a difference between the squatters who are willing to negotiate and those who refuse to do so. The ones willing to negotiate are offered rental contracts. The Senate speculated that the *occupation* mentality might eventually metamorphose into an *owner* mentality. The Berlin rules were also taken up by the Christian Democrats, who won the election in May 1981, partly as a reaction against the squatters. In the meantime virtually all squatters have made tenancy agreements with the city districts and renovated the houses by their own efforts and Senate funding.

A new generation has grown up which accuses the old squatters – meanwhile owners themselves – of being speculators. Thus, the 150 occupants of the oldest self-adminstered buildings in Berlin had to look on as their unused attics were stormed by 20 young people in April, 1990. After a couple of days the building owners called in the police.

Newly Squatted Houses in East Berlin

Endless reruns, or something entirely new? In the eastern section of the city there was a new edition of the squatters' movement in the spring of 1990. With 25,000 unoccupied apartments in a situation of unclarified ownership, a legacy of the former Communist state, the squatters forced their way in. The scattered remains of the West Berlin counter-culture scene and their younger successors also made their way to the east. Along with them came all sorts of young people from Bavaria and Baden-Württemberg who were revealed – with relish – by the media to be "sons of the middle class with daddy's money in their pockets."

The squatters from the east rapidly became a minority. 126 buildings were oc-cupied, the largest part of them in the Friedrichshain district, the remainder in Prenzlauer Berg and Lichtenberg.

The focal point of the protests was Mainzer Strasse, a block of 13 occupied buildings in a "state of emergency" with sofas and tables on the sidewalks, information cafés and in-house militias. The squatters had high-flying plans: they wanted to combine living and working together in one building with self-managed alternative businesses in the courtyards and womens' apartments in the front buildings. The city council offered the squatters who were willing to negotiate individual rental contracts. However, there was division in the "scene," and a portion refused to negotiate. On November 14, 1990, the situation escalated; squatters, autonomist elements and police wound up in a bloody street battle when the Senate decided to have the houses forcibly vacated. Since then the squatter scene in eastern Berlin has hardly been heard of.

Alternative Culture: A Village Idyll

Pragmatism is perhaps the decisive catchword to best describe the changes in the squatters' scene. Great ideals are no longer the primary concern; small concrete projects are. Meanwhile, there are some 2500 of these projects underway in Berlin, mostly in cultural or social areas. The alternative movement has, over time, moved into every nook and cranny of the general culture. However, even in the public eye the "scene" locations were soon no longer decried as meeting places for rabble-rousers, but were welcomed as spots of color in the grey uniformity of the city; as an appealing attribute for an open-minded Berlin. After reunification, however, many of the projects faced doom since they depended on a steady trickle of subsidies. Not much remains of the original concept of creating an area free of rulership, in which everything

Right: Punks and their favorite pets, still trying to shock even the Berliners.

was to be decided with equal voting rights – except for the uniform wages, which many of the projects have retained.

The **ufafabrik** (Tempelhof, Viktoriastr. 10-18, tel. 75 50 30) is one of the few projects which is making the challenge of living and working together into a reality. On a plot of land nearly 200,000 square feet (18,000 sq meters) in size, where UFA films were produced in the 1920s, there are now an organic bakery, a circus school, a theater, cinemas, a café, workshops and the residential buildings of the 60-member UFA commune. However, with its recognized cultural offerings, the ufafabrik has long been part of the establishment. Berlin, as a cultural capital, found the major European Theater Festival which the commune organized in 1988 worthy of a public boast; even the bread from the UFA bakery has become a household word in Berlin, which is by all accounts no small feat.

With 227 individual projects, the **Mehringhof** (Kreuzberg, Gneisenaustr. 2a, tel. 691 50 99) is also a major self-

administered project with a bookstore, a bicycle shop, an ecological bank, a bar and a theater. Demonstrations are planned in the Mehringhof, discussions are held, and people threatened by legal proceedings consult with each other here.

In the former eastern section of the city there is a self-administrated cultural center, the **Tacheles** (Mitte, Oranienburger Strasse 54-56), situated in the **Camera**, which was, until 1981, the only program-cinema of the former GDR's capital. During the last five years the Tacheles has developed into the leading address of the alternative art scene. Parties and performances are held, and the people who look on forget that all of this, just like the entire counter-culture scene on Oranienburger Strasse, is merely an interlude. Negotiations with the investor who wanted to build on the grounds dragged on for years in order to find some kind of solution for the Tacheles issue. In the meantime, after numerous negotiations and eviction notices, an investor has finally been found.

THE MULTICULTURAL CITY

There is no other German city where as many different nationalities live together as in Berlin. This is not just a fact of the recent past, either: the history of Berlin is also the history of waves of immigration that began in the 17th century. At that time it was especially the Huguenots, who, by 1700, numbered 5800 people and composed one-fourth of Berlin's population; in the 18th century about 2000 Bohemians also migrated to the city. Both of these peoples were persecuted for their religion in their native countries. The difficulties the Huguenots and Bohemians had in becoming accepted were rather slight in comparison to the Jews, who emigrated from Vienna to Berlin at the end of the 17th century: the Jews, branded as "murderers of Christ" by the Church, suffered from discrimination and weren't allowed to work

in most professions. In the fields remaining to them, such as trade and finance, they learned how to find loopholes in the market beyond the reach of the guilds and corporations. In the course of time, however, the economic success which many of Berlin's Jews achieved also increased the distrust – and sparked the envy – of the remaining population. The Jews were not given equal rights until 1812, after which they could participate relatively unhindered in Berlin's economic and cultural development. Not only were many well-known Berlin firms founded by Jews, they also produced an above average number of the most progressive artists and scientists of the day.

Toward the end of the 19th century more Jews, mostly poor, came from Russia to Berlin, fleeing the brutal pogroms in their homeland. And, as the last immigrants before World War Two, some 300,000 exiled Russians settled in Berlin, although they almost all left the city again after 1923. The Nazi's seizure of power in 1933, with their brutally en-

Above: The Prenzlauer Berg synagogue.
Right: Turkish Muslim before prayers.

forced ideologies and their mass murders, particularly directed against the Jews, brought the diversity of religion and nationality in Berlin to an end.

Berlin without the Allies

With its occupation by the victorious powers, Berlin became perforce somewhat more multi-cultural. Of course, at the beginning any contact between the Allied soldiers and the Germans was strictly forbidden. Nonetheless, the needs of both sides brought them closer together. Not only were the long-deprived troops surrounded by the widows of war, but the American GI's were in possession of goods, such as whiskey and cigarettes, which were sorely missed in the devastated city and which served as valuable mediums of exchange. The American Allies brought about the triumphal advance of the Anglo-American lifestyle. While in Berlin the radio broadcasters continued to slog away with German pop-songs, the programming for US soldiers by AFN (broadcasting from Zehlendorf) was already lighting quite a fire in their listeners with rock'n'roll music. Any Berlin kid with a claim to being "with it" only listened to AFN and the British BFBS. Because of the Allies' presence, Berliners were the first to develop an enthusiasm for American sports like football, baseball and basketball. When the Allied forces left Berlin, despite the festive spirit, many Berliners, especially the older ones, had lumps in their throats. Not only was a chapter in history closed but also many ties of friendship and culture sundered. The 4000 or so apartments which thus became free in West Berlin were moved into by students, and the German armed forces took over the empty Allied barracks.

In the old US Army cinema, the Outpost, an Allied Forces Museum opened in June 1998, commemorating this chapter of Berlin's history. Its fitting name is

"More than a Suitcase Remains" (Clayallee 135, tel. 81 81 99-0).

Turks and Other Foreign Workers

Whereas the soldiers lived in seclusion in their housing areas, the recruitment of guest workers has left behind an indelible mark on the texture of Berlin's population since the mid-1970s. That the integration of Italians and Greeks (of which there are some 13,000 and 10,600 respectively living in Berlin) is considered particularly successful is due especially to their home countries, which are members of the European Union and are familiar to the many Germans who vacation there. A large number of people who came as simple laborers have worked their way up the ladder and are now respected businessmen. Berlin's second-strongest group of foreigners, the roughly 39,000 former Yugoslavs, have a harder time as non-EU citizens. Permits for residency and employment are more complicated to obtain.

The largest group of foreigners in Berlin – the some 137,000 Turkish people – still faces a struggle for acceptance. In contrast to most other immigrants, they are Muslims (as are a number of immigrants from the former Yugoslavia) and are bound by the strict rules of the Koran. Especially the first generation arrivals, who have often come from remote villages, are conspicuous because of their way of life, which has been shaped by an unbroken patriarchal tradition. They have tried to preserve their cultural identity by residing close to each other in districts such as Kreuzberg, Wedding and Neukölln. As a result, the Turkish minority makes up 20 percent of the Kreuzberg population. A typical infrastructure has also developed, with Turkish restaurants, banks, physicians, travel agencies and countless shops. The religious involvement of the Turks is much less conspicuous than their economic activities.

Above: Turkish children. Right: Monk at the Buddhist monastery in Frohnau.

In Berlin, Islam is now the second-largest religious community after Christianity, even though the city's roughly 35 mosques are often hidden away in former factories and apartments above shops. Since the Turkish community has neither been able to reach agreement among themselves nor with the Senate on the matter of religious instruction in public schools, many children and youths attend Koranic schools in the afternoons after their regular classes. This means that the second and third generations of young Turks, who, as far as their interests go, see themselves more as Berliners than as foreigners, are thrust yet again into a separate role. Young Turkish people experience more than enough exclusion in their day-to-day lives. Their opportunities on the job market are fewer; even an innocent visit to a discotheque may often run aground on the resistance of the doorman. It's no wonder that many young Turks withdraw in frustration and sometimes join more-or-less aggressive youth gangs.

Discriminated Minorities in the East

In contrast to the western part of the city, the presence of foreigners has hardly had any impact on daily life in east Berlin, or in the former GDR as a whole. The approximately 11,000 guest workers – primarily from Vietnam, although also from Angola and Mozambique – who were working in the eastern part of the city on bilateral contracts, lead isolated lives in cramped apartment complexes. The "peoples' friendships" decreed by the GDR regime existed only for official occasions. After the opening of the Wall it became clear how damaging this separation had been to the psyches of many citizens of the former GDR.

With the absence of restrictions, many citizens and right-wing extremist groups that have suddenly sprung up are allowing their resentments to run free. Also, on the official side, labor contracts still in force have been frequently cancelled with little or no notice. After only a few months of "freedom," an increasing number of foreigners left the east. To be sure, several of the youth clubs are making efforts to foster understanding between quite different cultures. However, as long as foreign residents have to fear being attacked by right-wing hoodlums, especially at night, they feel more comfortable in the west.

Last Hope Berlin: The Refugees

Since the end of the 1970s the increasing number of people seeking asylum here have brought about the formation of new communities of foreigners. Until 1986 the refugees went to West Berlin via Schönefeld Airport, since they didn't need to present a visa for their further travel into West Berlin and the Federal Republic. Until the Bonn government managed to get the former GDR to apply stricter regulations, Berlin was the major gateway to the West, especially for

asylum-seekers from the Middle East and Africa.

Since Berlin didn't have much interest in this form of immigration, the applicants' living conditions were made harder during the often several-year-long waiting period for a decision on the petition for asylum.

It will probably be primarily the refugees who determine the composition of nationalities in Berlin in the future as well. A first indication of this already began dawning at the beginning of the 1980s, as an increasing number of Poles fled to Berlin because it was the closest Western city. After the fall of the Wall they were followed by the "consumer tourists" who sought to improve their meager incomes by working illegally or retailing goods purchased in the West. That foreigners are welcome in Berlin – despite the increasing violence of the radical right – is shown by the frequently forgotten but very friendly way different cultures live alongside each other in the city.

233

SCIENCE AND RESEARCH

Berlin's scientific landscape at the end of the 1990s is still undergoing radical change: the old institutions in the east have been dissolved and reintegrated, but the future of Berlin as a center of research is still unclear.

And yet Berlin, like no other city in Germany, can look back on a great scientific tradition: between 1870 and 1933 scientists such as Dr. Rudolf Virchow and the Nobel Prize Laureate Robert Koch worked here. Physicians such as Max Planck, Max von der Laue and Albert Einstein revolutionized the world; Otto Hahn and Lise Meitner did research on radioactivity in Berlin.

Although Berlin has never been one of the old university cities, its modern and enlightened atmosphere has attracted countless scientists since the beginning of the 19th century. However, after twelve years of National Socialism not much remained of this fruitful era, as many Jewish scientists were forced to emigrate or were brutally murdered.

The Mass Universities

Today the unified city of Berlin has a difficult time tying back into such grand traditions. The two oldest universities in Berlin, the Friedrich Wilhelm University, which was founded in 1810 and today is called Humboldt University, and the *Technische Universität* (Technical University – TU), which was founded in 1879, have had to undergo many changes during the course of their histories.

Nowadays the TU and the *Freie Universität* (Free University) represent Berlin's university image. The FU was founded in 1948 by former students of Humboldt University, who, for political reasons, were personae non gratae.

Right: The Siemens research laboratory, one of the high-tech centers in the city.

Spoon-fed with funds from the American Henry Ford Foundation, this copybook university of the Free West turned into a center of the student movement at the end of the 1960s.

Today more than 145,000 students are enrolled at the three Berlin universities, four artistic schools, nine vocational schools and the *Europäische Wirtschaftshochschule* (European Business School), making it university town number one in Germany.

But the mass universities, the FU (48,000 students) and the TU (35,000 students), are under budgetary constraints and are having a hard time maintaining research and teaching. By 2003 the two universities will have to cut 135 million marks from their budgets, and the number of students will have to be reduced to 100,000. As a consequence of Berlin's status as a divided city, some faculties were represented at two or even three universities. They are now being combined.

Humboldt University (HU) is the only one of the three universities that was able to increase its enrollment during the past few years in spite of restructuring. 29,000 students are working now at this honorable institution.

For a long time Berlin's universities, above all those in the western part of the city, had the reputation of expelling radical students who supposedly were more interested in demonstrating than in studying. But that is not the whole truth: even though the situation at both the Technical and the Free University is catastrophic, the two universities publish more scientific publications than anywhere else in Germany.

Many faculties, such as machine construction and industrial engineering at the TU, or biochemistry and history at the FU, are internationally renowned. Quite a few fields of study, such as culture management and ecotrophy, can only be studied in Berlin.

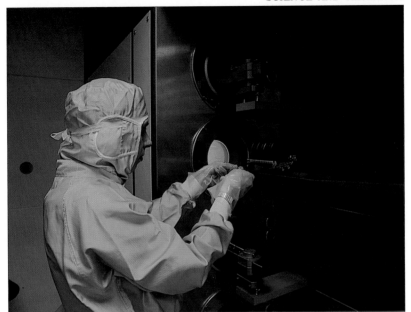

The City and its State-of-the-Art Technology

Meanwhile, almost unnoticed by the public, Berlin has worked its way up to becoming Germany's high-tech capital: in the whole city 50,000 scientists work at 250 different research institutions. The Max Planck Institute and its Hahn Meitner Institute, the Berlin Scientific Center and the German Institute for Economic Research are particularly renowned.

During the early 1980s, cooperative projects betweeen state-funded research, universities and industry gave new stimuli to the city. The *Produktionstechnisches Zentrum* (Production Engineering Center) is a classic example of this cooperation.

In the meantime, Berlin has become the German leader in genetic engineering and computer technology: accordingly it was scientists from the Rudolf-Virchow-Klinikum who, in 1994, launched the first treatment of cancer using gene therapy in Germany. And in cooperation with the German chemical firm Schering, the FU started its first open-air reseach with genetically manipulated plants. Berlin is also the leading location for laser and materials research.

The institutions of the former GDR regime, which were "wound down," will play a leading role in the future of Berlin as research capital. Both private and state institutions are benefiting from the huge potential of the former research academies of the GDR.

At least two places in Berlin are demonstrating what research may be like in the next century: at the Research and Technology Park Adlershof, 160 companies and institutes are jointly testing new technologies. And at the Innovations Park in Wuhlheide, research and industry have come together in innumerable projects. The construction and testing of new solar collectors is only one example among many.

Thus Berlin in the late-1990s seems to be right on course to pick up where its last great era left off.

BUSINESS AND INDUSTRY

Even years after the Wall came down and Berlin was reunified, it is still a city with an unusual industrial and economic structure. However, the unique industrial history of the city, which has always been the power behind its development, is not quite what it once was.

In 1996 Berlin turned over DM 150.5 million, representing 4.3 percent of Germany's GNP, but, seen against the backdrop of general growth development, Berlin is way behind and, since 1993, has been the poorest of Germany's 16 federal states. The process of structural change is far from adequate, and more jobs are being lost than are being created.

Berlin's Changing Economy

Berlin is still in a difficult period of transition years after the fall of the Wall: the industrial sector is, as yet, far from being reunified, and West Berlin's industry is presently experiencing a painful weaning process. This is because, until the Wall came down, the Western part of the city was always considered a capitalist showroom which was, on the whole, kept alive on a diet of generous federal subsidies, tax benefits and direct investment contributions.

Berlin lacks the production chains that developed naturally elsewhere, and its economic structure today still has something of that artificial quality due to its old island-like situation in the sea of the GDR. Hence the Berlin cigarette industry supplies almost 80 percent of Germany's requirements.

East Berlin, formerly the capital of the GDR, used to be the pride of East German industry. But that is all part of the past now.

Right: Once upon a time, Berlin was a major industrial bastion of the electrical industry – lamps being made at Osram.

The eastern half of the city has still not recovered from the after effects of 40 years of socialism. In the next few years the unemployment rate will be considerably higher here than in the rest of Germany, and thus will be a burden on the Berlin public purse. Almost all large industrial companies in east Berlin, mainly those that specialize in micro and electrical engineering, have been "finalized," sold and privatized by the governement. Of course, the east with its reasonable property and land prices, has great development potential.

Gradually, east and west have grown together to form a united economic entity, which, nevertheless, still has some problems with its geographical location and image. Thus, Berlin's industrial landscape is still dominated by the old industries: electrical (38,000 jobs), machine-building (15,400 jobs) and streetcar construction (8300 jobs). Taken together, they account for 45 percent of Berlin's blue-collar jobs.

Berlin – the Booming Metropolis?

Unlike other major West German cities such as Hamburg, Frankfurt and Munich, the service sector in Berlin is still completely underdeveloped. Commerce, banks and insurance companies – after a brief boom during the first few years after the Wall came down – have virtually stopped moving to Berlin. Business, too, is waiting for the government's relocation from Bonn to Berlin.

The few large projects in this area, such as the building of the service center of *debis*, the Mercedes Benz subsidiary, on Potsdamer Platz, or the construction of Sony's European headquarters, also on Potsdamer Platz, are simply trend-setters. Whether they will find companies willing to imitate them is still an open question.

Although foreign investors have been streaming into Berlin since reunification of the city, whether most of these pro-

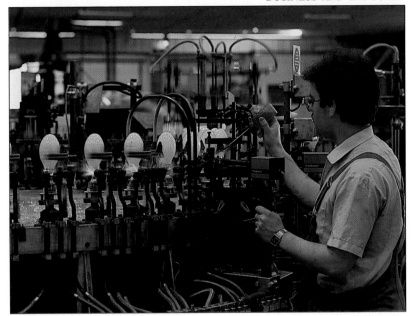

jects, such as the **American Business Center**, will decisively alter the city's economic future remains to be seen.

The current logistical problems in Berlin are probably an additional reason for potential investors to shun the city. Keeping the deadline for the renovation of the city and the timely move of the federal government to Berlin could possibly be of assistance.

Some investors who have been drawn to Berlin end up settling outside the city in Brandeburg to save on expenses. Some politicians in the city are already afraid that over the next few years Berlin will be surrounded by a belt of prosperity. Furthermore, unlike other German cities, such as Cologne and Hamburg, for example, Berlin can now feel the geographical proximity of the low-wage countries of eastern Europe, especially Poland. Berlin's function as the connecting point between East and West will soon decline to the city being simply a transit station which brings little profit to Berlin and its people.

The Future Beckons

All is not just gloom and doom in the economically troubled city. Berlin does have a few trumps up its sleeve. The city and its surroundings constitute a concentrated force of five million people; a major human resource asset. Global corporations like Siemens and Schering not only wish to keep their headquarters in Berlin, but they are intending to further expand there as well.

Berlin has the scientific and industrial potential to grow into a leading center of technology, and to establish itself as a hub of East-West economic cooperation. Significant for the city is its strength as a locus of science and research. One of Europe's most modern technology parks is being built in the eastern side of town, the *Wissenschafts- und Wirtschaftsstandort Berlin-Adlershof* (WISTA) on 185 acres (75 ha). Mainly innovative companies involved in environmental, information, and communications or photo technology are planning to settle here.

237

BERLIN'S TEMPO:
Public Transportation

"What on earth gives this city its charm? In the first place, its tempo. No city is as restless as Berlin. Everything is in motion." So wrote the English journalist Harold Nicolson, who spent the 1920s in Berlin. The rhythm of life in this city was set by its industrialization in the late 19th century. After the invention of the electric motor in 1879, it took about 20 years before all the horse-drawn train routes had been electrified and the horse-drawn omnibuses had been replaced by motorized buses. Simultaneously, between 1871 and 1877, the Stadtbahn (urban railway) was constructed; unique in Europe at the time, it connected the various Berlin train stations in a loop laid around the inner city. By 1925 this 7.5-mile (12-km) stretch had been electrified.

Above: Berlin's extensive rail network – here the U-1, connecting Zehlendorf, Kreuzberg and Friedrichshain.

Against resistance from the city's inhabitants and officials, Werner von Siemens managed to prevail with his idea of an underground railway, and in 1902 the first U-Bahn (subway) line was opened between Zoo and Stralauer Gate.

The Division and New Perspectives

Shortly after the end of World War Two, the S-Bahns (suburban train lines) and U-Bahns were in operation again, as were the streetcars and buses. However, the construction of the Wall in 1961 divided public transportation into two separate systems. Many lines ended as dead tracks at the Wall, and the stations in East Berlin remained closed to trains traveling through from the West. Only the S-Bahn in West Berlin was operated by the GDR's Reichsbahn, until it was sold to the BVG (West Berlin's office of transportation) in 1984. The Reichsbahn had already shut down its operation on the city ring line four years earlier, after a tenacious strike by S-Bahn employees.

Since the reunification of Berlin's two halves, the public transportation systems of both parts of the city have also been rejoined. In 1990-91 all the ghost stations were put back into service, the entire bus network was reorganized, and dead-end tracks were reconnected. Today Berlin has a total of 89 miles (143 km) of subway tracks, 110 miles (176 km) of streetcar lines and 185 miles (296 km) of S-Bahn tracks.

The reestablishment of service on the entire city ring is more problematic. The BVG has been renovating these routes since 1984, but it will hardly be able to complete the billion-mark improvement by the year 2000. Berliners have a sort of love-hate relationship with it: they complain halfheartedly when the trains are late, but, especially in summer, they enjoy riding in the wobbling cars, several of which have been rumbling over the tracks since before the war. The VBB (the government corporation responsible for public transportation in Brandenburg) is responsible for bus and rail rides into Berlin's surrounding countryside.

Berlin: Europe's Intersection

Since September 22, 1838, when the first Prussian railroad went into operation between Zehlendorf and Potsdam, tracks have been laid to Berlin from just about every point on the compass. As a result, in the late 19th century a series of grandiose rail terminals were built at the ends of these routes. Only the Hamburger Bahnhof, today an art gallery, is still standing.

Because of the division of Germany, rail traffic to and from Berlin diminished considerably. The new plans for Germany's transportation network include the expansion of existing railway lines to Hannover, Hamburg and Munich; furthermore, three new long-distance and local traffic train stations will be opened in the city center: **Lehrter Bahnhof**, **Potsdamer Platz**, and the station on **Papestrasse**. Travel is currently through **Bahnhof Zoo** (points west), and **Bahnhof Lichtenberg** and the **Ostbahnhof** (points east). The latter will be expanded to suit Germany's high speed ICE trains. To take some of the burden off the Ostbahnhof, many long-distance and regional trains stop at Bahnhof Lichtenberg.

Air travel, on the other hand, has developed at breathtaking speed. The great nostalgic zeppelins were built from 1915 in Staaken. In 1923 a small airport was inaugurated on the Tempelhofer Feld, which at that time was still outside of town. In 1926 **Deutsche Lufthansa** was founded with the **Tempelhof Airport** as its home base. In 1936 Ernst Sagebiel designed the current semi-circular complex, which was taken over by the US Army after the war. During the 1948-49 blockade of Berlin, the pilots of the Air-lift landed here.

The city's status under the Allies forbade German airlines to fly into Berlin. Thus, when **Tegel**, the new airport, was dedicated in 1974, only foreign airlines were on hand. Since the reunification of Germany, Lufthansa has flown from Tegel to its destinations all around the world. At present, 330 flights per day take off from the airport, and Tempelhof now has European regional airport rank. The airport was controversial no sooner had the first jets started taking off and landing: local residents complained bitterly about noise and air pollution. Hence, Tegel and Tempelhof will ultimately be closed after a new major airport is built.

After long discussion, it was decided to make the former GDR's central airport **Schönefeld** Berlin's new airport project. Actual construction work will most probably begin after the turn of the millennium. Schönefeld Airport will put the city right in the crosshairs of Europe's air routes, which indeed makes Berlin the fastest-moving city on the continent.

PREPARATIONS

Climate and Travel Times

Berlin is located in the middle of Europe in the center of the North German Plain. Therefore, Berlin's weather is determined by the continental climate. The Atlantic's influence only prevails now and then. There are few great variations in the climate throughout the year. The best times for travel are between March and June or between late August and October. It's either too hot or too cold in the other months. In addition, during the winter, the biting east wind and the smog are bothersome.

Clothing

In Berlin you can wear anything that is practical, pleasing or downright crazy. If you really must get to know Berlin in the winter, you can hardly bring enough warm clothing along, whereas in summer it can't be airy and light enough. But in spring and summer, too, you shouldn't forget to bring a raincoat and a warm sweater. If you like going out in the evening, you can dress more or less as you please, from casual to elegant, from fancy to wild. Only a few bars, restaurants and discotheques require a more formal attire or evening dress, suit and tie. Berlin's nightlife leaves enough room for fashion extravagance

Berlin in Statistics

Berlin is the largest German city, with an area of 338 square miles (890 sq km), almost as large as the entire Ruhr region. It extends 24 miles (38 km) from north to south; all of 28 miles (45 km) from east to west.

The greatest elevations in the city are the 368-foot (115-meter) Teufelsberg and the Grosser Müggelberg also 368 feet (115 meters) in eastern Berlin.

Currently there are 3,366,585 inhabitants residing in the city's 23 districts (as of October 1998). Only a bare 14 percent of the population is over 65 years of age. By the way, there are 106,500 more women than men.

ARRIVAL / TRANSPORTATION

Arriving by Air: Since the reunification of Germany, Berlin's skies are wider open than ever before; Lufthansa flies to the Spree again. In addition, many other airlines have acquired landing rights in Berlin.

Berlin's three airports each perform different functions: people flying in from western German cities and countries of western Europe, as well as other parts of the world, land in **Tegel** (TXL), in northern Berlin. Smaller regional and European airlines land their aircraft at **Tempelhof** (THF); and some international flights and travelers from eastern Europe land in **Schönefeld** (SXL).

The city center can be reached from all three airports by public transportation. From Tegel, **bus 109** runs to Bahnhof Zoo; **bus 128** to the U-Bahn station Osloer Strasse, and the **X9** express bus goes to Tiergarten via Bahnhof Zoo. From Tempelhof **bus 169** (or the **U 6** from Platz der Luftbrücke) brings travelers to the center; the **S-Bahn 9** connects **Schönefeld** with the city, stopping at Alexanderplatz and Zoologischer Garten, from where you can get U-Bahns.

By Train: The ride to Berlin has become increasingly comfortable. There are rapid connections to German and European cities. Train travelers arrive either at **Bahnhof Zoo** (from points west), the **Ostbahnhof** (from points east) or **Bahnhof Lichtenberg** (inter-regional and regional trains). Three more long-distance train stations are being planned for the next century: Lehrter Bahnhof, Bahnhof Potsdamer Platz and Bahnhof Papestrasse. Connections between Berlin and Hamburg, Cologne (high-speed ICE trains) and Aachen (IR train) have improved since 1997.

By Car or Bus: Those wishing to get to Berlin quickly can drive on the Autobahn from Hamburg, Hannover, Frankfurt or Nürnberg. For the next few years, however, factor extra time into car travel, as the Autobahns in the former GDR are one big construction site.

The Autobahns all end at the Berliner Ring, a peripheral road around the city. If arriving from the north, drive via **Stolpe** right onto the *Stadtautobahn* and straight into the city center, or via the A 114 to Pankow. From the west you take the A 5 via **Staaken** onto Heerstrasse.

Drivers coming from the south cross the former border checkpoint **Dreilinden** to reach the inner city and then take the **AVUS** to the junction at the **Funkturm** (radio tower). The B 1 highway comes from the east over **Dahlwitz-Hoppegarten** (harness-racing track) into the city.

The **bus station** (*Omnibusbahnhof ZOB*) at the *Funkturm* (radio tower) is where the bus lines connecting Berlin to the rest of the world arrive (Charlottenburg, Masurenallee 4-6, tel. 301 80 28). The ZOB connects to over 250 destinations in Germany and Europe. The U-Bahn 2 goes from the *Funkturm* (Kaiserdamm station) to the center in a few minutes.

Transportation in Berlin

The best thing to do in Berlin is leave your car parked somewhere. Typical big-city traffic clogs the streets of the capital. The inner city and Spandau have paid parking areas, and other districts will soon be equipped withthem as well.

Taxis present an alternative: in the entire city there are about 7000 cabs; even so, it's not always easy to flag one down. **Taxi Phones**: 690 22; 26 10 26; 21 01 01; 21 02 02; 96 44; 194 10.

Velotaxis, bicycle-pulled, environmentally friendly rickshaws, have been running since 1997 in summers only. Three fixed lines are currently open: Adenauerplatz – Wittenbergplatz, Zoologischer Garten – Pariser Platz and Pariser Platz – Alexanderplatz.

Public Transportation: Berlin's public transportation network is the most spread out and complete of any German city. New fare zones and fares were introduced in 1997 by the BVG (Berlin Transit Authority), the S-Bahn Berlin GmbH and the BVV (Brandenburg Transit Association) for Berlin and the region. However, fares are subject to change on short notice.

The two main traffic juntion points are the **Zoologische Garten** and **Alexanderplatz**. Several bus lines, suburban train (S-Bahn) and subway lines (U-Bahn) cross at both locations.

The BVG has set up an extensive nighttime bus network (*Nachtbusnetz*) for nighthawks. In addition, the U12 and U9 U-Bahn lines run all night on Fridays and Saturdays, as does the bus no. 100. For the most part, the last U-Bahn and S-Bahn trains stop between midnight and 1 a.m.

Berlin and environs are divided into three tariff zones: Zone A is within Berlin's S-Bahn ring, Zone B includes the rest of the city (and some of the train and bus stations from the region) and Zone C consists of the rest of the immediate surroundings. There is one fare for two neighboring zones and a supplement for a ride to the third zone.

PRACTICAL TIPS

Accommodation

Berlin has over 48,000 hotel beds to offer the weary visitor, and by the year 2000 that figure will rise to 60,000. Duringarge festivals and trade fairs (like the ITB at the beginning of March), rooms may be booked out weeks in advance; therefore we recommend you reserve as early as possible.

LUXURY and TOP HOTELS: Berlin's finest places to stay (with correspond-

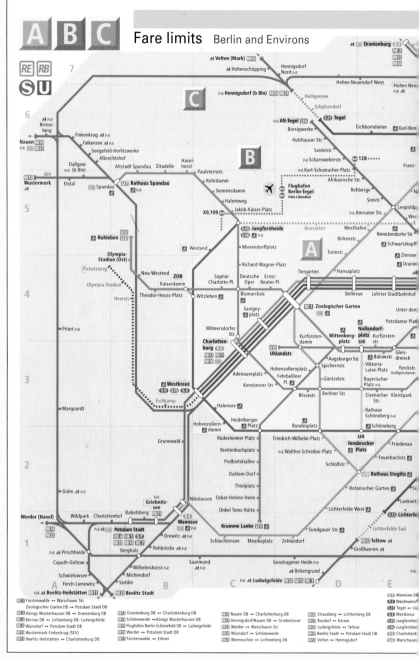

Fare limits Berlin and Environs

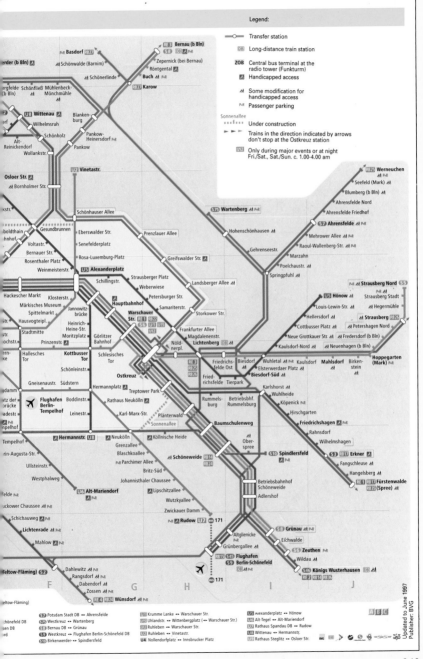

ingly high prices) are: **Berlin Hilton**, Mitte, Mohrenstr. 30, tel. 20 33-0; **Four Seasons Hotel**, Mitte, Charlottenstrasse 49, tel. 20 33-8; **Grand Hotel Esplanade**, Tiergarten, Lützowufer 15, tel. 26 10 11; **Grand Hyatt Berlin**, Tiergarten, Potsdamer Platz, tel. 2553 1234; **Hecker's Hotel**, Charlottenburg, Grolmanstr. 35, tel. 88 90-0; **Holiday Inn Crowne Plaza Berlin**, Schöneberg, Nürnberger Str. 65, tel. 210 07-0; **Hotel Adlon Kempinski Berlin**, Mitte, Unter den Linden 77, tel. 22 61-0; **Hotel Berlin**, Tiergarten, Lützowplatz 17, tel. 26 05-0; **Hotel Brandenburger Hof**, Wilmersdorf, Eilslebener Strasse 14, tel. 214 05-0; **Hotel Inter Continental**, Tiergarten, Budapester Strasse 2, tel. 26 02-0; **Hotel Mondial Berlin**, Charlottenburg, Kurfürstendamm 47, tel. 88 41 10; **Hotel Palace Berlin**, Charlottenburg, located in the Europa Center, tel. 25 02-0; **Hotel Seehof Berlin**, Charlottenburg, Lietzenseeufer 11, tel. 32 00 2-0; **Kempinski Hotel Bristol Berlin**, Charlottenburg, Kurfürstendamm 27, tel. 88 43 40; **Maritim proArte Hotel Berlin**, Mitte, Friedrichstr. 151, tel. 203 35; **Radisson SAS Hotel Berlin**, Mitte, Karl-Liebknecht-Strasse 5, tel. 238 28; **Savoy Hotel**, Charlottenburg, Fasanenstr. 9-10, tel. 311 03-0; **Ritz Carlton Vier Jahreszeiten Berlin**, Wilmersdorf, Brahmsstr. 10, tel. 895 84-0; **Steigenberger Berlin**, Charlottenburg, Los-Angeles-Platz 1, tel. 212 70; **Westin Grand Hotel**, Mitte, Friedrichstr. 158, tel. 20 27-0.

GOOD and *VERY GOOD HOTELS:* **art'otel Ermelerhaus Berlin**, Mitte, Wallstr. 70-73, tel. 240 62-0; **Bleibtreu Hotel**, Charlottenburg, Bleibtreustr. 31, tel. 884 74-0; **ESTREL Residence Congress Hotel**, Neukölln, Sonnenallee 225, tel. 68 31-0; **Mercure Alexander Plaza Berlin**, Mitte, Rosenstr. 1, tel. 240 01-0; **Sorat Art'otel Berlin**, Charlottenburg, Joachimstaler Str. 28/29, tel. 88 44 70.; **Sorat Hotel Spree-Bogen**, Tiergarten, Alt-Moabit 99, tel. 39 92 00.

NICE SMALLER HOTELS and *PENSIONS:* **Die Fabrik**, Kreuzberg, Schlesische Str. 18, tel. 611 71 16; **East-Side Hotel**, Friedrichshain, Mühlenstr. 6, tel. 29 38 33; **Frisco**, Wilmersdorf, Warnemünder Str. 8, tel. 823 47 62; **Hotel Alt-Tempelhof**, Tempelhof, Luise-Henrietten-Str. 4, tel. 756 85-0; **Propeller Island City Lodge**, Wilmersdorf, Pauslborner Str. 10, tel. 891 87 20.

YOUTH HOSTELS: An alternative to hotels and pensions are Berlin's youth hostels. More information from the **Deutsche Jugendherbergswerk**, Kreuzberg, Tempelhofer Ufer 32, tel. 264 95 20. Central reservations: Tiergarten, Klucksstr. 3, tel. 262 30 24.

PRIVATE ROOMS AND APARTMENTS: One of the best ways to get to know dyed-in-the-wool Berliners is to rent a room or an apartment from one of them through one of the city's so-called *Mitwohnzentralen*, a system of renting private accommodations. Usually good for a few days or even more:

Agentur Wohnwitz, Wilmersdorf, Holsteinische Str. 55, tel. 861 82 22 or 861 82 42; **Casa Nostra**, Schöneberg, Winterfeldtstr. 46, tel. 23 55 12-0 **Erste Mitwohnzentrale**, Charlottenburg, Sybelstr. 53, tel. 324 30 31; **Mitwohnzentrale Ku'damm-Eck/ Home Company**, Charlottenburg, Joachimstaler Str. 17 (in the "Ku'dorf" shopping arcade), tel. 194 45.

CAMPING: The **Deutscher Camping-Club e.V.**, Geisbergstr.11, 10777 Berlin (Schöneberg), tel. 218 60 71, has information on camping and camping sites in and around Berlin.

Airlines

Aeroflot, Mitte, Unter den Linden 51, tel. 22969 81 11; Schönefeld Airport, tel. 60 91 53 70; **Air France**, Tegel Airport, tel. 0180/536 03 70; **Alitalia**, Tegel Airport, tel. 21 01 81; **British Airways**, Europa Center, tel. 254 00 00; Deutsche BA, Europa-Center, tel. 254 00 00, Tegel

Airport, tel. 41 01 26 49; **Delta Airlines**, Charlottenburg, Budapester. Str. 41, reservations/information tel. 0180/333 78 80; **Eurowings**, Tempelhof Airport, tel. 695 128 32; **Hamburg Airlines**, Tempelhof Airport, tel. 695 138 64; **Iberia**, Kurfürstendamm 207, tel. 882 74 77, reservations tel. 261 7001; **KLM Royal Dutch Airlines**, reservations/ information tel. 0180/21 42 01; **Lufthansa**, city office at Kurfürstendamm 220, reservations/sales/information tel. 88 75 88; **Malev Hungarian Airlines**, Tiergarten, Budapester Str. 10, tel. 264 95 45; **Sabena**, Tempelhof Airport, tel. 69 5138 50/51; **Singapore Airlines**, Charlottenburg, Kurfürstendamm 206, tel. 88 59 22 13; **Swissair**, Charlottenburg, Kurfürstendamm 206, tel. 883 90 01; **Turkish Airlines**, Schöneberg, Budapester Str. 8, tel. 262 40 33.

Airports
Tegel: tel. 410 11; **Tempelhof**: tel. 695 10; **Schönefeld**: tel. 609 10.

Banks
There are numerous automatic teller machines (ATMs) in the city. The following banks (a small selection) offer late service: **Commerzbank** (Europa-Center, Tauentzienstr. 9), Uhlandstr. 181/183, Mon 9 a.m.-4 p.m., Tue and Thu 9 a.m.-6:30 p.m., Wed 9 a.m.-3 p.m., Fri 9 a.m.-1:30 p.m. ATMs of the bank are at Kurfürstendamm 59 and 102, and at Uhlandstr. 181-183, in Mitte, at Friedrichstr. 130.

Berliner Sparkasse, late service at: Rankestr. 33/34, Mon-Fri 9 a.m.-6 p.m., Sat 10 a.m.-1 p.m.; Wilmersdorfer Str./corner Kantstr., open Mon-Fri 9 a.m.-6 p.m. ATMs at Rankestr. 33/34, Kurfürstendamm 165, in the ICC and at Alexanderplatz 2.

The **Deutsche Bank** offers a late service at its branch on Otto-Suhr-Allee 6/16: Mon, Wed 9 a.m.-3:30 p.m., Tue, Thu 9 a.m.-6 p.m., Fri 9 a.m.-12:30 p.m.

ATMs at Kurfürstendamm 28 and 182, Tauentzien 1, Hardenbergstr. 27, Bismarckstr. 68, Alexanderplatz 6 and Karl-Marx-Allee 60/62.

Breakdown Assistance
ADAC Breakdown Service: tel. 01802 / 22 22 22; **ACE Auto-Club Europe**: tel. 211 90 31; **VCMD Verkehrshilfe**: tel. 331 80 08.

Car Pools
You can ride with someone for a small fee to the agency and to the driver.

ADM Mitfahrbüro in the Zoo U-Bahn station (Platform 2, toward Vinetastr.), tel. 241 58 20, Mon-Fri 9 a.m. to 8 p.m., Sat, Sun 10 a.m.-6 p.m.; in the Alexanderplatz U-Bahn station (at the transfer point from U8 to U2), tel. 241 58 20, Mon-Fri 10 a.m.-6 p.m., Thu 10 a.m.-8 p.m., Sat, Sun 11 a.m.-4 p.m.

Mitfahr-Zentralen Citynetz, Charlottenburg, Joachimstaler Str. 17, tel. 194 44 and 882 76 04, daily 8 a.m.-9 p.m., and in Kreuzberg, Bergmannstr. 57 (U-Bahn station Südstern) tel. 693 60 95, Mon-Fri 10 a.m.-8 p.m., Sat, Sun 10 a.m.-4 p.m.

Car Rentals
Avis, Int'l Reservations office, tel. 06171/68 18 00; Charlottenburg, Budapester Str. 43, tel. 261 18 81; Tegel Airport, tel. 41 01 31 48; **City Auto Verleih**, Schöneberg, Lietzenburger Str. 29/ Nürnberger Str., tel. 882 11 83 / 883 42 52; **Hertz** Reservation Center, tel. 0130 533 35 35; Schöneberg, Budapester Str. 39, tel. 261 10 53; Tegel Airport, tel. 41 01 33 15; **Europcar**, Mitte, Karl-Liebknecht-Str. 19-21 (Alexanderplatz), tel. 240 79 00; Charlottenburg, Messedamm 8 (bus station at the *Funkturm*), tel. 306 9590; Tegel Airport, tel. 417 85 20; Schöneberg Airport, tel. 634 91 60; **Sixt Budget**, Schönefeld Airport, tel. 60 91 56 90; Tegel Airport, tel. 41 01 28 86; Tempelhof Airport, tel. 69 51 38 16.

Consulates

American Consulate General, Mitte, Neustädtische Kirchstr. 4-5, tel. 238 51 74; **British Consulate General**, Mitte, Unter den Linden 32/34, tel. 20 18 40.

Currency Exchange

Money can be exchanged in all banks or at the Reisebank at the Bahnhof Zoo train station (tel. 881 71 17, Mon-Sat 7:30 a.m.-10 p.m., Sun and holidays 8 a.m.-9 p.m.). Reisebank in the Hauptbahnhof (main train station, tel. 296 43 93, Mon-Fri 7 a.m.-6 p.m., Sun 8 a.m.-4 p.m.). Or at the **Berliner Bank** at Tegel Airport (tel. 417 85 40, daily 7 a.m.-10 p.m.).

Emergencies

Police Emergency (Notruf): tel. 110; **Fire Department** (Feuerwehr): tel. 112; **Rescue Service** (Rettungsdienst): tel. 112; **Emergency Pharmacy Service** (Apotheken-Notdienst): tel. 011 41; **Emergency Physicians** (Ärztlicher Notdienst): tel. 31 00 31; **Emergency Dentist** (Zahnärztlicher Notdienst), tel. 89 00 43 00; **Drug Emergency** (Drogen-Notdienst): tel. 192 37; **Emergency Phone for Women** (Frauen-Notruf), tel. 615 42 43; **Emergency for Raped Women**, tel. 251 28 28; **Emergency Phone for Homosexuals**, (Schwulen-Notruf) tel; 216 33 36. **Poison Emergency** (Giftnotruf): 302 30 22; **Emergency Veterinary Service** (Tierarzt): tel. 011 41; **Telephone Counseling**, tel. 111 01.

Festivals, Trade Fairs, Exhibitions

January/February: Grüne Woche, International Film Festival.
March/April: International Tourism Fair (ITB), Music Biennale, Lützowplatz Spring Festival.
May: Theater Fair, German Open, Carnival of Cultures.
June/July: Free Berlin Art Exhibition, Franco-German Folk Festival, German-American Folk Festival, Love Parade, Christopher Street Day.
June/August: Schaustelle Berlin/SommerZeit Berlin (art festival).
August: International Broadcasting Exhibition (bi-annual), International Dance Festival.
September/October: Berlin Festival Week, Oktoberfest, Berlin Marathon.
October/November: International Boat Fair, Automobile Fair, Young Authors' Conference, Jewish Cultural Days.
December: Christmas Markets.

Further information available from: Austellungs-Messe-Kongress GmbH, Messedamm 22, 14055 Berlin (Charlottenburg), tel. 303 80, and from Berliner Festspiel GmbH, Budapester Str. 50, 10787 Berlin (Schöneberg), tel. 25 48 90.

Guided City Tours

Traditional tours of the city, both small and large day tours, excursions to Potsdam and nightclub tours are offered by the following enterprises:

Berliner Bären Stadtrundfahrt (BBS): Departures from Rankestr. 35/ Kurfürstendamm and from Alexanderplatz in front of the Forum Hotel (tel. 35 19 52 70); **Berolina Sightseeing**: starts at Meinkestr.3/Kurfürstendamm (tel. 88 56 80 30); **Busverkehr Berlin** (BVB): starts out at Kurfürstendamm 225, diagonally opposite of Café Kranzler, and at Alexanderplatz in front of the Forum Hotel (tel. 885 98 80); **Severin und Kühn**: Kurfürstendamm 216/Fasanenstr. (tel. 880 41 90).

In the last few years a series of independent associations and businesses have begun specializing in special tours. Instead of taking a bus, you go on foot, by bicycle or by public transportation. Often the groups are small, so there is enough time to ask questions of knowledgeable guides. The historians of **Statt-Reisen Berlin** (Wedding, Malplaquestr. 5, tel. 455 30 28) guide tourists onto unusual paths on foot or by subway. The **Kultur Büro Berlin** (Prenzlauer Berg, Greifenhagener Str. 62, tel. 444 09 36) organizes recommendable cultural, museum, city, architectural and park tours. Meeting points and times for the tours are published in city magazines.

Historic boat tours on the Spree and the Landwehrkanal through seven inner city districts (every Sunday from the Hansabrücke bridge at the Bundesratsufer in Moabit) are offered by the **Berliner Geschichtswerkstatt** (Schöneberg, Goltzstr. 49, tel. 215 44 50); group tours or chartered tours are possible on request. **pluspunkt Weiterbildung** (Steglitz, Steglitzer Damm 105, tel. 774 40 81) does cultural, architectural, historical and social tours on foot, by bicycle, by bus and by train. It even has a criminal tour, "Crime Scene Berlin – Criminal Cases that Shook the City."

The specialty of **art:berlin** is up-to-date strolls through the cultural, artistic and urban landscape, including tours of exhibitions, architectural tours and nocturnal art adventures (Schöneberg, Kufsteiner Str. 7, tel. 85 72 81 82). **Berlin by bike**, as suggested by the name, has tours by bike (can be rented) or by rickshaw (if you wish to be driven). The bike station is in the Hackesche Höfe, Hof 7, Mitte, Rosenthaler Str. 40/41, tel. 28 59 98 95.

Sightseeing in the Berlin of the year 2000 is possible at the INFO BOX on Leipziger Platz (Mitte, tel. 226 62 40). Since 1995 the unmistakable red steel construction has been giving information on the huge building projects on Potsdamer Platz through models, films, 3-D animation and computer simulations. The exhibition ends on December 31, 2000. The view from the rooftop terrace is truly magnificent.

Help for the Handicapped

In Berlin the **Telebus** offers transportation for handicapped and disabled persons: **Berliner Zentralausschuss für Behinderte im Land Berlin e.V.**, Pankow, Esplanade 17, tel. 47 88 20. Further services are offered by **Service-Ring Berlin**, Wilhelm-Hauff-Str. 1, tel. 859 40 10, and **MOVADO e.V.**, Weissensee, Langhansstr. 64, tel. 471 51 45. For issues concerning the handicapped contact **Landesbeauftragte für Behinderte** (a government office), Schöneberg, An der Urania 14, tel. 21 22 29 17.

Lost and Found Offices

BVG-Fundbüro, Charlottenburg, Frauenhoferstr. 33-36, tel. 25 62 30 40; **DB Fundbüro**, at S-Bahn station Schönefeld, Mittelstr. 20, tel. 29 72 96 12; **Zentrales Fundbüro West**, Tempelhof, Platz der Luftbrücke, tel. 69 95.

Media

The heyday of the Berlin Press has now been consigned to the past. After a brief boom in 1989-92 the newspaper market has again quieted down and the reader-paper bond of the individual newspapers has settled. Today there are nine dailies in the city – a European record. Numerous **city magazines** are published regularly, 30 radio stations are on the air, and five TV stations also keep the Berliners informed.

Berlin has three serious daily papers, the *Tagesspiegel*, the *Berliner Morgenpost* and the *Berliner Zeitung*, which is the last great East Berlin newspaper to survive from the old days. Far less liberal or serious are the Springer papers *BZ* and *Bild*, as well as the *Berliner Kurier*.

There is actually one Berlin newspaper that *does* transcend regional boundaries, the leftist-alternative *Tageszeitung (taz)*, which, despite all financial emergencies and internal quarrels, is as much a part of Berlin as the Victory Column.

If you want information on the current program in the cinemas and theaters, then read the city magazines *tip* and *zitty*, which appear every two weeks. The third city magazine is *030*, distributed free-of-charge in pubs, bars and restaurants.

The *flyer*, which offers the best overview of the party scene and clubs, is also distributed free-of-charge. The tourist office publication *Berlin Programm* also provides a good monthly survey of what's up. *Checkpoint* is a very successful city magazine in English.

Multicultural City of Berlin

Foreigners visiting Berlin or people wanting to learn about the foreign cultures existing in the city can turn to the following addresses: **Anti-Racist Initiative e.V.**, Kreuzberg, Yorckstr. 59, tel. 785 72 81; **Senate Commission on Foreigners**, Schöneberg, Potsdamer Str. 65, tel. 26 04 23 51; **German-Polish Association Berlin e.V.**, Steglitz, Albrechtstr. 7, tel. 793 47 15; **Jewish Community of Berlin**, Charlottenburg, Fasanenstr. 79, tel. 88 02 80; **Turkish Community of Berlin** (this is also the parent organization for various other Turkish associations), Kreuzberg, Adalbertstr. 4, tel. 615 59 67 and 614 00 06; **House of World Cultures** (the former Kongresshalle), Tiergarten, J.-Foster-Dulles-Allee 10, tel. 39 78 70, exhibits, festivals, and lectures; **Neighborhood House for Inter-Cultural Encounters ORA 34**, Kreuzberg, Oranienstr. 34., tel. 614 28 93; **Vietnam House**, Neukölln, Hobrechtstr. 8-9, tel. 623 40 77; **Europe-Africa Kulturzentrum e.V.**, Schöneberg, Nollendorfstr. 21a, tel. 216 20 89.

Postal Services

Postal Information, tel. 01802 / 33 33; **Post Office in Bikini-Haus at the Zoo**, Charlottenburg, Budapester Str. 42, day-and-night counter, Mon-Sat 8 a.m. to midnight, Sun and holidays, 10 a.m. to midnight); **Post Office 519, Tegel Airport**, Mon-Fri 7 a.m.-9 p.m., Sat, Sun, holidays, 8 a.m.-8 p.m., tel. 417 84 90.

Telephone

The area code for Berlin is 030. The telephone numbers supplied in this *Nelles-Guide* were brought up to date in early 1998. However, some of the telephone numbers may have changed again in the meantime. If in doubt, contact directory assistance at 11833.

Tourist Information

For comprehensive tourist information, for everything from sightseeing to hotel reservations, contact: **Berlin Tourism Marketing** (BTM), Am Karlsbad 11, 10785 Berlin-Tiergarten, tel. 030 / 25 00 25, fax. 25 00 24 24, Internet: http://www.berlin.de. Branch offices are located in the Europa Center (entrance Budapester Str. 45), open Mon-Sat 8 a.m. -10 p.m., Sun 9 a.m.-9 p.m.; in the Brandenburg Gate, daily 9:30 a.m.-6 p.m., and in the A.S. Airport Service at Tegel Airport (exit, main hall, opposite Gate 0, daily 5 a.m.-10:30 p.m.). Offices also in the Dresdner Bank, Unter den Linden 17, Mon-Fri 8:30 a.m.-2 p.m., Tue, Thu also 3:30-6 p.m.; in the KaDeWe Reise Center, ground floor.

Train and City Travel

Deutsche Bahn, DB Service Points: in Bahnhof Zoo, tel. 29 74 93 50; at the Hauptbahnhof (main station), tel. 200 73; in Berlin-Lichtenberg, tel. 29 71 29 17. Central train information, tel. 194 19. Bus Station at the Radio Tower, tel. 301 80 28. BVG (Public Transportation) information service: 194 49.

GLOSSARY

General Vocabulary

guten Tag	good day
guten Abend / gute Nacht	good evening / good night
tschüss / auf Wiedersehen	goodbye
Entschuldigen Sie bitte?	Excuse me?
Haben Sie...?	Do you have...?
Wieviel kostet...?	How much does ... cost?
bitte	please
danke(schön)	thank you (very much)
wann	when
wo	where

Ich brauche...	I need...
Ich suche...	I'm looing for...
sofort / später	right away / later
heute / morgen	today / tomorrow
Ich möchte...	I'd like...
zum Bahnhof / zum Hotel / zur Bank	

to the station / to the hotel / to the bank

Geld	money
viel	many, much
wenig	few, little
groß	big
klein	small
links	left
rechts	right
geradeaus	straight ahead
schnell / langsam	fast / slow
Ich verstehe nicht!	I don't understand!
ja / nein	yes / no
Wo finde ich...?	Where do I find...?
Bushaltestelle	busstop
Ausstellung	exhibition
Kirche	church
Denkmal	monument
Schloß	castle, palace
Stadtrundfahrt	city sightseeing tour
Ausflug	excursion
Imbiß	snack bar
Kneipe	bar, café
Straße	street
Brücke	bridge
Tankstelle	service station
Benzin	gasoline
Fundbüro	lost and found

What's on the Menu?

Vorspeise	appetizer
Wurst	cold cuts, sausage
Brot	bread
Fisch	fish
Rindfleisch	beef
Geflügel	poultry
Hühnchen	chicken
Schweinefleisch	pork
Lamm	lamb
Gemüse / Beilage	vegetables
Käse	cheese
Kuchen	cake
Obsttorte	fruit tart
Eis	ice / ice cream

Mineralwasser	mineral water
Wein	wine
Die Rechnung bitte!	The bill, please!

Berlin Specialties

Berliner	jelly donut
Berliner Schlachtplatte	cold cut

platter (liverwurst, blood sausage, etc.)

Berliner Weiße	wheat beer served

with raspberry or woodruff syrup

Currywurst	bratwurst with curry
Eisbein	pickled pork knuckle
Bulette	meatball
Molle mit Korn	beer and a shot
	of grain spirits
Rollmöpse	marinaded herring

Berlin Dialect

eine Fluppe	a cigarette
ein paar Groschen	a couple of cents
icke (for "ich")	I
jut (for "gut")	good, okay
schniecke	chic
Schrippe	white bread roll
Schusterjunge	rye bread roll
wat (for "was")	what

Note: Nouns are always capitalized in German. The letter "ß" (Schloß, Straße) is the same as "ss"; "J" is pronounced as "y"; "tsch" is pronounced "ch"; "ie" and "ei" vowel combinations are pronounced "ee" and "aye" respectively.

AUTHORS

Eva Apraku studied German and art history; she worked for the Berlin *dpa* office and today she is editor of the magazine *tip* ("The Multicultural City").

Manuela Blisse, Berlin-born, studied communications. She is a freelance journalist in Berlin. She updated this edition.

Ellen Brandt studied history and began working freelance in the cultural desk of *Radio Free Berlin;* she also writes for *tip* and the *Tagesspiegel* ("World Theater and Theatrical Berlin," "Operas, Orchestras, Variety, Cabaret").

Matthias Eckoldt, born in Prenzlauer Berg, studied biology, German and history. He works as a freelance journalist for the weekly newspaper *Freitag* and the Berlin city-magazine *zitty* ("From Unter den Linden to Alexanderplatz").

Reginald Hanicke studied history and political science in Berlin. He works as a freelance journalist and specializes in the individual districts ("The North," "The West," "The South" and "Spandau").

Adrienne Kömmler grew up in Prenzlauer Berg and was an editor at Berlin *Radio aktuell* following her studies in philosophy. Today she works for the *Berliner Morgenpost* ("The East").

Armin Lehmann, who is a native Berliner, studied history and German; he has written for the *Spandauer Volksblatt, dpa* and *tip*. Today he works for the *Tagesspiegel* ("Sports in Berlin").

Regina Mönch studied journalism and social therapy in Leipzig, wrote for the paper *die andere*, which came out of the GDR civil rights movement, and was legal reporter for the *Morgen*. She is now local editor for the *Tagesspiegel* ("Prenzlauer Berg").

Constanze Salm worked as an interior architect before becoming editor of the magazine *Feine Adressen Berlin*. Today she writes for the Berlin society magazine *topBerlin* ("Kurfürstendamm," "Shopping in Berlin").

Jürgen Scheunemann studied history in Berlin and Washington D.C., and now works as a freelance journalist and translator. He was a staff writer on the *Tagesspiegel* and writes for national and international magazines and newspapers. He was project editor of the *Nelles Guide USA* ("History and Culture," "Around the Brandenburg Gate," "Culinary Discoveries," "Bars," "Film City Berlin," "Business and Industry," "Berlin's Tempo" and "Oases of Nature").

Birgit Schönberger moved from West Germany to Kreuzberg, did an internship at *Radio Free Berlin* and now works as a freelance journalist ("Kreuzberg," "The Alternative Scene").

Martin Schrader worked in Berlin for broadcasters *Hit 103*, *RIAS* and *RIAS-TV*, for *ZDF Studio Berlin* and for *Ostdeutscher Rundfunk (ORB)* ("Making the Scene – Day of Night").

Petra Steuer studied filmmaking at the Potsdam Film College. Today she works as a freelance journalist ("Potsdam," "Landscapes of the March")

Hans-Joachim Wacker was co-founder of the Berlin cultural pages in the *tageszeitung* and has been cultural editor at *tip* since 1990 ("Art and Literature").

PHOTOGRAPHERS

Explore the World

AVAILABLE TITLES

Australia
Bali / Lombok
Berlin and Potsdam
Brazil
Brittany
Burma → Myanmar
California
  Las Vegas, Reno,
  Baja California
Cambodia / Laos
Canada
  Ontario, Québec,
  Atlantic Provinces
Canada
  Pacific Coast, the Rockies,
  Prairie Provinces, and
  the Territories
Caribbean
  The Greater Antilles,
  Bermuda, Bahamas
Caribbean
  The Lesser Antilles
China – Hong Kong
Corsica
Crete
Croatia – Adriatic Coast
Cyprus
Egypt
Florida
Greece – The Mainland
Hawai'i

Hungary
India
  Northern, Northeastern
  and Central India
India – Southern India
Indonesia
  Sumatra, Java, Bali,
  Lombok, Sulawesi
Ireland
Israel - with Excursions
  to Jordan
Kenya
London, England and
  Wales
Malaysia - Singapore
  - Brunei
Mexico
Morocco
Moscow / St. Petersburg
Munich
  Excursions to Castles,
  Lakes & Mountains
Myanmar (Burma)
Nepal
New York – City and State
New Zealand
Paris
Philippines
Portugal
Prague / Czech Republic
Provence

Rome
Scotland
South Africa
South Pacific Islands
Spain – Pyrenees, Atlantic
  Coast, Central Spain
Spain
  Mediterranean Coast,
  Southern Spain,
  Balearic Islands
Sri Lanka
Syria – Lebanon
Tanzania
Thailand
Turkey
Tuscany
U.S.A.
  The East, Midwest and South
U.S.A.
  The West, Rockies and Texas
Vietnam

FORTHCOMING

Canary Islands
Costa Rica
Greek Islands
Maldives
Norway
Poland
Sweden

Nelles Guides – authoritative, informed and informative.
Always up-to-date, extensively illustrated, and with first-rate relief maps.
256 pages, approx. 150 color photos, approx. 25 maps.